FROM BAKER STREET
TO BINARY

THE ANALYTICAL ENGINE

FROM
BAKER STREET
TO
BINARY

An Introduction to Computers and Computer Programming with Sherlock Holmes

Henry Ledgard

E. Patrick McQuaid

Andrew Singer

McGraw-Hill Book Company

New York St. Louis San Francisco Auckland Bogotá
Guatemala Hamburg Johannesburg Lisbon London
Madrid Mexico Montreal New Delhi Panama Paris
San Juan São Paulo Singapore Sydney Tokyo Toronto

Acknowledgments appear in the "Postscript" on page 273.

First McGraw-Hill Edition, 1983
3 4 5 6 7 8 9 DOCDOC 8 7 6 5 4 3

A BYTE Book

ISBN 0-07-036983-6

LIBRARY OF CONGRESS CATALOGING IN PUBLICATION DATA

Ledgard, Henry F., 1943-
   From Baker Street to binary.
   Includes index.
   1. Computers. 2. Programming (Electronic computers)
I. McQuaid, Patrick. II. Singer, Andrew, 1943-
III. Title.
QA76.L415 1983   001.64   83-928
ISBN 0-07-036983-6 (pbk.)

CONTENTS

PREFACE   ix

ELEMENTARY CONCEPTS

I   THE ANALYTICAL ENGINE   2
     Commentary   5

II   THE ADVENTURE OF THE ABACUS (Part I)   8
     Representing Data   16
     Computer Memory   19
     Storing Data   20

III   THE ADVENTURE OF THE ABACUS (Part II)   28
     The Insides of a Computer   38
     A Small Hypothetical Computer   40
     A Binary Adder   44

PROGRAMMING

IV   THE ADVENTURE OF THE CARRIAGE WHEEL   52
     (Part I)
     Programming   60
     Algorithms   62

V   THE ADVENTURE OF THE CARRIAGE WHEEL   66
     (Part II)
     The Programming Language Basic   73
     Programming Languages   77

APPLICATIONS

VI	A VICTIM OF INDISCRETION	84
	Word Processing	96
	A Visit with a Word Processor	100
	The Dazzling Marketplace	106

VII	THE ADVENTURE OF THE TOY TRAIN (Part I)	108
	Personal Computers	115
	Three Interviews	118
	Video Games	125

VIII	THE ADVENTURE OF THE TOY TRAIN (Part II)	128
	Many Users, One Computer	135
	Communication with Remote Users	138
	Computer Networks	140

IX	UPON THE VARIOUS SHORTCOMINGS OF THE ANALYTICAL ENGINE	145
	Behind the Glossy Brochure	151
	Taming the Beast	155

HORIZONS

X	THE AFFAIR AT THE GOLDEN EAGLE	160
	Turing Machines	173
	The Nature of Mechanical Computation	181
	Unsolvable Problems	182

XI	THE ADVENTURE OF THE RED QUEEN'S RACE (Part I)	185
	Artificial Intelligence	198
	An "Intelligent" Program	200
	Machine Learning and Other Directions	207

XII	THE ADVENTURE OF THE RED QUEEN'S RACE (Part II)	214
	Can a Machine Think?	230
	On Some Common Misconceptions	234
	Some Social Implications	237

APPENDIX A
ASCII Character Set   239

APPENDIX B
Basic: Its Grammar and Meaning   241

APPENDIX E
Exercises in Basic   256

APPENDIX H
The Halting Problem: Proof of Unsolvability   263

APPENDIX R
References and Further Reading   266

APPENDIX V
Vocabulary of Terms   269

POSTSCRIPT   273

INDEX   275

PREFACE

Despite the appearance of Sherlock Holmes in these pages, this is a serious text on contemporary computers and computer programming. Its aim is to teach people about a new technology that has come of age.

The computer technology, for all of its promise, has brought with it a sense of confusion and intimidation. Its reach is so large and its uses so varied that we are often humbled in attempting to deal with it. Some of the apparent complexity of computers is due to their speed. Were computers a hundred times slower, they might appear just like the mechanical devices that we have come to understand and appreciate. But their real challenge is that they can perform tasks often thought suitable only for people. They have become an amplifier of thinking, and therefore they can appear threatening.

This text seeks to allay these fears by explaining precisely what a computer can and cannot do and how it works. It assumes no background on the part of the reader. In fact, for the most part, the chapters can be read in any order. The objective of each chapter is to answer some basic questions about computers and computer programming.

The first three chapters are about the makeup of the computer itself. What are some of its basic properties? How does a computer "know" things? How does a computer "compute" something?

The next two chapters are about programming. How does a person give instructions to a computer? What is a computer (or programming) "language"?

The next chapters answer questions about how computers are used. What is a word processor? How does it actually work? What is a personal computer? Why do people buy them? How can many people use a single computer? How easy are computers to use?

The final three chapters are concerned with how far the computer technology can go. Are there limits to what a computer can be programmed to do? Is it possible to program a computer to learn things or to communicate in English? Is it reasonable to ask if a computer can "think"? What are some of the long-range social issues in computers? In all of the chapters the emphasis is on a thoughtful understanding of basic concepts.

At certain points the serious student of computing may wish to go a bit deeper into a given topic. The appendices provide this opportunity. They include a small reference manual on the programming language Basic, a guide to further reading, and a dictionary of technical terms.

But why Sherlock Holmes? Because we wanted to make the idea of the computer technology as unthreatening and as appealing as possible. What better way than to present the great detective, the supreme logician and deductive reasoner, as the means both to explain the computer to the reader and to demonstrate man's mastery over it? The Holmes episodes are not mere window-dressing. In each adventure Holmes and Watson introduce the topic at hand. The "computer" they employ is the Analytical Engine that Charles Babbage designed in the mid 1800's. While the Analytical Engine was never actually built, Babbage's work truly foreshadowed modern computer technology. The Holmes episodes in this book give the reader the opportunity to study the computer in its early stages of development. In the commentary that follows each story, we amplify the topic in a modern setting. Meanwhile Holmes, in his concise and articulate explanations to Watson, gives a straightforward explanation of how computers work, stripping away the layers of mystery and myth that have been heaped upon them, showing what they can do and, equally important, what their limitations are.

Finally, Holmes and Watson provide not only two entertaining individuals to whom to relate, but a focus on human need and ingenuity.

Elementary Concepts

CHAPTER I

‡

The Analytical Engine

N AN entirely inadequate fashion, I have endeavoured to give some account of the remarkable career of Mr. Sherlock Holmes as a criminal investigator and consulting detective. As the reader is undoubtedly well aware, my companion's interests were as broad as Nature herself. He often spoke on an amazing variety of subjects as though he had made a special study of each. In my modest chronicles of the cases that I had the privilege to share with Sherlock Holmes, I have often alluded to his numerous publications, but I have said nothing before of his unparalleled contributions to the development of the Analytical Engine.

My first introduction to the Analytical Engine was in the late spring, shortly after the conclusion of one of the most ghastly adventures we had ever shared, which I have chronicled under the heading, "The Adventure of the Speckled Band." The entire day Holmes was in a mood that some would call taciturn. He was unsettled, smoked incessantly, played snatches on his violin, sank into reveries, and hardly answered the casual questions that I put to him. We sat through a silent dinner together, after which, pushing his plate aside, he revealed the problem that preoccupied him.

"You can never foretell what one mind will come up with, Watson, but you can say with precision what an average person will do. Individuals vary, but percentages remain constant. While we have not yet grasped the heights that the human mind can attain, it has its distinct limitations. Only particular persons can be trusted to produce the same chain of logical argument from one occasion to the next."

"I certainly wouldn't argue with you, Holmes," I replied. "But as yet we have found no suitable replacement for human reasoning."

"On the contrary, Watson," he answered nonchalantly. "Have you ever heard of the Analytical Engine?"

"I know of no substitute for the mind of man."

Holmes chuckled. "Then you must learn of it. This ingenious mechanism has displayed a considerable talent for deductive reasoning, far superior to that of the average logician. You recall my recent intervention in the matter of the note-book floating in the River Cam?"

"I am not likely to forget the sight of that bloated face staring up at me, Holmes," I replied, grimly considering the sorry state of mankind that such events should come to pass. "What connection has the late Professor Blackwell with this Engine?"

"Well, as you may remember, my investigation led me to the Cavendish laboratories. There I had occasion to study the Engine, if only briefly. Since then I have been in correspondence with the mathematicians at Cambridge who have been conducting experiments with it. Watson, I do not exaggerate when I say that the Analytical Engine is capable of solving, within minutes, complex numerical problems that would keep five of London's finest mathematicians working for hours. Furthermore, it is adept at logic and has a perfect memory for detail.

"The Engine also has its limits," he continued. "It can undertake only problems whose solu-

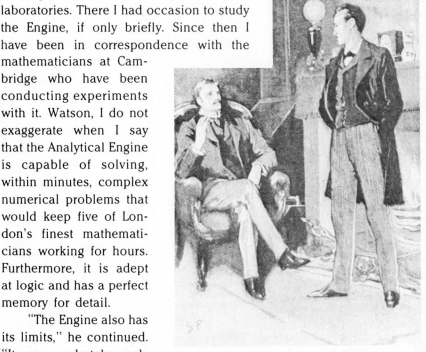

"HAVE YOU EVER HEARD OF
THE ANALYTICAL ENGINE?"

tions are spelled out in minute detail and presented in its own peculiar language."

"Really, Holmes, sometimes you go too far with my patience!" I exclaimed. "You expect me to believe that this device is capable of solving problems, has a perfect memory, and actually speaks a language of its own?"

"No, no, my dear Watson, you take me too literally. The Analytical Engine does indeed have a language of its own, but it does not speak, nor can it be spoken to; communications must be written out."

"Now you tell me it can read?"

"In a sense, yes."

I threw up my arm.

"I fear I am going too fast for you, Watson. Everything I say is true, but let me assure you that the Analytical Engine hardly resembles a human being. Its 'language' is actually a highly logical code, designed by mathematicians. This code is not difficult to master, but it does require considerable discipline. It has a very small vocabulary, which one arranges into statements according to a limited set of rules.

"The major problem in communicating with the Engine is that one must use the utmost care and precision in giving it instructions, for it has no imagination whatsoever and cannot correct even trivial errors in spelling or punctuation. It is, after all, like other machines in that it has no awareness of the tasks that it performs; therefore it will obey the most unreasonable instructions. For example, if it is told to print the number zero *ad infinitum,* it will continue to do so for hours on end, until a human being finally causes it to stop."

"But Holmes, how does one give instructions to this Engine?" I asked, scarcely crediting my companion's remarks thus far and wondering whether perhaps his penchant for cocaine had finally betrayed his reason.

"By writing a set of instructions in code and supplying them mechanically to the Engine. Such a set of instructions is called a *programme,* because it is an orderly and precise procedure for solving a problem. The art of writing programmes is called, reasonably enough, *programming.*"

"What relevance has this strange machine to you, Holmes?"

"I intend to employ the Engine whenever possible in my future criminal cases," he replied. "As you know, I have been rather overburdened with work in recent months. The Engine's speed and potential accuracy are most attractive to me. It has a great capacity for dealing with voluminous amounts of information as well."

"But, Holmes," I interrupted, "do you truly expect this device, if it is as unimaginative as you say, to solve crimes?"

"Not at all, my dear Watson," said Holmes with a laugh. "It is by no means clever enough to replace my brain; but it will be useful for storing information and for performing certain repetitive tasks that absorb too much of my time. You know of my interest in finding a means for expressing my logical methods in a rigorous form. The Engine may be useful in communicating to others my modest attempts at formulating a Science of Deduction."

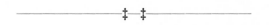

1.1 Commentary

Many people view computers as a product of our modern age. Actually, the English mathematician Charles Babbage and his collaborator, Lady Augusta Ada Lovelace (Lord Byron's daughter), between them worked out most of the fundamental principles upon which modern computing is based.

Babbage's Analytical Engine was designed in the mid 1800's but never actually built. It was intended for calculating mathematical tables. At the time, the Engine was considered too costly and the project was never funded. But its similarities to contemporary computers are striking. Babbage foresaw the use of punched cards to enter data, the internal mechanisms that perform computations, and a device for printing results. The Analytical Engine was indeed a direct forerunner of today's computers.

As Holmes observed, that primitive model already revealed the promises and pitfalls of the contemporary computer. The promises — the ability to handle great amounts of data, to remember even the tiniest detail, to make extremely accurate calculations, and to obey instructions over and over again — have all been fulfilled. So, alas, have the less well recognized pitfalls — the often endless details that must be resolved, the intolerance of error, the machine's annoying idiosyncrasies, and the need for unremitting rigor on the part of the user.

Your first attempt at using a computer is likely to be a frustrating experience. The precision to which Holmes alludes is quite unfamiliar to most people. You must struggle to piece together a variety of computer instructions, making changes almost randomly and hoping somehow it will work. You might enter a line like

```
PRINT THE ANSWER
```

and expect the computer to print the correct result. This will not happen. More than likely, the computer will respond with a message like

```
*** 'THE' IS NOT A LEGAL SEPARATOR; COMMAND IGNORED.
```

To get a computer to do your bidding, you must tell it precisely what you want it to do in exactly the right way.

When you instruct a computer properly, you have at your command a kind of modern genie. For example, this entire book has been typed on a specialized computer called a *word processor*. This made it possible for us to modify the text in small and large ways and then print out revised versions quickly for study and further improvement. When we finished revising the manuscript, it reproduced our text in a form that enabled another computer to typeset the book automatically. Babbage would be especially satisfied if he were alive today, for it was his desire to eliminate error from tide tables that led him to develop the Difference Engine from which the Analytical Engine evolved. In fact, this early computer was designed to set type for the printing of the tables.

In the chapters that follow, Holmes will introduce you to some elementary concepts about computers. You do not need to use a computer to understand these concepts. The objective is to help you develop a certain computer "literacy," an understanding of some fundamental aspects of the computer technology.

In the first episode, "The Adventure of the Abacus," you will be introduced to some of the basic elements of the computer itself. You will learn how a computer stores data and how its internal mechanisms work.

In the next episode, Holmes writes an algorithm. The concept of an algorithm is one of the most fundamental ideas in computer programming. Having introduced the subject, Holmes then presents his algorithm coded in Basic, one of the artificial languages created for writing computer programs.

CHARLES BABBAGE

LADY LOVELACE

The uses for computers vary widely. In the thirty or so years since modern computer technology was introduced, they have come closer and closer to our everyday lives. Today word processors, personal computers, and terminals that connect to large computer systems are commonplace. The rudimentary ideas behind these are taken up in Chapters VI through VIII. In Chapter IX Holmes discusses perhaps the largest failure of computer technology, the neglect in adapting computers to human needs.

Chapter X, written for those who are more theoretically minded, discusses Turing machines and the implications on the ultimate limitations of computers. We conclude with "The Adventure of the Red Queen's Race." This episode brings up two topics of general importance— some long range objectives of computer technology and a discussion of what computers can and cannot do.

CHAPTER II

‡

The Adventure of the Abacus

(Part I)

E WERE accustomed to receiving urgent letters and telegrams at Baker Street, but I have a particular recollection of one that reached us on a wet and gloomy September morning some four or five years ago. Holmes quickly scanned a sheet of thick note-paper and, with an exclamation of impatience, pushed it across the table to me. "This came by the morning post, Watson."

The note, postmarked "Cambridge," the preceding evening, read :—

Dear Mr. Holmes,

It is imperative that I meet with you on a matter of the greatest concern to the security of the nation. I shall call at your Baker Street quarters at noon, the 10th of September.

—James Manning, Professor of Mathematics

"Why, this fellow hasn't even the courtesy to ask for a reply," I said. "What will you do?"

"Meet with him, I suppose," replied Holmes. "After all, this appeal to patriotic duty leaves us little choice. It is now nearly eleven, and he writes that he will arrive by noon today."

I returned the note to Holmes. As he put it back into its envelope, another page dropped to the top of the table.

"Hullo, this is interesting," said Holmes, quickly examining the paper and passing it for my inspection. It was a rough chart of some sort and looked like this :—

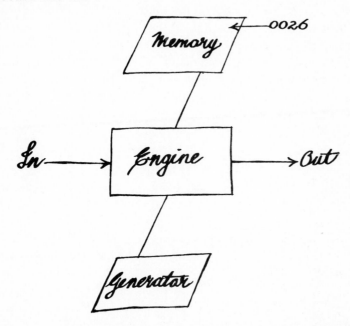

"This makes as little sense as his note," I replied. "He is certainly one for cryptic messages. Mind you, I wouldn't——" I began but was struck speechless as Holmes turned and, leaning out of his chair, transfixed the remainder of his unopened correspondence to the mantelpiece with his jack-knife.

"Mrs. Hudson will surely send us notice to quit," I protested, but Holmes held up his hand to command silence.

"Is our visitor an hour early?" he asked. "No, unless I miss my guess, we are about to receive our friend Lestrade, and on official business, I might add."

A moment later our landlady showed the sallow, sharp-faced Scotland Yard official into our rooms. As Holmes rose to greet him, I took up a position in front of the fireplace to conceal my companion's handiwork.

"Ah, good morning, Inspector. You're just in time for a cup of tea," said Holmes with bluff bonhomie, as Lestrade sat at the table and took out his official note-book. "You must have something remarkable on hand."

"Yes, nasty business. You've heard then?" queried the Inspector.

"No, but those splashes of mud on your trouser-legs and your hurried step would suggest this is not a social call."

"Indeed it is not," snapped Lestrade. "I've no time to waste. I believe in hard work, not in spinning theories. I'm here to request that you accompany me immediately to Cambridge."

"I'm afraid I cannot accommodate you, Inspector. I am expecting a client within the hour, a Cambridge man as a matter of fact. Perhaps you could shed some light on this business." Holmes handed the letter to Lestrade, who appeared as surprised as I that Holmes should seek his assistance.

"What the devil!" exclaimed Lestrade, once he had read the letter. "Why, this is the very man!"

Holmes strolled over to the corner of the mantelpiece where, carefully dried and collected, lay the plugs and dottles from his smokes of the previous day. With these he began filling his pipe.

"If you would take a moment, Inspector, to elaborate the circumstances of this extraordinary coincidence, I could perhaps be of some assistance."

"LESTRADE TOOK OUT HIS OFFICIAL NOTE-BOOK."

"The circumstances, Mr. Holmes," said the Inspector, "are that your Professor Manning was found this morning on the floor of his study by a colleague, Trevor Seabury. He'd been shot at close range. Now I don't think he'll be keeping that appointment. However, if you're unable to come along——"

"Well, Watson," said Holmes, turning to me, "there is, if I remember correctly, a hotel called the Garden House where the port used to be above mediocrity, and the linen above reproach. It would appear, Doctor, that our lot for the next few days might lie in less pleasant places."

And so it happened that two hours later we found ourselves in the corner of a first-class carriage, flying along, *en route* to Cambridge.

"It would clear matters up considerably, Inspector," said Holmes, "if you were to fill me in on the nature of Professor Manning's work. I assume he was conducting research for Whitehall?"

"I'm afraid that's not something I am authorized to discuss with you, Mr. Holmes," replied Lestrade.

"In other words, they didn't take you into their confidence."

"I can tell you this much, as you'll see once we arrive. Your brother is involved. It was at his wish that you've been invited into the case. We've no reason to suspect robbery since nothing appears to be missing. There are powder stains on his jacket, so we know he was shot at close range, possibly by someone he knew. Then there's the business of the abacus."

"The abacus?"

"Yes, very queer indeed," replied Lestrade, knowing that this singular feature would arouse Holmes's curiosity. "He was found clutching a small abacus, one of those Chinese figuring devices. I left explicit orders that nothing was to be touched. I know you like to examine things for yourself. But I can tell you, Mr. Holmes, I myself, along with my best men, have combed through everything and there's neither head nor tail to be made of it."

There was little further discussion between the two detectives for the remainder of our journey. We were met at the station by an exceedingly alert man, retaining the erect bearing of one accustomed to official uniform; I recognised him as Lestrade's colleague, Stanley Hopkins.

Inspector Hopkins had enquired into the matter of the abacus and discovered that it was a gift from an Italian associate. This led Lestrade to suggest the Italian as a suspect. After a brief discussion of the point, Holmes and I were escorted by Hopkins to a small antechamber outside Manning's private rooms. My companion's portly brother, Mycroft Holmes, opened the door and beckoned us to enter.

"Has the coroner had a look yet?" asked Holmes.

"No," replied Mycroft.

"We are fortunate, then, that you came along, Watson. Would you care to lend Her Majesty your medical expertise?"

"Most certainly," I replied, and Mycroft Holmes led us into the study.

The room, lined with old book cases, was littered with hundreds of small chits of paper. They were all of uniform size and a dull buff in colour. Sherlock Holmes stooped down and removed one, making certain not to disturb the others. It was heavier than ordinary paper; small holes, each the same size, were punched across it in a seemingly random fashion.

Before an unlit fireplace lay the body of Professor Manning, the abacus held tightly to his chest. There were no signs of injury save the fatal wound to his left breast. The wound was a clean one, and unusually small for a bullet hole. I remarked on this fact, whereupon Sherlock Holmes knelt beside the corpse and confirmed my observation.

"We shall have to wait for the coroner's report to be certain," said he, "but even our cursory examination leads me to believe that the murder weapon was a pistol of a smaller than normal calibre, perhaps an American .25 calibre Colt pistol, which is small enough to be concealed in a man's waistcoat pocket."

Holmes carefully pried the dead man's fingers loose from the abacus and its blood-stained leather case. He placed the curious little device on the late Professor's desk, which was covered with much larger papers containing mathematical equations and what appeared to be engineering calculations.

"Here," said Holmes, pointing to the abacus, "is one of the earliest tools for carrying out mathematical computations. Invented somewhere in Asia thousands of years ago, the abacus was introduced into Western Civilization ten centuries ago by Gerbert, who later became Pope Sylvester II. It is a base-ten calculator, similar to those found in ancient Egypt. Numbers were represented by pebbles in grooves. With the abacus, lead beads were strung on these parallel wires representing ones, tens, hundreds and so forth. Our very word 'calculate' comes from the Latin word *calculus,* meaning an abacus pebble.

"Roman numerals were very much in vogue during Gerbert's day, but they were difficult to use with basic mathematical operations. A number system was devised to represent the contents of the abacus and wires to facilitate the calculations. With the advent of Arabic numerals in Europe a short time later, calculating itself became easier and the abacus was considered a toy.

"Even with Arabic numerals, numbers were long considered important for what they symbolized rather than as numerals that could be combined in mathematical operations. Three and six, for instance, were thought to contain the secrets of Nature."

"This is all quite fascinating Holmes," I interjected, "but what does it have to do with the affair at hand?"

"That is precisely what we must discover, Watson," said my friend. "I'll want to examine this room very carefully. It is absolutely paramount to my investigation that this abacus remain exactly as it is now, untouched by anyone."

Holmes took a seat at a table and thoughtfully studied the case of the abacus. Hopkins and I stood behind him and gazed at it also, waiting for him to speak. Finally, he rose and with a pocket-lens began to survey the top of Manning's desk and the papers that lay scattered about, pausing to make several notations.

"HOPKINS AND I GAZED AT IT ALSO."

"Am I correct, Mycroft" he said at last, "in deducing that Professor Manning was engaged in the construction of the Analytical Engine?"

"You are."

"Surely, Mycroft, you know that the Professor has spelled out the name of his assailant in numerical code on this abacus, an elementary task for your talents. Why, pray, have I been summoned?"

"You've looked at the desk?" asked Mycroft.

"Yes. You chose not to inform Inspector Lestrade of the theft?"

"I thought it best to await your arrival before broaching that subject."

"Diplomatic papers?"

"The Russian or German Embassy would pay a princely sum for the document Professor Manning had encoded for us," Mycroft Holmes replied gravely.

"There is only a faint reminder in the air now," continued Sherlock Holmes, pacing around the cramped study like a foxhound flushing its quarry. "There are seventy-five perfumes. It is essential that a criminal expert be able to distinguish each from the others."

"The scent," said Mycroft, "was no stronger when I arrived than it is now."

Sherlock Holmes turned his attention to the floor. From his pocket he produced the card he had picked up earlier.

"I've read of these in my research. Herman Hollerith's mechanism for recording the American census, unless I am mistaken?"

"Indeed," said Mycroft. "Perhaps I should explain how they were used in the Professor's work." He picked up a card from the floor. Holding it in one hand, he pointed out its features.

"The information entered into the Analytical Engine—in this case international treaties and other diplomatic papers—is stored on these cards by use of a numerical code. The code itself is not very complicated, as you will see. All the data for the Engine, in fact, are represented by a sequence of zeroes and ones."

"Ha," said Sherlock Holmes. "Binary code."

"Precisely," said Mycroft.

"Excuse me," I put in. "That may make sense to you but it means absolutely nothing to me."

"You are aware, Watson," Mycroft continued, "that our number system, and that of the abacus, is a decimal one. That is, it is based on groups of ten. Ten separate symbols represent the basic numerals; these are combined to represent the larger numbers.

"In a binary system there only two numerals, zero and one; these numerals in combination represent all other numbers. Counting is done by groups of two instead of groups of ten. Here, let me show you." Mycroft Holmes took a sheet of paper and wrote out the following table:

0 — 0	7 — 111
1 — 1	8 — 1000
2 — 10	
3 — 11	16 — 10000
4 — 100	32 — 100000
5 — 101	64 — 1000000
6 — 110	

"The powers of increase in a binary system are not powers of ten, but rather powers of two: zero or one, then two, four, eight, sixteen, and so on. Six, for example, is represented as 110, meaning one times four, plus one times two, plus zero. Other values are represented as you see in the table."

"But," said I, "Professor Manning was working with worded documents, not numbers. How can words be used in this binary system?"

"Manning devised a cipher for that purpose, Doctor," said Mycroft. "The card, as you can see, is arranged in columns and rows. Each of these columns represents a sequence of bits. The word 'bit' is the mathematicians' abbreviation for 'binary digit.'

"The cipher gives each letter of the alphabet its own binary code. The letter 'A,' for instance, is represented by the sequence 1000001, 'B' as 1000010, and 'C' as 1000011, and so forth. Bear with me for a moment," he added as I sighed audibly.

"This code is depicted on the card by means of these holes punched into it. A punched hole represents a 1, and the absence of a hole represents a 0. The entire sequence of bits for a letter, a numeral, a punctuation mark, or any piece of data is thus spelled out on the card.

"When this enters the Engine, a light is flashed on one side of the card. Only where there is a hole will light come through. This is read as a '1,' while the absence of light is interpreted as a '0.' The light-sensing mechanism inside the Engine converts this information into usable data."

"Good heavens!" I cried, quite involuntarily. "Whatever will they think of next?"

"Some other mechanism to record data, I hope," snapped Sherlock Holmes as he let the card drop from his hand. It sailed a short distance across the room and then gently settled down among the hundreds more that covered nearly half the room.

2.1   Representing Data

A computer can store all kinds of data—a person's name, a telephone number, a hair color, the number of feet to the scene of a crime, or the fact that a bank balance is in the red. It can also store a program ready to run, the text of a book, or a code to turn off the lights at ten o'clock. Such information is as varied as you can imagine. The question is, how can the computer be made to know such things.

To get to the bottom of this matter, we turn to *binary* notation. Consider the following sequence of 0's and 1's.

10010 00111 00100 10001 01011 01110 00010 01010

This strange looking sequence is typical of the way many computers spell the name SHERLOCK. In computer parlance, this is a binary representation of the letters S,H,E,R,L,O,C, and K.

Most people, of course, don't use binary notation because it is nearly impossible to read and use. For the computer, however, binary is just the thing. At the heart of the circuitry of any computer is the mechanism of a "switch." Such a switch has many forms, but their essence is a device that can be in one of two states. You may think of such states as being "open" or "closed," "on" or "off," "positive" or "negative." This basic fact, and the ease with which a computer can set or reset a switch, leads quite naturally to the concept of a binary system, the system of 0's and 1's.

In the next chapter we will have more to say on how the computer makes use of a binary system. For now we make one basic point: *All* information and data stored in a computer can be represented in binary form. What this means is that there is no mystery about how the computer can know about such diverse things as people's names, telephone numbers, and hair color.

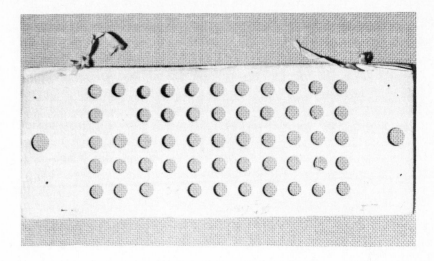

Original Punched Card of Charles Babbage

Take, for example, the following table:

A	00000	J	01001	S	10010
B	00001	K	01010	T	10011
C	00010	L	01011	U	10100
D	00011	M	01100	V	10101
E	00100	N	01101	W	10111
F	00101	O	01110	X	11000
G	00110	P	01111	Y	11001
H	00111	Q	10000	Z	11010
I	01000	R	10001		

Here the 26 letters of the alphabet are each given a different binary value, 00000 for A, 00001 for B, 00010 for C, and so on. The combinations from 00000 to 11111 allow 2^5 (or 32) possibilities, of which 26 are used above. Each binary digit is called a *bit* and the above scheme is called a five-bit code.

Consider, also, the following table:

0	0000	5	0101
1	0001	6	0111
2	0010	7	1000
3	0011	8	1001
4	0100	9	1010

Here each of the decimal digits 0 through 9 is given a different binary value, 0000 for 0, 0001 for 1, 0010 for 2, and so on.

Next consider:

Red	000	Blue	100
Orange	001	Violet	101
Yellow	010	Brown	110
Green	011	Black	111

Here eight different colors are again represented as binary values.

Finally, consider the following innocuous table:

In the red	0
In the black	1

in which the state of a bank balance is coded in binary. The next step in refining this would be to express how much we are in the red or black by giving a suitable code representing the amount.

Many applications require that computers "know" about the outside world through some sort of sensor. Such an application might control the temperature in a building or the flight path of a spaceship. To communicate to the computer what the sensor is "feeling" requires a special type of electronic device called a "convertor."

A convertor changes the sensor's signal to a voltage, which in turn is measured and used to generate a binary number representing the level of the signal sensed. This is done very quickly, taking less than 100 microseconds per signal for most devices of this kind. Some are much faster, and much more expensive. By using such convertors with a computer, actions can be controlled to a very high degree of precision, resulting in economies of time and resources that could be only dreamed of before.

The ASCII Standard Binary Code

The tables above suggest that there are all kinds of ways of using binary notation. If every computer had its own method of coding binary, we would be in a bit of a fix, just as we would if every electrical wall outlet were a different size.

Fortunately, there are a number of binary codes in common use; the most widespread of these is ASCII (*A*merican *S*tandard *C*ode for *I*nformation *I*nterchange). The next most common is EBCDIC (*E*xtended *B*inary *C*oded *D*ecimal *I*nterchange *C*ode), which is used on IBM equipment. Many other devices also use it so that data can be transferred to and from IBM systems. Older systems have very strange code conventions, such as the five bit Baudot code used on old teletypes.

Appendix A lists all of the ASCII binary codes, their decimal equivalents, and the characters they represent. Notice, for instance, that the numeric code for the uppercase letter "A" is 1000001, or 65 in decimal, and the code for the lowercase letter "a" is 97. The code for the character "1" is not 1, but 49. Notice, also, the appearance of nonprinting characters, such as BEL or CR. These characters have various uses, depending on your computer. For instance, the character BEL makes a bell ring on a terminal (if the computer has one) and CR is used for a carriage return.

Normally, you need not be particularly concerned with the details of ASCII, unless you are doing some fancy programming. The important thing is that you have a standard scheme for representing information in a form suitable to a computer.

Most coding schemes are implemented by using 8 bits. This is because modern computers move multiples of 8 bits at a time, normally 8, 16, or 32 bits. The amount of data moved at one time is usually called a "word."

The use of 8 bits is so common that it has the special name "byte." Most small computers move one byte at a time so it is convenient to use a full byte to represent a character. Devices using ASCII or EBCDIC generally use the full byte; ASCII machines often use the eighth bit, which is not needed for the character codes, as a redundancy bit for detecting errors in transmission.

2.2   Computer Memory

A central feature of every computer is its ability to store data. There are many kinds of data—that provided by the user, tables of information needed by the computer itself, or the millions of instructions that control the computer's behavior. Computer data fall into one of two categories: *external,* which means they are needed only when a particular program is run and thus may be stored elsewhere; or *internal,* which means they are needed inside the computer. Methods for storing external data will be treated in the following section. Here we concentrate on internal data, that stored in the computer's "memory."

Early computer memories were made from magnetic core rings, and many still are. Such computer memory is constructed of thousands of doughnut-shaped magnetic cores threaded in a grid of tiny wires. They can be made so minute that over five thousand cores fit in a thimble. Figure 2.1 illustrates four such cores. Each core is magnetized in either a clockwise or counter-clockwise direction, giving us either a 1 or a 0. The cores are arranged in a computer's memory so that a given sequence of bits (the data) can be obtained immediately.

Despite their widespread use, magnetic core rings have given way to the rapidly changing solid state technology and the now famous "silicon chip." A silicon chip is a very tiny configuration of transistors arranged in a grid. A binary 1 is represented by a small electrical charge, and a binary 0 by its absence.

The chip's advantage in storage capacity is one of astounding proportions. A Mostek MK 4116 silicon chip, about the size of a piece of confetti, can store 16,384 bits. Access to the data is so fast that a large-scale computer could read the contents of this book (assuming it were suitably coded in binary) in less than a second. Newer chips can store 64K (computer jargon for 64,000) and even 256K bits. Eventually problems with material impurity, cracks, and so forth will limit this growth, but a 64K chip was not even a dream a decade or so ago when micro-processor technology was created.

Lest these facts dazzle you, keep in mind that this book was prepared on a small computer with a video screen. The text of the book was stored as external data on a "floppy disk" (a technology we will discuss shortly). Simply to read each page into the computer's memory and display each page on the screen would take a good half hour.

The technology of computer hardware, the internal machinery and computer memory, has changed dramatically over the years. It will probably continue to do so, but the underlying principles are still simple.

2.3   Storing Data

Binary notation is the basis for almost every method of recording data for computer use. A half decade before the advent of computer technology, Herman Hollerith invented a scheme for automating census tabulations. In this scheme, which was a modification of the code already developed by Samuel Morse, the census data was directly represented in binary form. The code quickly became a success, and when the computer technology was later developed, the Hollerith code was widely adopted for recording computer data.

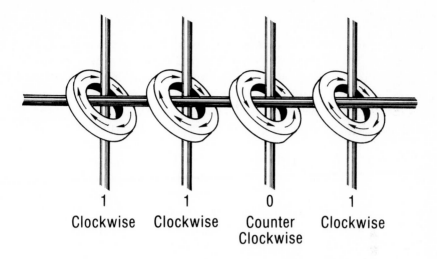

| 1 | 1 | 0 | 1 |
| Clockwise | Clockwise | Counter Clockwise | Clockwise |

Figure 2.1   *Magnetic Cores with Read-Write Wires*

Hollerith's Tabulator-Listing Machine, 1924

Punched Cards

In the early years of computing, Hollerith's code was most often associated with the famous "punched card." The card was about the size of a dollar bill so that money-handling equipment, widely and cheaply available, could be used to handle the large number of cards usually generated. Newer versions of the punch card, most notably those introduced by IBM, attempt to get more information on small cards.

With a punched card, the coding method is roughly as follows. The card is made of a thin piece of cardboard-like material, usually three inches by nine inches. It is divided into rows, say 10 rows; each row is further divided into columns, say 80 columns, making 800 different positions on the card. Each position can be punched out to make a small hole. A given position is either punched or unpunched, i.e., either 1 or 0.

Consider the simple example illustrated in Figure 2.2. Here columns 8 and 9 of row 2 record the sex of a person. A punch in column 8 identifies a female, a punch in column 9 identifies a male.

More typically, a standard encoding scheme like ASCII is used, as in Figure 2.3. Here the upper seven positions in each column record the binary equivalent of an ASCII character. The letter S, for example, has a binary code of 1010011, so holes are punched in rows 1, 3, 6, and 7 of the first column.

Once the data is encoded on a punched card, usually with a keypunch machine, it can be read into the computer's memory. For this operation a device called a card reader is used. The presence or absence of a hole is converted into electrical impulses representing 1's and 0's. Small wire brushes or a light-sensing mechanism do the required conversion. A fast card reader can read more than a thousand cards per minute.

The punched card system exemplifies the value of all methods for recording data. Once the form of the data is fixed, a suitable binary scheme for encoding can be devised. Data can then be recorded, preserved, and if need be, taken home and put into safe keeping. When desired, the data can be read by a computer.

Punched cards are, of course, bulky, heavy to carry, apt to be spilled on the floor, bent, torn, or easily burned. Users have been known to have boxes and boxes of them. The rise of sophisticated computer technology has led to other ways of recording data.

One of these is popular for applications that require immediate input. You have probably used these cards when you "darken the

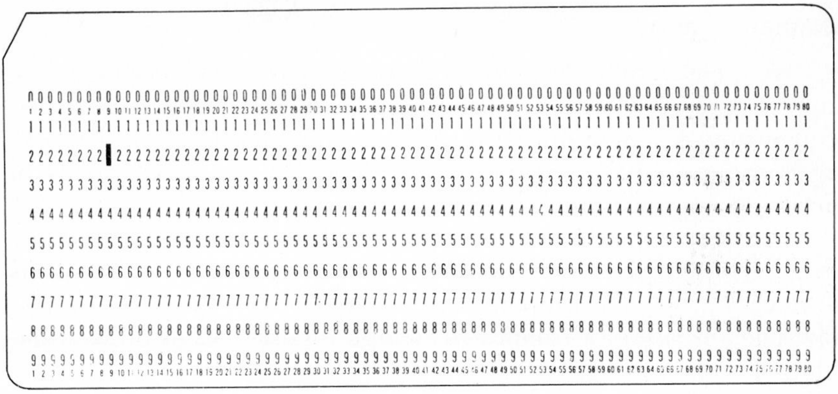

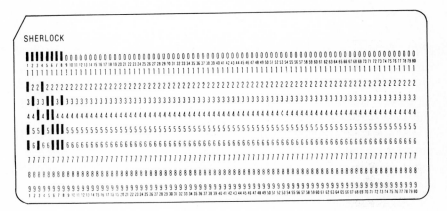

Figure 2.2   *A Punched Card*

Figure 2.3   *ASCII Codes on a Punched Card*

appropriate square" with a pencil. A photocell notices the difference between the light paper and the dark pencil mark, telling the computer which mark was darkened. Some personal computers use these cards, opening up many novel uses. Badge and credit-card readers, for example, read a strip of magnetic tape on the card itself, informing the computer of the content of the card without examining the print on the front.

On most computers, however, one of two other methods is used— magnetic tape or disks.

Magnetic Tape

We are all familiar with musical recordings on magnetic tape. The tape is organized into parallel tracks, and the music is recorded sequentially. A similar format is used for computer data, only the data are encoded digitally, in binary. Incidentally, digital recordings of music are not uncommon.

Consider Figure 2.4. This hypothetical tape fragment shows the word SHERLOCK encoded in ASCII. The 1's indicate tiny fragments in which the magnetic properties of the tape are set in a predetermined way. The absence of a 1 indicates the opposite setting. Again, you can think of a blank as representing a 0.

Like a punched card, or for that matter any other recording medium, a magnetic tape must be read into a computer with a special device. For large tapes this means a "tape drive," and for small tapes held in a cassette, a cassette reader similar to the tape player in a stereo music system.

Tapes can store large amounts of data in a fairly compressed form. Some systems can even store the equivalent of two million punched cards on a single tape. Different methods of encoding the information on the tapes have been used, each trying to achieve more storage space. At higher densities, however, more errors are likely, and the error-checking must be better.

One major drawback is that the tape must be read in sequence. If the data you want happens to be at the end, you may have to wait a few minutes to get it. When working on a computer terminal where you are accustomed to immediate responses, reading data from tapes becomes very tedious. This brings us to magnetic disks.

Magnetic Disks

In a magnetic disk system, a piece of data can be obtained without reading what has gone before. While the time needed to get a piece of data from a disk is much greater than it is to get data stored in the computer's internal memory, the time is much less than using punched cards or magnetic tape.

Consider Figure 2.5. The disk is divided into concentric magnetic rings, called tracks, similar to a phonograph record. As before, data are electronically recorded in binary form. The key idea is that data on a given track can be read directly, just as you can listen to a certain section of music by putting the phonograph arm on the middle of a record. Again, special equipment is needed, but that is always the case with computers.

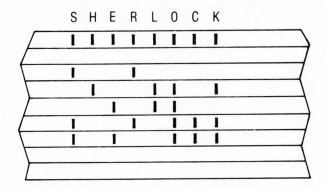

Figure 2.4 *Coding on Magnetic Tape*

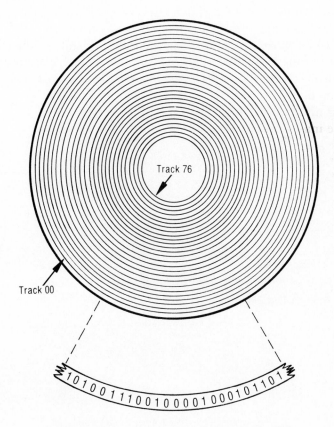

Figure 2.5 *The Surface of a Magnetic Disk*

A large variety of disk systems are now in common use. On a small computer, a disk may be the size of a 45 rpm record, and the disk reader may be part of the computer itself. This is the ubiquitous "floppy" disk, illustrated in Figure 2.6. On a large computer, there may be many disks inside a special disk unit the size of a large piece of furniture. Obviously, capacity for storing data and speed of access can vary just as greatly.

Table 2.1 lists some properties of the devices mentioned above. Some of the speeds and storage capacities may seem large by everyday standards, but not necessarily from a computer standpoint. Remember, if you're keeping track of all the accounts in a bank or writing a book on a computer, you will need a good deal of storage. And if you're using an airline reservation system or electronic mail system, even the programs needed to operate the system may be huge. Social Security, the IRS, and the FBI, for instance, all have large disk-storage systems with tens of billions of bytes available for immediate recall and usually a spare copy on magnetic tape.

All of this gets down to a single fact—any kind of data can be encoded in binary and recorded in computer readable form.

Figure 2.6 *Inserting a Floppy Disk*

Table 2.1
Typical Properties of Devices for Storing Data

Box of Punched Cards

Type of Access:	Sequential
Storage Capacity:	80,000 characters per box
Reading Speed:	two or three minutes per box
Notes:	Normally a box of punched cards contains a thousand cards

Standard Tape Cassette

Type of Access:	Sequential
Storage Capacity:	256,000 characters per cassette
Reading Speed:	several minutes per cassette
Notes:	Figures for standard audio-type cassettes on a personal computer

Reel of Magnetic Tape

Type of Access:	Sequential
Storage Capacity:	46 million characters
Reading Speed:	4 minutes per reel
Notes:	Figures are for a 2400 foot reel of tape on an IBM 3420 Model 5

Floppy Disk

Type of Access:	Direct
Storage Capacity:	300,000 characters
Reading Speed:	30 seconds per disk
Notes:	Figures are for an 8-inch floppy disk on a conventional word processor

Hard Disk Pack

Type of Access:	Direct
Storage Capacity:	20 to 40 million characters
Reading Speed:	2 minutes per disk
Notes:	Figures are for an 8-inch Winchester-type disk unit

CHAPTER III

‡

The Adventure of the Abacus

(Part II)

N HOUR later found us in a large, lofty chamber filled with broad, low tables, shelves lined with test tubes, and even a dining table that confirmed the Professor's rumoured habit of eating and calculating at the same time. We were led, in the company of Mycroft Holmes, to the far end of the room and into a much smaller space where charts covered with intricate calculations hung from the walls. At the centre of the room, as if on display, sat a contraption much like a weaver's device. It was made of wood and metal and topped with numerous gears and dials.

"The fruit of the Professor's labours and many great minds before him," said Mycroft by way of introduction.

"Babbage's Engine," said Sherlock.

"Yes, but with some amendments," replied his brother.

"And what, exactly, was Professor Manning's contribution?"

"He supervised the construction of the Engine, but his real work lay in its application," explained Mycroft. He took a note-book from a small table at one side of the machine and presented it to his brother. "Using the symbolic logic developed by George Boole, the Professor was working on a new system for communicating instructions directly to the Engine—machine language programmes, he called them."

Sherlock Holmes began dipping into the book when something caught his attention. "The Professor was a bachelor, I see." His brother nodded.

"The notes in this margin and at the bottom of this page were no doubt written by another," Sherlock Holmes continued. "The shape of the 'a' in 'and,' as well as the 'o' in both 'not' and 'or,' when compared with the same words written elsewhere on this page, indicate the work of another hand. Furthermore, I draw your attention to the crossing of the 't' and the overall appearance of these words. A brief analysis would suggest that they were written by a woman."

"By Jove!" I cried, looking in amazement at this man who was forever confounding me with some new phase of his astuteness.

"There are, at first glance, sixteen other deductions we could make, but they would be of more interest to handwriting experts. Any thoughts, Mycroft, on whom this woman might be?"

"I think that I can solve that mystery for you," said a woman's voice.

We turned. By the table stood an attractive young lady, tall, graceful, and dressed in the most perfect taste. "Mr. Sherlock Holmes? Yes, I see the resemblance. I knew you would be along sooner or later once your brother had taken an interest in this unfortunate affair."

We remained quite speechless until Mycroft made the introductions. She was Lady Diana Seabury. Her husband, Professor Trevor Seabury, was a close associate of the late Professor Manning as well as the unlucky soul who discovered the murder.

"SHE WAS LADY DIANA SEABURY."

"Professor Manning's notes were often quite illegible," she continued. "As my husband was working so closely with him, I offered to rewrite many of them. I sometimes served as a secretary and handled their correspondence."

"Yes, I quite understand," said Sherlock Holmes. "But it appears on this page you've added a few thoughts of your own. I don't see this algorithm in the Professor's notes."

"I sometimes added my husband's work to the Professor's," she replied.

Holmes seemed satisfied with the answer and we were soon discussing other matters.

"I wonder," said he, "being as intimate as you are with your husband's work, if you could point out some of the Engine's features?"

"I can try, but, of course, I have only a primitive understanding of these things. This machine has hardly been given a thorough testing and is already considered antiquated. One idea spawns another, and it is amazing that the Engine was ever built as the plans were constantly being revised. But throughout these plans there remained four constants. Both my husband and Professor Manning felt that, despite the mechanical adjustments that might be made, these four will remain the basic functions of the Analytical Engine.

"What you see before you, gentlemen," she continued, "is merely an elaborate collection of switching devices. As complicated as it may appear, that's all there really is to the Engine. Each switch is in either the on or the off position, depending upon the particular task it has been instructed to carry out. Of these four functions, the first is the insertion of coded information into the Engine. This information, which must be presented to the Engine in a binary format, is actually a set of instructions telling which switches are to be turned on and which will remain off."

"The instructions are punched onto these cards?" asked Sherlock Holmes, as he produced the sample from his pocket.

"Yes, but already there are plans for using paper tapes," she replied. "They are much less cumbersome. But to continue, the second of these functions is a storing mechanism that allows the Engine to hold instructions, data, and partial results from calculations.

"At the heart of it all is what Mr. Babbage called the 'Mill.' This is the arithmetic unit, which actually does the computations on data. Although the Engine appears to carry out intricate calculations, all mathematical procedures, even complicated ones like analytical geometry, are reduced to simple operations such as addition and subtraction. The results of these operations can be routed to the temporary storage unit for retrieval at a later stage, sent back to control the next step in the calculation, or ejected from the Engine in a usable form. This last operation is much like the first. The Engine takes the results, decodes them from their binary form, and presents them in a form that its operator can use."

"Excellent!" cried Sherlock Holmes. "The Royal Society would benefit no end by your membership, Lady Diana. But tell me, what is it that makes the Engine automatic?"

"A control unit, Mr. Holmes. It gives the Engine its power of judgment. It reads the instructions of the programme, calls up information from the storage unit, and orders the flow of numbers. It not only allows for these mathematical calculations to take place, it makes logical judgments based on their results."

"What have we come to?" said I in disbelief.

"A conclusion," answered Sherlock Holmes. "Lady Diana, would it be reasonable to diagram these functions like this?"

Holmes turned to a blank page in the note-book and taking up a pen that lay nearby made the following sketch:

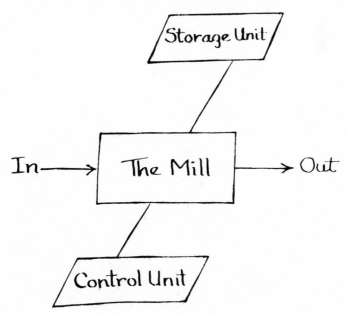

I recognised it immediately as similar to the diagram Professor Manning had enclosed in his communication to Holmes the morning of the murder.

"Yes," said Lady Diana, after examining the sketch, "this is very much like the design the Professor came up with himself."

"And if we were to diagram the workings of one particular unit, say, the storage unit, what might that look like?"

"Well," replied Lady Diana, "you might consider it as a series of post-boxes; each is assigned an address number and each contains a single piece of correspondence."

"Fascinating," said Holmes. "Now what would the order of these numbers be?"

"Nothing extraordinary," said she. "They begin with the number 0000 and run through 4095."

"It sounds childishly simple and yet so effective," said Holmes. "I wonder if we might have a demonstration and run through an illustrative number."

"Certainly. But I don't know how to operate the Engine myself. Perhaps my husband——"

"Splendid!" cried Holmes. "I'll leave those arrangements to you. Now I should like to return to Professor Manning's study. We can all meet here again in one hour if that is convenient."

"HE SIFTED THROUGH THE PAPERS."

This was agreeable to Mycroft and Lady Diana, and a short time later Holmes and I were once again at the scene of the crime. Manning's body had been removed, and his strong-box had been opened.

"Should you care to add this case to your annals, my dear Watson," said Holmes as he sifted through the papers, "I hope you will make very careful notes. We are dealing with a most intricate subject, this Engine. In the past you have erred, in my estimation, by attempting to put colour into your writings instead of setting to paper an accurate account of those incidents which have provided room for the faculties of deduction and logical synthesis."

Here was a sermon I had heard many times before, and with just cause, but I readily confessed that I observed neither cause nor effect between this Engine and Professor Manning's assassination.

"Yes, I suppose an apology and some explanation is in order," said Holmes. "I can barely expect to count on your continued assistance if I do not retrace our steps momentarily to show you the position from which we start. This is one of those particular cases, Doctor, where the art of the reasoner should be used for the sifting of details rather than for the acquiring of fresh evidence. I am convinced that the key to this entire mystery lies before us in this very room. Our task is to extract the framework of fact from the embellishment of theory in order to reveal the special points upon which this whole puzzle revolves."

Holmes set down the papers and picked up the abacus. "Let's begin with this novelty. It is a crucial piece of evidence as well as a perfect, though crude, example of the Professor's work.

"Though a much more complex mechanism, the Analytical Engine carries out the same basic functions as the abacus. Think of the Engine, Watson, as an extension of the human brain. A collection of carefully designed devices, it operates in two distinct ways. First, as a simple tool. Like our abacus, it carries out the basic computational functions such as addition and subtraction. Second, as an automatic tool. The Engine can direct those computations, taking over the function of control that the brain formerly supplied. This, of course, is well out of the realm of such a simple device as the abacus.

"These controls," he continued, "are carried out in one of two ways, depending upon the type of calculating device we are using. When physical quantities are used to represent numbers, such as the dials on Babbage's original Difference Engine or the positions on a slide-rule, we are speaking of an analog device. On the other hand, objects used to represent numbers, like the abacus, are known as digital devices. Such machines are universal and limited not to one function, but only by the particular programme in use at any one time."

"But why should we want something more elaborate when this simple calculator will suffice?" I asked.

"That is not always the case," replied Holmes. "For simple calculations of a reasonable length the Engine is a waste of time. It would, in fact, be wiser to use an adding machine, a slide-rule, an abacus, or even to do the work oneself. However, let us suppose we were faced with a recurring problem that could be solved over and over, using different sets of facts each time. We may want the Engine to complete a calculation, say, and return to the first step.

"Then there is the question of accuracy and human error. As our Engine is not prone to sentiment or distraction, we are guaranteed the highest accuracy. Let us say we wanted to produce nautical or trigonometric tables, both extremely long lists of figures. There is bound to be error if the task is left to some fellow equally concerned that his pipe will go out or that his tea will get cold. We also need to store large amounts of information on which we can call to carry out a particular calculation, or series of calculations.

"On an investigation such as this, once there is some slight indication of the course of events, I am able to guide myself by the thousands of other similar cases that will occur to my memory. Scotland Yard is not so fortunate, as each man is not so well versed in the history of our profession. With so many cases spread out among so many investigators there is little opportunity for comparing notes. Imagine, Watson, if all those facts could be committed to *one* memory, one memory that all criminal investigators could query at *any* time. Imagine, too, if we could pre-assemble the formulae for cracking the most intricate codes and puzzles and slip them into our Engine whenever needed."

"Why, you might find yourself without business, Holmes," I ventured.

"Oh, hardly, Watson. The Engine may take over the labour of synthetic reasoning. But in the end, decisions must be made by those who can reason analytically. Remember, Watson, that the Engine can work only with the particular facts that its operator has had the forethought to put into it."

We were interrupted by the appearance of Inspector Lestrade. "You come at a crucial moment, Inspector," said Holmes. "Perhaps you will accompany us to the Professor's laboratory and bring with you a note-book. I believe you may receive a confession of sorts before the afternoon is finished.''

It was now nearly five o'clock on a cold and dark September afternoon. A sharp wind brought with it a fine rain as we made our way across the University lawns to the conclusion of this case, which was as much a mystery to me as was this Engine upon which so much seemed to depend.

The stage was set, with Holmes, the master dramatist, loth to communicate his plans until the instant of their fulfillment. As we entered the laboratory his eyes shone with a steely glitter and his cheeks were tinged with colour.

Lady Diana was in the company of a thin, bespectacled gentleman many years her elder, who was introduced to us as her husband, Professor Trevor Seabury.

"I do hope I can be of some assistance to you, Mr. Holmes," said he, "though I cannot imagine how."

"A demonstration of the Engine's capabilities may prove invaluable to the solution of this case," said Holmes. "I am hoping you could run a random number through," he continued, scribbling something out on a sheet from his note-book, "to show us how the unit for storing data operates." Holmes tore the paper from his book and gave it to the Professor, who examined it momentarily and agreed to run it through.

"I'm not certain we'll find anything in this particular track," he cautioned as he seated himself before the Engine. We waited in silence.

"Why, this is extraordinary!" cried Seabury a few moments later as he looked over the results. "This track holds my name in storage!"

"No, Professor, it isn't your name," said Holmes. "The Seabury stored on this track refers to your wife. Isn't that correct, Lady Diana?"

"I am inclined to think, Mr. Holmes——" she began, but Sherlock Holmes cut her off.

"You should indeed do so, and with extreme caution before you say anything more," was his curt reply. "You see, Lady Diana, this random number that we have run through the Engine was provided by the late Professor Manning. He marked off the numerals on his abacus after you fled his study.

"I'll make this whole matter clear to you presently, Inspector," Holmes went on, turning to Lestrade. "If you dispatch one of your men to the lady's quarters, I would not be surprised if he were to discover in her fireplace whatever remains of the documents the Professor had encoded on the Engine. A *thorough* search might also yield up a small calibre pistol as the one by which the lady caused Manning's untimely end."

"Diana!" Professor Seabury's face was ashen pale. "You told me you had taken my small pistol to be cleaned."

If ever there was a clear confession of guilt upon a human countenance, it was there now in the perfectly sculpted features of Lady Diana's face. She fixed her gaze upon the floor, standing still and white as a marble statue. Her voice was low.

"The police will find both the notes and the pistol, Mr. Holmes, just as you have said. They might also find two letters from the Royal Society. Perhaps these will explain the motive for my deed. The first contains an invitation to a testimonial which was to be held in my honour for original contributions to mathematics. The subsequent letter informed me coldly, and without explanation, that the testimonial had been cancelled.

"I had no idea why the Society had changed their minds so abruptly. I naturally appealed to Professor Manning, who was a member. He informed me that it had been at his urging that the testimonial had been cancelled. He had told the Society that I had not, in fact, performed any original work at all. When I demanded to know the reason for this patent lie, he told me it was completely presumptuous for me, a mere woman, to aspire to any such honour. I had, he said, even overstepped my bounds by adding my own ideas to his notes. My role was simply that of an assistant, and I should be more than content with whatever meagre recognition he chose to give me. Outraged, I immediately declared that my services to him were at an end, and I left him.

"I was extremely keen to avenge him. I recalled that the Professor was encoding some secret government documents on the Analytical Engine—my husband had told me so by chance. It occurred to me that if I could destroy this work, it would prove a serious blow to him. I hurried to the Engine and tried to gain access to the documents. Finally I succeeded in getting them printed out, after which I erased the information completely from the Engine's memory.

"I took the printed documents home and burned them secretly, but my triumph was short-lived. The thought struck me that Professor

Manning might have another copy of their contents and the encoding information in his study. I took my husband's pistol and went to his home when I knew he would be alone, in order to force him to surrender the documents, should he possess them.

"The Professor was at his desk when I entered and made my demands. In his anger at learning of my actions, for it turned out that I had burned the only copy of the information, he leapt at me and threatened me with violence. I pulled the pistol from behind my cloak and shot him, then turned and ran."

Professor Seabury, who had jumped to his feet when Holmes accused Lady Diana of the murder, sank back into his chair with a stricken expression on his face. When Lady Diana finished speaking in those hushed tones which were all the more terrible for their restraint, his head fell forward, and he covered his face with his hands.

"My apologies, Professor Seabury," said Holmes in sincere compassion. "I never imagined the effects of this experiment would be so severe." Holmes placed a hand upon the man's shoulder and turning again to Lestrade gave him a quick, silent nod.

"I fancy that this is the time for our exit, Watson."

Holmes said not one word to me about this tragedy throughout the remainder of the day though I observed that he was in a most thoughtful mood. The following morning, while we made our way back to Baker Street, he made one final comment as he stared out the window of our railway carriage. "I must confess, Watson, that some of my sympathies lie with the criminal in this case," he sighed. "I am reminded of the Lady Ada Lovelace, without whom the work of Charles Babbage might never have seen the light of day. Like Lady Diana Seabury, she took the scattered notes of the inventor, clarified them, added her own thoughts, and in many ways improved upon them. Ada Lovelace will be remembered for her contributions, and, perhaps, one day will share the recognition that Babbage has earned. But such is not the case with Lady Diana. A remarkable woman, I'm sure she will present a brilliant argument at her trial."

3.1   The Insides of a Computer

At the beginning of "The Analytical Engine," Watson remarked to Sherlock Holmes, "I know of no substitute for the mind of man." Certainly neither the Analytical Engine nor even the most sophisticated modern computer can approach the unfathomable complexity of the human brain. People who think of a computer as an artificial brain might be quite surprised to discover the very primitive functions of its internal components. Even a small home computer may require thousands of instructions just to print the time of day. It is the speed with which these primitive components operate that gives the aura of a modern genie. Most modern computers can execute thousands of primitive instructions in the time it takes to blink an eye, an extraordinary change from the relatively slow and huge computers of the early fifties.

A greatly simplified sketch of a computer system is shown in Figure 3.1. Here we see an input device for supplying data to the computer. This may be a deck of punched cards, a keyboard, a tape cassette, or any of the other varieties of input media. The output device is the place where results are recorded. This may be another tape cassette, a video screen, a printer, or again, any device capable of recording data. The memory is internal to the computer. As explained earlier, it holds the programs being run and the required support data.

The concept of putting the instructions in the computer memory as opposed to the method of wiring the circuits for the program was conceived by John von Neumann, a mathematician and one of the great pioneers in computing. This concept paved the way for the modern computer and its many programming languages. People may complain of the difficulty of programming a computer, but the old method was *much* more time-consuming and difficult.

At the heart of the computer is the central processing unit (CPU). This unit has a lot of work to do. It has to obtain data from the input device, send data to and from the memory, process the output, and make the calculations. On top of all this, it must coordinate everything that happens.

The inside of a computer (including the CPU) is usually a maze of electronic circuitry. There are units for performing arithmetic, registers for storing values, circuits for accessing data in the computer's memory, electronic timers for coordinating events, mechanisms for decoding bit strings, and what have you. This collection of electronic gadgets is called *hardware.*

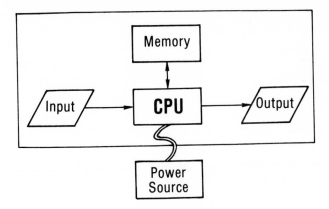

Figure 3.1   *Simplified Sketch of a Computer System*

*The "Mill" of the Babbage's Analytical Engine, precursor of the "Central
Processing Unit" of Modern Computers*

To program this circuitry, the computer hardware comes with various formats for giving instructions to the machine. The computer is "hardwired" to interpret such instructions. That is, the computer is built to understand these instructions directly. The instructions, of course, differ from computer to computer. In a simple programmable calculator, for instance, the instructions will tend towards common arithmetic operations. In a large computer designed for data processing, like those for census tabulations or corporate payrolls, many of the instructions will deal with organizing and checking files of data. These instructions, when used according to the rules that govern them, for a language of sorts, are called *machine language*.

3.2   A Small Hypothetical Computer

While the technology of computers has changed dramatically over the years, a number of key ideas have remained commonplace. To understand these issues in some detail, let us turn to a small hypothetical computer typical of those in popular use. The details of this machine are based on Sam, a simple mini-computer described by Ira Pohl and Alan Shaw.

Internal Organization

The internal organization of this computer is illustrated in Figure 3.2. The computer is said to be a *16 bit* machine, which means that it operates on bit patterns of length 16. As mentioned earlier, this sequence of 16 bits is said to form a word. Both the memory and internal components of the computer are set up on a word basis.

By convention, a computer's word length is the number of bits it can move at one time. A little thought will show that the longer the word length, the more information that can be processed in a single operation. Also, computers with larger (32 or 64 bit) word lengths tend to have denser components, which have shorter paths for electricity to follow and thus further speed up processing. Some of today's fastest computers are arranged in a circular fashion to reduce connection length as much as possible. In one, the CRAY-2, the longest connecting wire is only 16 inches long, and from the top it looks like a thin snowflake. It is common to see wires many feet long in commercial computers.

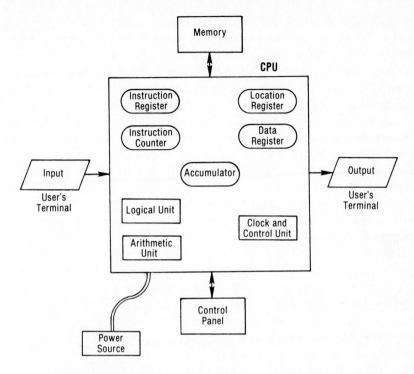

Figure 3.2 *Internal Components of a Hypothetical Computer*

The memory consists of storage for 4,096 words. This apparently magic number is 2^{12} (2 to the 12*th* power), which means that 12 bits are needed to specify a location in the memory. For instance, the lowest location is

0000 0000 0000

and the highest is

1111 1111 1111

This latter number is $(2^{12} - 1)$, i.e. 4095. Thus the memory locations are numbered 0 through 4,095. In more ordinary computer jargon, we say that the computer has a *4K* memory, meaning roughly 4,000 words.

In order to get values in and out of the memory, the central processing unit of Sam contains two *registers*. The first is a 12 bit register called a *location register;* it holds the binary value of a location in the memory. The second is a 16 bit register called a *data register;* it holds a word to be stored in the memory or a word to be obtained from the memory. Every word transfer in and out of the memory is via these two registers. When a word is to be obtained from the memory, for instance, the location of the word is established in the location register, and then the word is copied into the data register.

As we have said, all program instructions are stored in the memory. For our hypothetical computer, all instructions have a 16 bit format. The *instruction register* holds the instruction currently being executed. It is supported by the circuitry needed to carry out the instruction.

Unless a specific branch is made to another instruction, the instructions are executed in sequence. For this purpose, the CPU contains an *instruction counter.* The instruction counter holds the location of the current instruction. Except for a specific branch to another instruction, the instruction counter is automatically incremented by 1 after completing a given instruction; otherwise, the instruction counter is set to the location of the instruction to which a branch is made.

To perform basic computations, we have an *arithmetic unit* and a *logical unit.* The arithmetic unit contains the circuitry to perform the addition and subtraction of binary numbers. The logical unit implements the comparison of numbers and some elementary bit-by-bit processing.

Almost all of the work inside the computer makes use of the *accumulator,* a rather ubiquitous 16 bit register used to store intermediate results. For example, the result of an addition is placed in the accumulator.

All of the action inside the central processing unit is coordinated with the *clock-and-control unit.* This device sends signals to initiate the retrieval of a word from the memory and monitors the status of other units to determine when an instruction is completed. The clock-and-control unit is connected to an external control panel, which contains an on-off switch for the computer, a mechanism for getting programs into the computer, and miscellaneous buttons, switches, and status lights. If you have ever used a programmable calculator, most of these functions will be familiar.

Memory Organization

As mentioned above, the memory is organized as a sequence of words. Words may contain instructions or data, as illustrated in Figure 3.3.

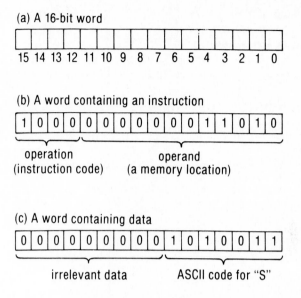

(a) A 16-bit word

(b) A word containing an instruction

operation   operand
(instruction code)   (a memory location)

(c) A word containing data

irrelevant data   ASCII code for "S"

Figure 3.3   *16 Bit Words*

All instructions have the form

operation-code   operand

where the operation code requires 4 bits and the operand 12 bits. If the instruction requires no operand, the operand is given as a sequence of 0's.

For instance, consider the instruction

0010 000000011010

The operation code 0010 denotes an add instruction; the operand, the binary equivalent of 26, specifies a location in the memory. The instruction means

Get the value stored in memory location 26, and
add it to the value in the accumulator.

Some machine language instructions perform detailed machine operations. For instance, consider the instruction

```
0111 000000000010
```

Here the operation code 0111 denotes a "left shift" operation; the operand, the binary equivalent of 2, specifies a number of bits. The instruction means

> Shift the value in the accumulator 2 positions to the left.

Machine instructions are normally written in a more humanized form, giving names to the operations and decimal numbers in place of binary numbers. For example, the instructions above might be written

```
ADD 26
LSHIFT 2
```

rather than spelled out in binary.

Data items are also stored in the memory as 16 bit words. For instance, the word

```
000000000 1010011
```

contains the ASCII binary code for the letter "S." Here the first 9 bits, which are irrelevant to a 7 bit ASCII code, are set to 0.

Normally the words in memory are organized as in Figure 3.4. Here, for example, locations 0000 through 0019 contain instructions, locations 0020 through 0025 contain data, and the remaining locations are unused.

The use of special machine features is quite tricky in practice. Understanding these features, however, is revealing and highly educational. The reader who wishes to explore these inner depths of computers may find a good source of material in the book by Pohl and Shaw given in the references.

3.3   A Binary Adder

As mentioned earlier, the primitive components of a computer are indeed primitive. To appreciate this fact and to provide an example of how such primitive components are constructed, consider the design of a binary adder. Arithmetic operations, addition in particular, are an important part of any computer system. The binary adder described below is one way to build the circuitry needed for the ADD instruction on a computer or the + key on a common calculator.

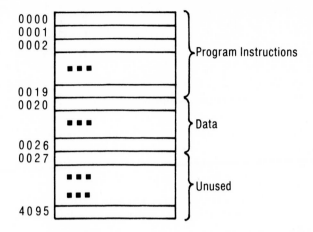

Figure 3.4   *Organization of Memory*

Consider the problem of simple binary addition. When we add in binary, 0 plus 0 is 0, 0 plus 1 is 1, 1 plus 0 is 1, and 1 plus 1 is 0 with a *carry* of 1. For example, using 8 bits we have:

Decimal	Binary
42	00101010
33	00100001
75	01001011

Notice that the number of bits used limits the range of numbers that can be handled. With 8 bits we can have numbers up to 255 ($2^8 - 1$), with 16 bits we get 65,535 ($2^{16} - 1$), and with 32 we get 4,294,967,295. A given computer will have some fixed number of bits for representing whole numbers (normally 16 or 32 bits).

Consider also:

Decimal	Binary
31	00011111
1	00000001
32	00100000

In this case the addition in binary causes a carry of 1, five times, just as adding 1 to 99999 does in decimal.

Returning to our original issue, how does a computer, a piece of electronic hardware, do it? We start with Figure 3.5. This diagram displays three logical elements, called *and, or,* and *not* gates. An *and* gate takes two binary signals, 0 or 1, and produces the signal for 1 as output if both inputs are 1, and 0 otherwise. The *or* gate also takes the two binary signals 0 or 1. It produces an output of 1 if either input is 1, and a 0 if both inputs are 0. The *not* gate uses only one binary input signal, 0 or 1, and changes it in the output to the opposite signal. Such gates can be readily implemented electronically as tiny transistor switches. Somewhat surprisingly, these innocuous three gates are enough to produce a full binary adder, as follows.

Consider Figure 3.6. Here we see a configuration of *and, or,* and *not* gates. The gates are arranged so that two binary signals can be "added." For instance, if input line A is 1 and B is 0, then the output line for the binary result R is 1 and the carry line is 0. If A and B are both 1, the result line R is 0 but the carry line is 1.

The real step up comes in Figure 3.7, where provision has been made for a third input, a carry signal resulting from a previous binary addition.

Understanding the circuit of Figure 3.7 is not easy. Let's look at some easy cases. If both input lines A and B are 0 and the carry-in is also 0, the result R and carry-out are also 0. In this case all the internal signals are 0 except the signal out of the *not* gate and following *or* gate. This 1 signal goes through the final *and* gate with another 0, giving a result R as 0.

The case where A, B, and the carry-in C_{in} are each 1 is equally easy. Here we have 1's everywhere, again except after the *not* gate. This 0 is put through the following *or* gate with a 1, giving 1 as the result R. All of this simply means that $1 + 1 + 1$ gives a result of 1 with a carry of 1.

The remaining cases are not so easy. Rather than review them, we have marked the circuit of Figure 3.7 with a sample input as well as some notes describing when the internal gates produce a 1 as output.

Now for the final blessing, Figure 3.8. Here the full one-digit adders of Figure 3.7 have been duplicated, one duplicate for each binary digit. The carry-out signal of one adder is connected to the carry-in line for the next. The initial carry-in signal is set to 0. The net result is full four-digit binary adder, and the extension to 8 or 16 bit adder is trivial.

The design of the adder of Figure 3.8 is typical of many computer components, where a few simple mechanisms are replicated over and

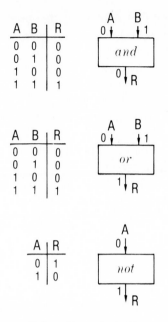

Figure 3.5 *Binary Logic Elements*

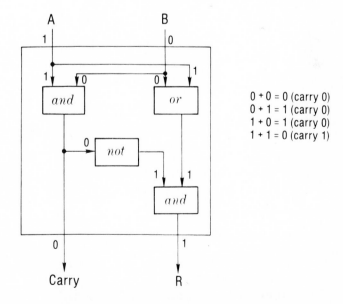

Figure 3.6 *A One-Digit Binary Adder*

over to produce some effect. It is worth underscoring this point. The computer technology is, in part, one of great replication. If computers held only a hundred characters in memory and executed only one instruction per second, the technology would be largely a curiosity. But computer memories can now hold, not thousands or even tens of thousands, but millions of characters—all through replication of a single idea. Furthermore, while machine instructions are primitive, the computer can execute thousands of instructions in an instant. For instance, on most computers a binary adder can perform at least ten thousand additions in a second.

Some electronic chips have on 1/8th of a square inch the equivalent of 400,000 individual components, and there can be thousands of these chips in a modern computer. Think about it!

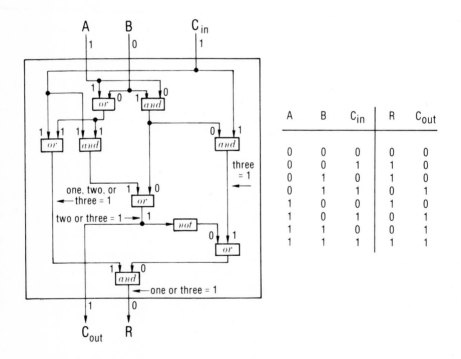

Figure 3.7   *A Full One-Digit Binary Adder*

One special observation on the adder of Figure 3.8. If the last carry signal is a 1, we have a condition generally known as *overflow*. An overflow occurs whenever the computed result does not fit in the prescribed number of bits. If you run a program that causes this to happen, it is likely that the computer will come to a dead halt, after issuing some strange cease and desist order.

There are many such anomalies in every computer; they happen any time its limits are exceeded. This indicates one (not so uncommon) way in which computers can fail. The best systems are those in which all such anomalies are handled in advance by the programmer. Unfortunately anomalies do get through, and computers do fail.

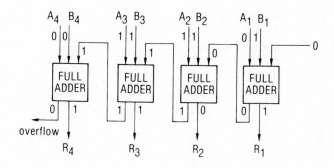

$$A_4 \quad A_3 \quad A_2 \quad A_1 \quad = \quad 0\ 1\ 1\ 0$$
$$B_4 \quad B_3 \quad B_2 \quad B_1 \quad = \quad 0\ 1\ 1\ 1$$
$$R_4 \quad R_3 \quad R_2 \quad R_1 \quad = \quad 1\ 1\ 0\ 1$$

Figure 3.8   *A Four-Digit Binary Adder*

Programming

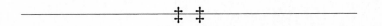

CHAPTER IV

---‡---

The Adventure of the Carriage Wheel

(Part I)

T WAS a busy summer when the minor but exceedingly instructive episode of the carriage wheel took place. Mr. Sherlock Holmes and I were again visitors at Trinity College, Cambridge. Over the three preceding months, he had worked no less than fifteen hours a day on a case of shocking dimensions, the details of which I am not at liberty to discuss here. Under such strain his iron constitution had broken down. He was barely able to conclude his investigation before, as his physician, I urged him to take restorative measures. Perhaps, I suggested, he should apply his mind to the problems furnished by the Analytical Engine, rather than those more superficial ones for which the criminal world of London was responsible. It proved the correct prescription.

Almost daily the postman delivered some new reading matter relevant in some degree to Holmes's current interest. As the hours of intellectual pleasure accumulated, his vigor returned, and his expertise with the mechanical mind broadened considerably. On a number of occasions Holmes was asked to step in on some case or other but always, to my relief, he replied that he was much too engaged.

"I really must insist on as little distraction as possible from the work I have undertaken," he told one visitor. "My advice is that you summon the aid of your local police, who, I am certain, are quite capable of handling such a small affair."

One morning, having risen earlier than usual, I was surprised to find Holmes already busy with his breakfast. It had become his habit of late to sleep until ten or later. The sight of him munching on his toast, while he carefully studied the morning papers, told me that something was in the air. Upon informing the landlady that I, too, was ready for breakfast, I joined my colleague in our small sitting-room. My first few attempts at conversation failed to disengage Holmes from his reading, so I began leafing through a few of the scientific journals strewn over the furniture, floor, and mantel. One I found open, with numerous comments pencilled in the margins. Naturally, I began to run through the article so copiously annotated.

It was a monograph on the impressions made by carriage wheels and bicycle tyres. I chuckled when, on one page, I found a table measuring the number of threads a bolt can be expected to loosen over time, given a certain number of rotations.

"You are amused, Watson," observed my friend.

"Indeed," I said. "This is the most preposterous collection of trivia and useless figures I have ever seen. The work of some university scholar, clapped down in his secluded study, where he has nothing better to do than con- coct these neat little for- mulae.

"I BEGAN TO RUN THROUGH THE ARTICLE SO COPIOUSLY ANNOTATED."

"Useless, you say?"

"Absolutely," I responded, slapping the magazine to the floor beside me.

Holmes glanced down from his breakfast table. "Ah, the piece on carriage wheels. Illuminating, I think."

"You must be joking, dear fellow. Of what possible use is this disquisition on minutiae to you?"

"How many times have I told you, Watson, that the little things, the things most often overlooked by others, are infinitely the more important? In my work a man's life may hang on the testimony of his coat-sleeve, a bootlace, or, perhaps, a carriage bolt. Did you notice, by the way, the name of the author of that little treatise? I thought I might drop him a note of thanks for such a useful bit of work."

Holmes's nonchalance caught me off my guard, so that I was quite unprepared for the name I found after flipping through the journal to the article in question. "Why, Holmes, you wrote this!"

Sherlock Holmes smiled broadly.

"We have, perhaps fortunately, perhaps not, a perfect example of the usefulness of the careful observation of trifles here in the morning papers," he said, tapping an article with his egg spoon. "A most valuable institution, the press, if one knows how to use it. Here is an account of one Quincy Pritchard, a young man accused of burglary in the town of Woking. He claims that he wasn't even in Woking yesterday afternoon and that he had come directly from Aldershot to Guildford, where he was arrested some three hours later. This was an hour or so after the theft was reported."

"Why is this Pritchard fellow suspected?" I queried.

"The papers don't say too much. But I gather there were no witnesses and that the stolen property was found in his possession."

"Well that seems fitting don't you think?"

"Yes, if that's all there were to it. Mr. Pritchard claims to have had his carriage repaired in Aldershot just before setting out. He was *en route* to Dover by way of Guildford when the wheel came loose, nearly falling off. While repairs were being made again, the police found him having dinner in Guildford and took him into custody.

"The police have confirmed that he did have the carriage repaired first in Aldershot. They theorize that Mr. Pritchard first rode to Woking, some ten miles north, and then on to Guildford, another, let's see, yes, six and two-tenths miles."

"You're not proposing to follow his tracks from one location to the next are you?" I asked incredulously.

"Oh, dear me, no, Watson. But we can determine what route he took by a careful examination of the carriage bolt. Obviously, whatever work he had done in Aldershot was faulty. What would you theorize, Doctor?"

I thought for a moment, and something struck me. "Why, Holmes, do you think there could have been something wrong with the wheel bolt? Defective, perhaps?"

"Precisely, Watson," Holmes replied. "I knew I could count on your keenness of mind to spot the crux of Mr. Pritchard's defense. We must determine how far the defective carriage could have travelled from Aldershot. Now, if you would be so good as to hand me that piece of rubbish you found so amusing earlier," he said, indicating the journal. He opened it to one of the many tables in his article and began to study it intently. I took advantage of his preoccupation to make a start on my breakfast tea.

Holmes turned to me again, "Watson, dear chap, could you find some paper and a pencil? We shall need to make a few notes." When I brought him these, he began to sketch a crude map of the towns and their connecting roads, which I have duplicated below.

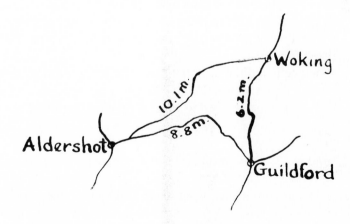

"A problem of this kind is easily solved by the simple and expedient process of reasoning backwards—a process which, simple as it is, the otherwise capable minds of the police often fail to use. Let us begin with the fact that Quincy Pritchard had his carriage fixed in Aldershot three hours before he was apprehended in Guildford. So we shall first list any facts we can deduce from this and refer to them as the 'givens.' Then we shall list the information to be determined, which we shall call the 'finds.'

"Now, Watson," he went on, handing me the pencil and the rest of the paper, "if you would be good enough to transcribe as I direct, we may begin.

"First given: according to the newspaper, Mr. Pritchard was driving a gig of standard size. Its wheels each have a circumference of ten point four feet."

I made note of this.

"Our next given is that there are twenty-eight threads on the standard wheel bolt. You may refer to my article for this datum, and I can attest to its reliability."

Holmes rattled off a few more figures, flipping to one table after another in his obscure study for details. When he was finished, I could not help smiling at the completed list :—

The Givens:

    a.   Wheel circumference 10.4 feet.
    b.   28 threads on standard wheel bolt.
    c.   A defective bolt loosens one-tenth of a turn during the first 100 rotations.
    d.   With each additional 100 turns, rate of loosening increases by six per cent.
    e.   Suspect apprehended one hour after crime reported.

The Finds:

    a.   Number of miles travelled by the carriage.

"Now," Holmes went on, "some easy arithmetic tells us that with the first 100 rotations the carriage will have travelled exactly 1,040 feet, bringing the bolt 0.1 turns loose. The rate of loosening is thus 0.1 plus six per cent times 0.1, or 0.106 turns per hundred rotations.

"The next 100 rotations, then, will bring the carriage a total of 2,080 feet. Our bolt is now 0.206 turns loose, and the loosening rate is 0.106 plus six per cent times 0.106, or 0.11236. Do you follow?"

"The formulae seem easy enough to set up, Holmes, but this is going to be a tediously lengthy calculation."

"I could not agree more, Watson. Were we to continue in this manner, we would undoubtedly err at some point due to confusion or fatigue. There is, however, an ingenious mechanical device which can assist us."

"Of course—the Analytical Engine!" I exclaimed.

"Yes, the Engine, my dear fellow," Holmes rejoined. "It is not subject to the weaknesses which would beset us in this instance. Unfortunately, it too has a weakness; the Engine can only carry out its function if the problem at hand is stated in a very precise form. It remains, therefore, for us to phrase our problem with the clarity which the Engine requires, so it may take over where we cannot, or rather, where we would not proceed for fear of error.

"Our task, Watson, is to design a set of instructions the Engine can follow. As you know, they must advance in step-by-step fashion, and they must be expressed in terms which the Engine comprehends. Now jot this down, please."

I took down the following agenda :—

1. Establish the knowns.
2. — Calculate the distance travelled.
    Let distance = 0.
    As long as more threads remain to be turned:
        add 100 times the circumference to the distance, and
        record the number of threads that have been turned.
3. Print the distance in miles.

I stared at what I had written in both amazement and skepticism.

"Holmes," I observed, "the Analytical Engine must be an incredibly sophisticated machine to be able to understand such a set of instructions, for I must confess some doubts in my own ability to complete them."

"Set your mind at ease, Watson," Holmes replied with a smile. "These are merely preliminary instructions for our own guidance. For the Engine, we need to represent our data in far more explicit terms.

"It is our second instruction, Doctor, upon which this experiment will turn, if you will excuse an unfortunate pun. The mathematicians call this step a *loop,* by which they mean a series of instructions to be repeated. As long as there remain threads to turn, the calculation will continue. How often have I said that when you have eliminated the impossible, whatever remains, however improbable, must be the truth? In this case, the Engine runs through this exercise repeatedly, and, when there are no more threads on the bolt, we will have our answer as to the veracity of Mr. Pritchard's statement."

"But, Holmes," I protested, "this is hardly explicit enough for me. Is the Engine so much more intelligent that it can comprehend what I cannot?"

"Watson," Holmes laughed, "the Analytical Engine's intelligence, if it can be called such, consists solely in its ability to carry out a set of definite instructions, which must be compiled in a fixed form if they are to be intelligible. Here we are simply attempting to establish a framework from which to formulate those instructions. Now then, what can we add to our first item about the knowns?"

He took the paper from me and began to write, reading his figures aloud as he did so.

"The total number of threads is 28, the loosening factor is 0.1, the increment is 6 per cent, the circumference of the wheel is 10.4 feet. Have we overlooked anything?"

"Travel time, one hour approximately," I offered.

"Ah, yes, thank you. Now for our next instruction, 'let DISTANCE equal zero.' Nothing more to add there. The loop of step three needs elaboration, however. As long as the number of turns is less than the total number of threads, we shall do the following.

"Add 100 times the circumference to the distance.
"Add the loosening factor to the number turned.
"Increment the loosening factor by six per cent.

"I think, too," he continued, "that we can dispense with the given of the travel time, one hour. True, it is a known fact, but in this instance it is also an extraneous detail."

"Why is that, Holmes?" I asked, puzzled by my friend's intent to disregard what seemed to me necessary information.

"Because, my dear Watson, at the moment Mr. Pritchard's rate of speed does not concern us, but simply the distance he has covered."

"Ah, now I see," I said. "Is there anything else?"

"Oh, yes, Watson, we need to go further yet. This requires an *algorithm,* an explicit and written set of instructions. We begin with a definition of our terms, so there will be no chance for ambiguity. Next, we outline the exact sequence of operations, namely each calculation which the Engine must perform. We have assembled all of the facts. Now it is simply a matter of putting it into formal mathematical language."

He turned to a fresh page and diligently prepared the agenda that I have reproduced as Figure 4.1. I studied this curious document for some time, unable to decipher its intent. "What exactly are your plans for this, Holmes?"

"We may discuss them, Watson, when you have consumed the two hard-boiled eggs with which our new cook has favoured you," he answered.

I looked down at the handsome cuisine which had arrived unnoticed and which I had completely neglected throughout our fascinating discussion.

"When you have finished, Watson, I shall put to you the whole situation. Pray, renew your energies now before we make fresh demands upon them."

Definitions:

TOTAL_THREADS   :   the total number of threads per bolt
NUMBER_TURNED :   the number of threads turned
LOOSEN_FACTOR :   basic loosening factor for a defective bolt
INCREMENT   :   increment in loosen factor each 100 wheel rotations

CIRCUMFERENCE :   circumference of a wheel
DISTANCE   :   distance travelled in feet
MILES   :   distance in miles

Algorithm:

— Establish the knowns
Let TOTAL_THREADS = 28
Let LOOSEN_FACTOR = 0.10
Let INCREMENT = 0.6
Let CIRCUMFERENCE = 10.4

— Calculate the distance travelled
Let DISTANCE = 0.0
Let NUMBER_TURNED = 0.0
As long as NUMBER_TURNED < TOTAL_THREADS do the following:
   let DISTANCE = DISTANCE + CIRCUMFERENCE·100
   let NUMBER_TURNED = NUMBER_TURNED + LOOSEN_FACTOR
   let LOOSEN_FACTOR = LOOSEN_FACTOR
                              + INCREMENT·LOOSEN_FACTOR

— Print the distance in miles
Let MILES = DISTANCE / 5280
Print MILES

Figure 4.1   *Algorithm for the Carriage Wheel Problem*

4.1   Programming

Even Sherlock Holmes, whose insistence on accuracy in details won him his reputation, fell prey to an occasional lapse. In *The Hound of the Baskervilles,* Holmes forgot to tell Sir Henry Baskerville to cross the Grimpen Mine before the fog set in. As a result, in addition to the threat posed by the fiendish hound, Sir Henry only just escaped losing his way in the fog and being swallowed up in the Mire.

With a computer, everything must be spelled out. A computer would be nothing but a piece of electronic furniture without the instructions needed to make it operate. The instructions direct its behavior. Even when you prepare a letter on an electronic mail system, millions of instructions may be executed just to make things work correctly. All you may see are letters appearing on a screen and a terminal that is ready to accept your input. But underneath this simple facade are all the instructions that make the device do what it appears to do.

The instructions and associated data for operating a computer are called *software*. The terms "hardware" and "software" form a computer-ese dual—hardware refers to the "hard" parts of a computer system, the physical devices; software to the "soft" or changeable parts, the instructions and data. These are soft in the sense that we can replace one set of instructions with another and thereby give the device an entirely different purpose. It is possible, for instance, to buy a word processor, replace its software, and turn it into an accounting system.

The writing of software comprises the single largest share of the computer industry. Every personal computer, every word processor, every special purpose system, and every computer application requires software, often lots of it.

The software of a computer system is divided into units. Some of the units are data, such as a set of names and addresses; others are programs, perhaps a program to print a list of names in alphabetical order. It is the programs that direct the operation of the hardware, interpret the data, and, in general, control the computer "behavior" that the user sees.

Programs are written not only to make a computer function properly, but to perform tasks users deem practical. A student may buy a personal computer and write a program to draw pictures or play a game. A teacher with access to a large computer may write a program to record student grading information. A scientist may write a program to compute statistics from laboratory test results.

Programming is the process required to produce a computer program. It is one of the most demanding activities associated with computers. It is also one of the most exciting, for it lets you be the genie behind the computer.

People often take many things for granted when they give instructions to others. With a computer, nothing can be left out or assumed. The instructions must be extraordinarily detailed, spelled out in a special language, and given with an exacting rigor that, for many, makes programming a difficult challenge.

4.2   Algorithms

In programming, the most fundamental concept is the *algorithm*. An algorithm is a sequence of instructions to solve a problem. The rigor necessary for a computer algorithm is the essence of programming, no matter which programming language is used. To understand this matter let us review the algorithm developed by Holmes. Then, in the next chapter, it will be presented as a program in Basic, one of the many special languages for computers.

To begin with, Holmes's algorithm is organized in two parts:

> Definitions:
> *name and description of relevant items*
>
> Algorithm:
> *steps for carrying out the computation*

One important characteristic of a computer algorithm is that each item in the computation must be explicitly identified. If the algorithm concerns suspects and room numbers, or miles traveled and a loosening factor on a carriage bolt, loose statements about implicitly understood things will never suffice. The items in question have to be "smoked out" and identified. Holmes, in his algorithm, names and describes each item mentioned in the computation.

An algorithm always reflects some sequence of instructions that could, if needed, be carried out by hand. Accordingly, it must be arranged in some meaningful way. Notice the overall organization of Holmes's algorithm.

1.   Establish the knowns.
2.   Calculate the distance traveled.
3.   Print the distance in miles.

This simple organization is meaningful to a reader.

One of the most difficult aspects of algorithms is the need to give instructions on a step-by-step basis. Each step must be an imperative statement, and upon completion, the next step in the solution should be clear. In Holmes's case, each statement is executed in order; first the number of threads per bolt is set to 28, next the loosening factor is set to .10, and so on, until the final statement where the number of miles is printed.

The loop given in the algorithm,

> As long as NUMBER_TURNED < TOTAL_THREADS do the following:
>   let DISTANCE = *new-value*
>   let NUMBER_TURNED = *new-value*
>   let LOOSEN_FACTOR = *new-value*

can also be considered as a single step, consisting of three component steps, each setting a new value for one of three items. These three component steps are executed repeatedly until the number of threads turned equals or exceeds the established number of threads per bolt. When this condition is met, the next step,

> let MILES = *new-value*

is executed.

Notice that Holmes's algorithm is quite precise. A computer algorithm must leave no room for ambiguity; the statements can have only one interpretation. Ideally, any two persons who follow the algorithm should arrive at exactly the same result. Notice also that the algorithm contains no extraneous information. It describes only those computations needed to obtain the answer. It does not include, for example, the irrelevant fact about the time taken by the suspect to make the journey in question.

To make sure Holmes's algorithm is fully understood, we give a quick review of its operation. The lines preceding the loop establish values for several named items. These are

TOTAL_THREADS	28
LOOSEN_FACTOR	0.10
INCREMENT	0.06
CIRCUMFERENCE	10.4
DISTANCE	0.0
NUMBER_TURNED	0.0

Next, the condition given in the heading of the loop,

> NUMBER_TURNED < TOTAL_THREADS

is tested. Since 0 is less than 28, the statements within the loop are executed. This gives the following values:

DISTANCE	1,040
NUMBER_TURNED	0.1
LOOSEN_FACTOR	0.106

The condition in the loop heading is again tried, that is, the condition

0.1 < 28

is tested and again fulfilled. So, the statements within the loop are once more executed, giving

DISTANCE	2,080
NUMBER_TURNED	0.206
LOOSEN_FACTOR	0.11236

Now, with a condition of

0.206 < 28

the loop continues.

As is evident, at some point the test

NUMBER_TURNED < TOTAL_THREADS

will become false, and the loop will terminate. A final value for DISTANCE will have been established, so that the statements following the loop will be executed. In particular

Let MILES = DISTANCE / 5280

will determine the distance in miles, and

Print MILES

will print the resulting value.

Consider the following simple change to Holmes's algorithm, replacing the line

Let DISTANCE = 0

by

Let DISTANCE = 10

The algorithm is now incorrect. The distance calculated will be off by 10 feet. Consider next the replacement of the line

let NUMBER_TURNED = NUMBER_TURNED + LOOSEN_FACTOR

by

let NUMBER_TURNED = NUMBER_TURNED + 0.10

Now the number of threads turned will be uniformly incremented by 0.10 rather than progressively incremented with a six percent increase. It's hard to say how much this will affect the final answer without examining the entire algorithm, but the answer will definitely be incorrect.

Notice that the first error mentioned above probably is of trifling concern, especially considering that 10 feet is not really of much interest in a program whose result is in miles. Notice also that the second, more subtle error, can make a big difference in the result. This range of effects is typical.

Correctness is of capital importance in computer programming. Writing correct programs, especially large ones that are hundreds of pages long, is one of the most talked-about, expensive, time-consuming, and difficult tasks in producing commercial software.

Summing Up

The essence of a computer program is an algorithm. Algorithms are written to solve a given problem or carry out a given task. An algorithm has certain characteristics:

1. It is organized as a sequence of instructions.
2. The instructions are given step by step.
3. Each item of data is explicitly identified.
4. There is no room for ambiguity.
5. There is no extraneous information.
6. It must be correct.

With these in mind, let's have a look at an actual program.

CHAPTER V

‡

The Adventure of the Carriage Wheel

(Part II)

T WAS one o'clock when we left our small but comfortable lodgings. Sherlock Holmes had remained completely absorbed in this newest adventure. He was bright, eager, and in excellent spirits as he led me to the nearest telegraph office, whence he dispatched a long cable to the Chief of the Surrey Constabulary.

Our destination was the laboratory which housed the Analytical Engine. It may be recalled that the mystery surrounding the death of the mathematician James Manning was brought to light here by the use of this remarkable machine.

"I take it you are planning to run this problem through the Analytical Engine?" I asked as we entered the familiar room with its rows of laboratory tables and bottle-lined shelves.

"Exactly, Watson," he said. "I have here a translation of the problem which the Engine will be able to decipher." He offered the document for my inspection. It displayed a programme in the machine's special language, Basic, and I have duplicated it here in its entirety as Figure 5.1.

"Surely you do not expect me to make sense of this extraordinary mumbo-jumbo?" I exclaimed. "This is the oddest assortment of words, numbers, and stray punctuation marks I have ever seen. What does it all mean, Holmes?"

"I have written out the problem in the Engine's special code," he commented. "You explained it rather well, I thought, in your exaggerated commentary concerning the affair of the abacus."

```
0010 REM  -- THIS PROGRAMME READS IN FOUR CHARACTERISTICS OF A
0020 REM  -- DEFECTIVE CARRIAGE WHEEL BOLT: THE NUMBER OF THREADS,
0030 REM  -- ITS INITIAL LOOSENING FACTOR, THE INCREMENT IN THE
0040 REM  -- LOOSENING FACTOR EACH 100 TURNS OF THE WHEEL, AND THE
0050 REM  -- CIRCUMFERENCE OF THE WHEEL.
0060 REM  -- THE PROGRAMME PRINTS THE DISTANCE TRAVELLED BEFORE
0070 REM  -- THE WHEEL WILL FALL OFF.
0080 REM
0090 REM  -- DICTIONARY OF NAMES:
0100 REM
0110 REM  -- T  TOTAL NUMBER OF THREADS PER BOLT
0120 REM  -- N  NUMBER OF THREADS TURNED
0130 REM  -- L  LOOSENING FACTOR AT INITIAL
0140 REM  -- I  INCREMENT IN LOOSENING FACTOR
0150 REM  -- C  CIRCUMFERENCE OF WHEEL, IN FEET
0160 REM  -- D  DISTANCE TRAVELLED, IN FEET
0170 REM  -- M  MILES TRAVELLED.
0180 REM
0190 REM
0200 REM  -- ESTABLISH THE KNOWNS:
0210      INPUT T, L, I, C
0220 REM
0230 REM  -- CALCULATE THE DISTANCE TRAVELLED:
0240      LET D = 0
0250      LET N = 0
0260      IF N >= T THEN 0330
0270         LET D = D + C*100
0280         LET N = N + L
0290         LET L = L + I*L
0300         GOTO 0260
0310 REM
0320 REM  -- PRINT THE DISTANCE IN MILES:
0330      LET M = D / 5280
0340      PRINT "DISTANCE IN MILES IS ", M
0350      STOP
0360 END
```

Figure 5.1   *Holmes's Programme for the Carriage Wheel Problem*

"Maybe so, my dear Holmes. But these seven lines here, for instance," I said, tapping the papers with the stem of my pipe, "these at the beginning. They hardly appear to be written in code at all while the remainder of this document is a mass of hieroglyphics!"

"Those are *remarks,* Watson. They are used to make observations on the contents of the programme and are composed solely for the attendant's enlightenment. They contain no instructions for the Engine and in no way affect the exercise. You might consider them as aids to communicating in ordinary English any details the attendant may wish to include."

"Well, that makes sense," I allowed. "But you seem to have gone to great lengths to confuse the reader. It might as well be the Rosetta Stone as far as I'm concerned."

"Ah, but you are fortunate, my dear Watson, in having the services of the writer to decipher these hieroglyphics, as you call them.

"You see, the succession of lines beginning with 0090 and running through 0200 are also remarks. You will observe that each name used in the programme is listed along with a comment describing its purpose."

"But, Holmes," I asked, "how does this make a pennyworth of difference to us?"

"In writing a programme, Watson, one must choose names for all the entities of the algorithm. Here, for example, T is the programme name for the total number of threads on a bolt, D the programme name for the distance travelled. These names are called *variables* because the values associated with them can vary as the programme progresses. For instance, the value associated with the distance D will be gradually increased until the final value is determined.

"Now, Watson, rather than establish the known facts directly, as in our algorithm, they can be supplied by the operator. In this way our programme can be used with different data—for example, the data for a different carriage bolt or for a carriage wheel with a different circumference."

"This seems a bit much to digest all at once, Holmes," I protested.

"It will all become clear to you, Watson, as we work further with the Engine. For the moment, let us study the structure of a programme, using our work on the affairs of Mr. Pritchard as a guide.

"Allow me to summarize for you exactly what the main body of the programme accomplishes. It begins with the line:

```
0210 INPUT T, L, I, C
```

When this line is executed, the Engine will request the operator to enter four values: one for the total number of threads T, one for the initial loosening factor L, one for the increment in the loosening factor I, and one for the circumference of the wheel C.

"The lines,

```
0240 LET D = 0
0250 LET N = 0
```

establish the initial distance D and the initial number of threads turned N as zero.

"The following line,

```
0260 IF N >= T THEN 0330
```

expresses the way in which a decision is made. If the current value of N is greater than or equal to the value of the total number of threads T, a branch is made to line 0330. Since N is initially 0, the test is initially false and the programme continues in the normal fashion, that is, with lines 0270 through 0300. Notice that this last line,

```
0300 GOTO 0260
```

causes a direct branch back to line 0260, where the process I have just described is repeated.

"You may recall in our earlier discussions that this repetition of instructions is called a *loop*. As long as the value of N is less than the value of T, the three lines 0270 through 0290 are executed repeatedly. When N becomes equal to or greater than T, the loop terminates. At this point a value for the distance D will have been established—precisely the distance travelled by the carriage wheel."

Although this exposition of the programme seemed to follow readily from our algorithm, I remained confused by the odd grammar and vocabulary. Ordinary words like LET and IF seemed to take on entirely new meanings in Basic and I questioned Holmes on this point.

"The words that baffle you, Watson," he explained, "are known as *keywords*. They are the framework for constructing logical operations within the language itself. Once you have learned more of the grammar of Basic you will be able to write simple programmes of your own with little difficulty."

"Very well, Holmes, but what of the names T or D? As you chose these names yourself, I surmise they are not part of the Engine's special lexicon. Yet are there not some restrictions as to how such names may be conceived?"

"Certainly," agreed Holmes. "There are specific rules governing the formation of names. A name must be written as a letter, or as a letter followed by a digit.

"Unfortunately, these names are hardly illuminating, especially to someone other than the programme's author. Some mathematicians are developing versions that allow for longer names, like TOTAL_THREADS or DISTANCE, to be used. I hope they succeed, for such names will greatly enhance their clarity."

"The line numbers make little sense to me," I protested. "Some are referenced in the programme, and others are not. Why, it is quite impossible to see what happens after one instruction branches off to another."

Holmes seemed a trifle disconcerted at this last remark. "Oddly enough, Watson, the reference to line numbers *is* somewhat confusing and impossible to encapsulate here. I suggest that we leave this document with the Engine's capable attendant and return in a few hours to see how he has progressed. For now, let us head into town and sample the fare at the University Arms. Programming is certainly a subject that is best absorbed in moderate doses at the outset."

"HE TOUCHED ON THE ANALYTICAL ENGINES
OF THE FUTURE."

We shared a pleasant and leisurely meal of oysters, a brace of grouse, and a choice white wine, all to the accompaniment of an easy flow of conversation. We touched on miracle plays, mediaeval pottery, the Buddhism of Ceylon, Stradivarius violins, and the Analytical Engines of the future. My dear friend discoursed on each as though he had made a special study of it. In the case of the latter, I was convinced that this was so.

As we made our way back to the college laboratory, Holmes stopped for an evening paper, which reported that Quincy Pritchard had been cleared of any guilt in the Woking burglary case.

"Ha! There is occasional want of imagination and intuition in our county constabularies," he said, "but the Surrey police seem to have been thorough with this case. I think we can wait till morning to see what the Engine has come up with, but I'll lay you a thousand to one that our little exercise will show that, had Mr. Pritchard driven to Woking and then on to Guildford, his carriage would have broken down along the way."

I had no keener pleasure than following Sherlock Holmes in his professional investigations and admiring the rapid deductions—swift as intuitions yet always founded on a logical basis—with which he unravelled the problems that were submitted to him. Or, as in the present instance, in which he chose to involve himself.

Holmes's deductions, with the help of the Analytical Engine, were not needed to clear Mr. Pritchard's good name. But, in writing to thank my friend for his help, the Chief Constable of Surrey was good enough to relate the extraordinary manner in which Pritchard's innocence was established.

"AS THEY ENJOYED PORT AND CIGARS TOGETHER"

The reason for Mr. Quincy Pritchard's journey was to submit to the appraisal of an interested buyer on the continent a valuable stamp collection, which Pritchard had inherited but did not choose to retain. By a remarkable coincidence, the album containing the collection was identical to that which was the object of the theft in Woking. When the unfortunate traveller happened to show his album to his dinner companion, as they enjoyed port and cigars together, he came under the eye of a plain-clothes detective. Pritchard's evening was quite spoiled by his ensuing apprehension and interrogation, after which the owner of the stolen album was fetched from *his* dinner and offered Mr. Pritchard's album, supposedly a miraculous return of stolen goods. The police were understandably disappointed when it was quickly discovered that his was not the missing album. For Pritchard, however, the outcome was happy since, shall we say, the turn of the wheel had led him to a wealthy philatelist who offered to buy his album at a price higher than that proposed by the Swiss collector. Furthermore, he was spared the expense and inconvenience of a journey he had had no great desire to take.

"BEFORE A CRACKLING FIRE."

"Hmm," said Holmes thoughtfully, as we smoked a late evening pipe and sipped whisky and soda before a crackling fire, "carriage wheels—luck—roulette—Cannes might produce some interesting problems for the Analytical Engine."

5.1   The Programming Language Basic

Writing a sequence of instructions for a computer cannot be done arbitrarily. The instructions must be written in one of the special languages available on the computer. The programming language *Basic* is one such language, probably the most widely utilized on small computers. Basic, like all programming languages, is governed by rigid rules. Unlike English, the grammatical forms are extraordinarily limited and have a single, unambiguous meaning.

Learning how to write programs is a major task in itself, far beyond our intent here. But it is probably safe to say that of all the issues related to computers, the writing of programs is practiced by more persons, is the source of more employment, is more expensive, and is discussed more than any other issue. Every day, on every major computer system, programs are being written or modified.

For these reasons, and to help demystify the art of programming, we concentrate on a more limited objective—understanding one simple program. Let us look at the program conveniently at hand, the one Holmes wrote, set out in Figure 5.1. Even this brief program is highly illustrative of some basic (or should we say, Basic?) principles of programming.

Holmes's Program

A program is designed to be executed on a computer. What this means is that after you type the text of a program on a computer terminal and save the text in the computer's storage, you can give a command to the computer to carry out the program's instructions. While the program is being executed, the program controls the behavior of the computer.

programming—programming implies the more difficult task of designing algorithms.

There were many problems with this method of expressing algorithms. For instance,

- The programs were exceedingly difficult to write. They were often long, tedious, and filled with special codes.

- The close association between a program and a particular machine design not only permitted but encouraged the invention of all kinds of tricks to get maximum performance from the computer. The correctness of such programs was very difficult to verify, and it was nearly impossible to discover the algorithm behind a program coded by a colleague.

- The language in which the program was written contained practically no textual redundancy that could be used to detect errors. Almost any combination of characters could be executed. To tie an error back to the faulty code was difficult and time consuming.

With these difficulties in mind, in 1954 John Backus formed a group to develop the Fortran (*For*mula *Tran*slator) language aimed at the automatic translation of mathematical formulas into machine instructions. The group hoped to bring about a radical change in the economics of scientific computing. They hoped to make programming much cheaper through a drastic reduction in the time it took for a working program to be prepared. Because of the atmosphere of skepticism, the group's emphasis was on the efficiency of the translated program rather than on language design. At that time, little was known of many issues now considered important in language design. For instance, Fortran was viewed as applying to just one machine. Little thought was given to the implications of making a machine-independent programming language.

Fortran was just one of several programming languages that appeared in 1956 and 1957. This period was the beginning of a programming revolution; it almost seemed that each new computer, and even each programming group, was spawning its own programming language or favorite dialect of an existing one. Most of these languages were aimed at helping the scientific programmer and were restricted to a particular machine. Their designers were generally a small group of implementors, rather than users, drawn from a single company. A primary design objective was to produce efficient machine code, even if it meant sacrificing some clarity of expression in the language.

```
program DEFECTIVEBOLT (INPUT, OUTPUT);

{  -- This program reads in four characteristics of a
   -- defective carriage wheel bolt: the number of threads,
   -- its initial loosening factor, the increment in the
   -- loosening factor each 100 turns of the wheel, and the
   -- circumference of the wheel.
   -- The program prints the distance travelled before
   -- the wheel will fall off. }

   var
      TOTALTHREADS, NUMBERTURNED,
      LOOSENFACTOR, INCREMENT,
      CIRCUMFERENCE, DISTANCE, MILES:   REAL;

begin
   {  -- Establish the knowns }
   READ (TOTALTHREADS, LOOSENFACTOR, INCREMENT, CIRCUMFERENCE);

   {  -- Calculate the distance travelled }
   DISTANCE := 0.0;
   NUMBERTURNED := 0.0;
   while NUMBERTURNED < TOTALTHREADS do begin
      DISTANCE := DISTANCE + CIRCUMFERENCE*100;
      NUMBERTURNED := NUMBERTURNED + LOOSENFACTOR;
      LOOSENFACTOR := LOOSENFACTOR + INCREMENT*LOOSENFACTOR
   end;

   {  -- Print the distance in miles }
   MILES := DISTANCE / 5280;
   WRITE ('DISTANCE IN MILES IS', MILES)
end.
```

Figure 5.2   *Pascal Program for the Carriage Wheel Problem*

The objectives of the designers of Cobol (*Common Business Oriented Language*) were different. In 1959, a committee of representatives from several organizations was formed. Their objective was to design a *machine independent* programming language suitable for use by the business community. The committee decided that the language should make the maximum use of simple English so that managers who had no programming experience would be able to understand the programs. Many committee members felt that arithmetic operations should be specified by words like ADD and MULTIPLY rather than by the symbols + and * because these words would be more readily understood. The important thing is not whether the committee was right, but that a serious effort was being made to design a language for communication between people and computers.

Fortran and Cobol are only two examples of the many, many languages that have been developed in order to program computers. Each time a new language is proposed, reasons are given to justify its design. Basic, for instance, was designed to be extremely easy to learn. It is not considered suitable for most practical applications. Pascal, in many ways a more expressive language than Basic, was designed to teach certain fundamental concepts in programming. A specialized application area is often given as justification—the programming language Apt, for instance, is used to write programs to control machine tools.

In most cases, however, programming languages are still far from satisfactory. This is demonstrated in two major ways:

- Languages have often been designed according to what is thought to be the easiest form for computer analysis rather than what is most natural as a means of expression.

- Economy and simplicity of design are rarely seen.

The profusion of programming languages and their design weaknesses severely hinder valuable communication between programmers. We are still in the state described in Genesis as leading to the failure of the Tower of Babel project. This is despite the efforts of many very talented people working individually, in groups, in small and large committees, and even in international committees. Some have attempted to design a "universal" language. There have been several candidates for this position, but none has achieved widespread acceptance and use.

Implementation Schemes

As mentioned above, a programming language is a higher form of communication than the machine language expressing the built-in operations of a computer. The way in which a programming language is realized is called the *implementation*. A programming language may be implemented in one of two ways: *compilation* or *interpretation*.

Compilation: The program written in the programming language is translated into an equivalent program in the machine language of a given computer. The machine language version is then executed directly by the computer.

The translation of a program to machine language is performed by another program, generally referred to as a *translator* or *compiler.* Pascal is a language that is often implemented in this way.

Interpretation: The program is translated into an intermediate form that cannot be executed directly by an actual computer. Instead, execution of the intermediate form is achieved by another program that reads and takes action much like executing the original program by hand.

The program that reads and takes action on the intermediate version of the original program is generally known as an *interpreter.* Basic is often implemented in this way.

The use of an interpreter allows for greater flexibility than direct execution of a compiled program. However, the penalty is that interpretation is generally much slower than direct execution.

There is no hard line of differentiation between compilation and interpretation. Even in systems where the compiler produces machine code for a real machine, an extensive library of supporting programs is usually required for execution. As the implementation moves more in the direction of interpretation, the library becomes bigger and less is done by execution of compiled codes.

Applications

CHAPTER VI

---†---

A Victim of Indiscretion

HE YEARS from 1885 to 1890 appear to have been active ones for criminals of the more refined and subtle type who so often came to the attention of my friend Sherlock Holmes. There is in my files a wealth of notes on cases he handled, occasionally with modest help from myself, and I have been much exercised to cull from the riches the most intriguing to chronicle. One such is the case of the death, apparently by his own hand, of the Honourable Spencer St. Martin. Holmes was successful in preventing who knows how many of St. Martin's former associates from following him precipitously from life into death. The prime mover, however, has never been brought to justice. In fact, this person unknown was saved, by Holmes's enlightened use of the Analytical Engine, from his own criminal tendencies and deprived of considerable ill-gotten gains which, taken together with several probable suicides and ruined lives, could only have weighed most miserably on his conscience. I will set forth the circumstances of the case and the reader may judge whether or not Holmes's swift action was the only course open to us.

Spencer St. Martin had become a prolific social commentator since his retirement from the bench a year before his death. Scarcely a week went by in which one of his many letters to the editor did not appear in *The Times*. It is even possible that his wide-ranging interests and opinions contributed to his downfall. Regular appearances in print brought his name to the attention of a much wider readership than his pronouncements from the bench. He never reached the eminence of hearing cases at the Old Bailey, which would have ensured his name becoming a household word to all those who savour sordid sensationalism. It was, then, by way of St. Martin's one-sided correspondence with the editor of *The Times* that his name was familiar to Holmes and myself. We were shocked one morning in 1887 to find him represented twice in the pages of that paper. No, more than twice—three times—for there was a brief obituary notice in addition to his latest, and last, letter to the editor and a short column at the foot of the front page describing his death.

St. Martin owned a large house in Leatherhead, a community much favoured by professional men and industrial magnates for its salubrious position on the North Downs and its proximity to both London and Brighton. It was to this house that he retired, to spend his days contentedly pottering in his garden, hybridising cinerarias in his greenhouse and writing copiously in his library. And, sadly, it was in this peaceful milieu that he died a violent and lonely death. He was found by the maid when she entered his bedroom with hot water for his morning shave. Only briefly mentioned in the press was the fact that she had to be extensively treated for scalding. St. Martin had hanged himself from a lamp hook with a length of rope he had removed from the laundry and, being versed in the law and the ritual of hanging, he had taken care not to bungle the job.

Since he was a bachelor and without living kin, St. Martin, prolific letter writer though he was, apparently felt no urge to leave a farewell note explaining his sudden departure from life—an oversight that might have given rise to questioning whether the hand of another was involved. However, the local police described his death as "a deliberate affair," an ambiguous term which could mean murder just as readily as suicide. The latter was the police reading of the case and generally accepted.

All the more surprising then was the visitor we received at Baker Street some weeks later, a young man articled to a firm of solicitors. Mr. Bancroft Henderson had been retained to handle the late magistrate's affairs on behalf of St. Martin's solicitor.

"The police, for once, seem to have done a thorough job," said Holmes as young Henderson took a seat by our fire. "Have you reason to suspect foul play?"

"I must confess, Mr. Holmes," said our visitor, "that I really don't know what to think."

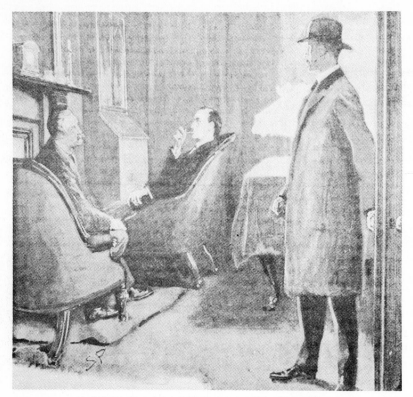

"A YOUNG MAN ARTICLED TO A FIRM OF SOLICITORS."

Henderson began by explaining his own role in administering the estate. He had, until recently, remained somewhat at arm's-length. But after an unsuccessful attempt to identify possible heirs through research in London, he decided to search through the magistrate's personal papers and so paid the great house a visit.

"It was a lovely morning and I was glad to get out of town. There I was," he told us, "humming the theme of the first movement of Beethoven's Sixth Symphony. If I'd only known—— " he trailed off, gloomily.

"Your experience in Leatherhead seems to have been disquieting, Mr. Henderson," said Holmes in those easy, soothing tones which he employed so often and so well.

"I found a letter, sir, that seems to explain why our client took his own life. I brought it first thing this morning to the senior partner working on St. Martin's probate affairs. He advised me to bring it directly to you. Here it is." He opened his brief-case to produce an envelope which bore the name and address of Spencer St. Martin. He withdrew a single sheet of paper, carefully typed, and passed it to my friend.

I was, of course, unable to restrain myself from moving over to peer across Holmes's shoulder and read the letter with him. This is what we saw :—

My dear St. Martin,

 Do you think it would be of interest to the members of your club to learn that one of their own members, a respectable gentleman, staid in demeanour and circumspect in his habits, has lived a secret life? Such a tale, entitled "A Victim of Indiscretion," has been prepared for distribution, beautifully printed on Toned Paper, in a private edition of one hundred copies.

 As a courtesy to their subject, I offer them first to you at ten guineas per copy. Since this work does not lack literary merit, I am naturally eager to see it in the hands of London's most distinguished readers. Your reply, via t he personal column of The Times and addressed to MAX BRICE, is impatiently awaited by the author, who wishes, in all modesty, to remain anonymous.

"Shocking," said Holmes, as he lowered the letter to his knee and felt around his pockets for his pipe. "We never know, gentlemen, how shaky are the pillars of our respectable society."

There followed several minutes of silence, broken only by the sound attendant to getting Holmes's pipe drawing to his satisfaction. Accustomed as I am to my friend's ways of working, I waited calmly for the inevitable indication that the real mind was coming to grips with the problem. Mr. Henderson appeared to find the inaction a strain but was too much in awe of Holmes's reputation to venture any questions.

Finally, Holmes rose from his chair and subjected the letter to minute scrutiny, first against the sunlight at the window, then under the powerful lens at his desk. At last he turned to Mr. Henderson.

"Thank you, Mr. Henderson," said Holmes, "for giving me the opportunity to work on this case. I believe an early solution can be engineered without great difficulty. Don't you agree, Watson?" he added, turning to me with a suave smile.

"Oh, absolutely," I responded heartily, guessing from his choice of words the direction he meant to go in pursuing the search for the extortioner.

"Spencer St. Martin's professional associations must have been considerable. As a magistrate, he had connections with all levels of society. From what I have read, he had an unusually large number of close friends—over three hundred people attended his memorial service."

"What are you getting at, Mr. Holmes?" Henderson asked.

"There is something about this note that suggests it was intended for a much larger readership than St. Martin alone. These words indicate to me that whatever this 'indiscretion' our late magistrate was guilty of committing, he was not the only participant. You'll note, also, that while the message is cleanly typed out, in very neat workmanship, the salutation has been handwritten and, I might add, in a manner designed to disguise the identity of its author."

"But what can be done, Mr. Holmes?" pleaded Henderson.

"Your immediate task, Mr. Henderson, is to procure for me a list of the members of Spencer St. Martin's club and any other associations of which he was a member and give me their addresses. You must act exactly as I say and not discuss my instructions. It's a sizable task, but I assure you quite necessary. Do you understand?"

Mr. Bancroft Henderson had relaxed perceptibly as Holmes spoke. Now he sprang to his feet and extended his hand to us each in turn.

"Thank you ever so much, Mr. Holmes," he declared with a boyish fervour that must have survived from his schooldays. "I shall follow your instructions in every particular and call upon you in a day or two to report my findings." With his new commission, the articled clerk took his leave.

"You have, I take it, formed some definite conception as to the meaning of this?" I ventured when Henderson had left.

"You will remember, Watson, my remark during the case concerning the King of Bohemia that I was planning another little monograph some of these days on the typewriter and its relation to crime. Well, I dare say, I may have to modify my subject somewhat when this matter is resolved. For now, there can be no doubt that this communication is the first installment in a series that adds up to a case of, shall we call it, genteel extortion."

"Blackmail?" I cried.

"Yes, Watson. Have you considered how the letter to Spencer St. Martin may have been produced? Consider the squaring off of the right-hand margin. If we assume, as I believe we must, that copies of this letter have been sent to a large number of persons, it would be a formidable task indeed for a typist to see to it that each copy should be so precisely laid out. That is, for a *human* typist."

I stared at my friend. "But, Holmes, no typewriting machine can operate without a human being to make use of it—unless—— " My eyes grew wider as a thought came to mind. "Do you suppose that the Analytical Engine figures in this somehow? Could someone have written a programme instructing it to type out that letter?"

"Precisely, Watson," Holmes declared, clapping me on the shoulder. "Moreover, I am quite certain that St. Martin is not the only victim. He was, perhaps, the most deeply involved, since the mere mention to him of his past indiscretion—in which I suspect this blackmailer played an equal hand—was enough to send the poor man to his own private gallows."

"But what is the point of this charge you've given young Henderson?"

"My purpose is twofold, dear Watson. Though I suspect Henderson's role in this affair places him in no personal jeopardy, he will certainly remain safe enough these next few days locked in the vaults of his firm as he sifts through St. Martin's papers. Second, we need a list of the dead man's closest associates, especially those dating back to the early years of his career. Once we have this in hand, we begin the tedious task of following every possible avenue. And follow them we shall, for sooner or later some two or more paths will cross.

"But," he continued, "there is nothing more to be said or done until our client returns. So what do you say to something nutritious at Simpson's, and after, a visit with Thurston on Newcastle Street for a game of fifth-up?"

The next few days were made memorable by a visit from my literary agent, who was eager to receive my manuscript concerning the strange affair at Reigate a year earlier. Sherlock Holmes was distant and uncommunicative during this visit. After a short but uncomfortable spell, he excused himself to post a letter. When he returned, my agent had departed and we were again alone.

He scarcely acknowledged my amiable queries. Taking his violin from the corner, he started to play some low, dreary air and then without pausing launched a series of crude, unpleasant snatches. At last, he put down his bow and sank into his arm-chair, the violin in his lap.

"You have given some prominence in your chronicles, Watson," he began, "to the incidents displaying those faculties of deduction and of logical synthesis which I have made my special province."

"Well, I must say, myself—— "

"However," he said dryly, "I have noticed that your writings have developed a certain vein of sensationalism. You have exaggerated my performances, embellished these simple exercises in deductive reasoning, and embroidered even my personal habits."

"This is Conan Doyle's doing," said I, rising to my defense. "Literary license he calls it."

"Libel I call it, and I believe the courts would agree," answered Holmes flatly.

"Really, Holmes, you are exaggerating yourself now."

"And what of this ridiculous costume you have dressed me in? How often has a client walked through that door expecting me to be clad rather for a jaunt on the moor than for a stroll down the Strand?"

"Paget. That's Paget's work. You can't expect to hold me responsible for an illustrator's imagination."

Holmes was silent for a moment. Then, looking belligerently around the room, he pointed with his bow to the large 'V' he had fashioned upon our wall with my old service revolver one day during a dreadful period of inaction.

"On how many more occasions will you recount this incident for the delight of your readers?"

"I believe that I am one of the most patient and long-suffering of individuals, Holmes," I said severely. "But I must draw the line. I live with a man who keeps his cigars in the coal-scuttle, his tobacco in the toe of a Persian slipper, smokes incessantly, keeps the most ungodly hours, and each day invites new terrors into our home. Now I must admit to being slightly annoyed by this fit of pique."

Holmes seemed too absorbed in his own thoughts to make any immediate response to my remonstrance. Finally he rose from his position and paced the room, his chin sunk deep on to his chest. He nodded from time to time and then, reaching into the Persian slipper, began to fill his pipe with shag. "Surely you will permit me to indulge in one of my filthy habits?" he asked apologetically.

It was difficult to refuse any of Sherlock Holmes's requests, for he had, when he wished, an almost hypnotic power of soothing.

"I was only saying that the manuscripts I present to Conan Doyle undergo considerable change at his hand before they are submitted to his editors for even further work."

"Yes, well, but it would be good if I had the opportunity to review them before they were published," replied Holmes.

"That's a privilege even I don't enjoy, dear friend—or Conan Doyle himself, as I understand."

"It seems to me, dear Watson, a problem of logistics—how to enable a copy of the manuscript as it develops from one stage to the next to be placed into the many hands of all concerned."

"But surely you see how impossible that would be, Holmes," I pointed out. "Oh, it could be done, I suppose, if one had the services of a very efficient typist. But time would be lost whenever a mistake were made. And suppose a manuscript should need to be revised a number of times? Or should require changes here and there? The typist might have to redo the entire manuscript, or at least several pages, to take such changes into account."

"Your arguments are quite valid, dear fellow," said Holmes with a smile. "Let me see if I can muster a defense." He lit his pipe and, settling back in his chair, watched the blue smoke from his pipe drift to the ceiling. For some time his eyes remained vacantly fixed upon the corner of the room.

"You know, Watson," he said at last, "I fancy this to be a task well-suited to the Analytical Engine. Even in its current state of development, the Engine plainly can be used to produce a number of identical copies of some piece of writing—the letter to Spencer St. Martin and the other blackmail victims proves that."

"If there *are* other letters," I reminded him. "We know of no others thus far."

"Allow me to continue, Watson. Suppose it were possible for the Engine to be altered so that a manuscript could be somehow recorded in its memory in an unwritten form—that is, the manuscript would exist not on paper, but merely in the Engine's memory unit, just as any other type of data is stored. Our manuscript would not be entirely unwritten, for we would have a means by which we could see what the Engine's memory contains."

"That's preposterous, Holmes!" I broke in. "How could there be such a thing as a recorded yet unwritten manuscript? Next you'll be telling me it's written on air!"

"Indulge me in my fancy for a bit, Watson. Let me see—— Ah, perhaps this analogy will be acceptable to you. Let us pretend that we can write our manuscript on an imaginary slate so that we can change it as we please in an instant simply by telling the Analytical Engine to erase this or to write that. We could compose our entire manuscript on the slate, leaving the Engine to remember its contents and to make any emendations we desire. Once our manuscript is complete and correct in its ethereal form—for we could obviously correct any errors easily—we could then order the Engine to print it out on paper and to produce as many copies of it as we please."

" 'Pon my word, Holmes, I believe you've missed your calling in life," I chuckled. "You should be the one to work with Conan Doyle, not I."

"Scoff if you will, Watson," Holmes responded, "but bear in mind that inventions such as the locomotive, the steam ship, the typewriter, and yes, the Analytical Engine, too, were all once merely ideas in men's imaginations. But to return to the world of reality, my plans are to put the Engine to use in clearing up this matter with Mr. Henderson. I shall broach the subject with my brother Mycroft when our young client returns."

The following day Henderson was at our apartment before our breakfast dishes had been cleared. He brought with him several sheets of foolscap bearing the names and addresses of every individual and professional association to which he could link Spencer St. Martin.

"Allowing for human error and oversight, we probably have as complete a document as I might have wished," said Holmes as he ran his eye up and down the lengthy columns of names and addresses. "Tell me, sir, why have you marked off the name of Mr. Colin Monroe?"

"Did you not see the morning papers, Mr. Holmes?" answered Henderson.

"I read something the other day of his promotion to a senior position within his firm."

"And just yesterday he left the company without a word of explanation. The chairman of the firm says he is completely in the dark about it."

"Do you think there may be some connection, Holmes?" I asked.

"We must never trust to general impressions, gentlemen, but concentrate on the details. It is a capital error to theorize without sufficient data, for invariably one begins to twist facts to fit theories. However—— " He trailed off and turned his attention again to the document. "Hmm, First Battalion, the Royal Mallows."

"Formerly the 117th Foot," said I. "The Indian Mutiny, you know."

"This was St. Martin's regiment?" asked Holmes. Henderson nodded. "It appears as though a visit with Mr. Monroe will not be wasted energy. But first I must get a message to my brother at Whitehall. Could

"HE BROUGHT WITH HIM SEVERAL SHEETS OF FOOLSCAP."

you deliver it, Mr. Henderson, while Watson and I make our way to the West End?"

"Of course, sir," he replied.

"Excellent," said Holmes as he quickly scribbled something on the first of the many sheets Henderson had brought to him. He folded them together in one bundle and handed the package to the young lawyer. "Mycroft Holmes. You will find him in the Home Office. He will know exactly what to do."

Holmes and I left immediately to pay a call on Mr. Colin Monroe. Not a moment too soon, either, for we found him about to depart for who knows where. Holmes introduced us both, but Monroe made it patently evident that he had no wish to linger.

"I apologize, gentlemen. I have some personal affairs to attend to," said Monroe, whose demeanour and bearing showed him to be every inch the successful business magnate. "I'm afraid I must leave at once."

"WE FOUND HIM ABOUT TO DEPART."

"How much more harm could you possibly suffer?" said Holmes.

"I am sure I do not quite follow you, sir."

"There are certain crimes which the law cannot touch and which justify private action, Mr. Monroe. I am speaking of blackmail. I suspect you may stand in need of our help."

At this, Monroe turned about and wordlessly led us into his library, staggering as if about to faint.

"Now, sir," said Holmes, "after you have consumed some brandy and are restored, you will kindly tell us all that has happened. Meanwhile, I should like to have a look at the letter that is the cause of all this."

Holmes helped him to a chair while I went to the sideboard for brandy. From his breast pocket he produced an envelope and passed it with trembling hands to Holmes. He seemed too shaken to question why Holmes would know about this matter.

"To the letter," said the detective as he read through the page. "You see, Watson, that the additional space mistakenly inserted between the 'th' and the 'e' in the word 'the' is present in both letters. The right hand margin is also squared off in the same way."

I stood by his shoulder and examined the note. It was identical in every way to the correspondence St. Martin had received. At the top of the page Monroe's name had been written in by an unsteady hand.

Monroe's story began in Calcutta, some twenty years back. Obviously, to include any details enabling the reader to identify the incident or the particular personalities connected with it would be injudicious and offensive. So painful a scandal, which I can state was not criminal in nature, is best allowed to die.

"Your discretion is as well known as your remarkable abilities, Mr. Holmes," said Monroe, recovering some of his composure. "I beg you to do whatever you can, sir."

"I believe that an end to this has already been put in motion. You will be troubled no more, save by your own conscience," said Holmes.

"But this is incredible! Whom do you suspect?" he exclaimed.

"No one in particular. There are several points in this matter which shall remain unexplained. Yet, if the actions that I have taken bear fruit, you have received the last of these letters."

Holmes's reassurance was enough to put Monroe at ease, and we bade him goodbye. I remained completely confused about the entire matter as we set a brisk pace back to Baker Street.

"Yes, I owe you every atonement, Watson, for having allowed your curiosity to remain so long unsatisfied," said Holmes once we were back at our chambers with our feet stretched out before a cheery fire. "As you know, I suspected early on that the blackmailer was sending the same letter to each of his victims, but I needed, of course, at least one other copy to test that theory. I asked Mr. Henderson to draw up a list that would be likely to include some of the other recipients. Our stumbling upon Mr. Monroe was pure chance, though I suspect that our enquiry into the other names on that list would have produced similar results."

"What leads you to think that the blackmailer will stop sending out more letters?"

"Because I have written and asked him to do so," said my companion with an enigmatical smile.

"This is preposterous! What are you saying, Holmes?" I exclaimed.

"Shall I say it again for you? I have written to the blackmailer, and everyone else whose name is on that list—a point I should have made when you first asked."

"And what did you say?" I demanded curtly.

"That I was investigating the affair, that I was on to him, and he must stop at once or I shall be forced to take action against him."

"But, Holmes, there were several hundred names on that list. How did you manage? We haven't been apart long enough for you to have posted a single letter!"

"That's true, my dear Watson, but I wrote it here, before you and Henderson this morning, and he delivered it for me."

"To your brother?"

"Yes. I asked Mycroft to instruct the Analytical Engine to print copies and send them along to every name on the list. I suspect our blackmailer has used a very similar method, which certainly narrows down the field of candidates should we elect to pursue him."

"Extraordinary, dear Holmes," was all I could say.

"Not really, but it has potential. I should like to drop by Fleet Street some time soon, Watson, and discuss the matter of your fabulous chronicles and how we may all have a hand in their editing."

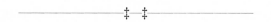

6.1 Word Processing

In "The Adventure of the Naval Treaty," Percy Phelps relates to Sherlock Holmes how his uncle, Lord Holdhurst, entrusted him with a vital commission for the Foreign Office where they both worked.

> " 'This,' said he, taking a grey roll of paper from his bureau, 'is the original of that secret treaty between England and Italy ... The French or Russian Embassies would pay an immense sum to learn the contents of these papers. They should not leave my bureau were it not absolutely necessary to have them copied.' "

While not all documents are as valuable as the Naval Treaty which Percy Phelps was to copy, they are nonetheless the lifeblood of many professions.

Underwood Typewriter, 1897

For an author, whether it be of a five-page report or a textbook, the document in preparation is the focus of attention. For a law firm, the primary function is not just counsel but documents as well—legal documents that should be letter perfect. For a bank, not only must monetary transactions be correct, but they must be supported in written form. For an insurance firm, reports, tables, and forms abound. Somewhat unfortunately, almost everywhere we turn, some organization has reason to send us a form letter, generated by a computer of course.

While the classical, early applications of computers centered on numerical processing, the production of documents by computer has become almost a way of life. This application has given rise to the development of computers specialized to this purpose, i.e., *word processors.*

At the outset, we should comment on the term "word processor." Words are only a part of this ubiquitous area. A word processor is a computer system whose primary role is the production of documents, including their size, layout, and organization. For effective use, a word processor may require specialized associated devices, access to large amounts of data, or specialized management procedures. But at the root of it all, the purpose of word processors is to help you prepare documents.

Documents produced by means of a word processor usually have one or more of the following characteristics:

■ They must be revised frequently. For example, it is not uncommon for a document such as a textbook or final report to be revised ten or twenty times. The author may prepare a rough draft, revise it for minor corrections, edit and add to it later, revise it again, show it to several people who make further suggestions, and so on.

■ Multiple variants of a master document are generated by "filling in the blanks." At the top of this category are the form letters; other examples are price lists, financial reports, and customer bills.

■ Perfect (or near perfect) copy is needed. Such cases include legal documents, important letters, mailing labels, or for that matter, any document that the preparer wishes to be error free.

The salient value of word processing is that the typing or editing process is cumulative. Once a correction is made, it stays made; a new correction does not disturb an old one, as retyping of the entire copy is not required. This means that the production of a "perfect" copy need not require a skilled typist. With enough patience anyone can do it. With a word processor, typing speed is more important than typing accuracy.

Most word processors have four basic components:

1. *Keyboard.* The keyboard is used to enter text and to control the operation of the system.

2. *Screen.* The video screen is used to display the text of the document and to provide status information (for example, the name of the document and the current page number).

3. *Storage Device.* The storage device holds the master copy of the user's document. Often storage is on a floppy disk that can be inserted directly into the word processor, although other methods, including the use of remote devices, are used.

A Commercially Available Word Processor

4. *Printer.* A printer is used to print a copy of the document when desired.

These four components illustrate the four essential functions of word processing:

1. *Entering text.* An electronic keyboard is the computer's replacement for a pencil.

2. *Observing results.* A screen is the computer's replacement for paper. The text can be reviewed, corrections can be seen, and the format can be observed by viewing the screen.

3. *Preserving the work.* With pencil and paper, you can save your work on the corner of a table or in a drawer. With a computer, the results are saved in some electronic form.

4. *Printing the final product.* When you are finished for the day, or finished with the entire job, you may want to take the result home or give a copy to someone. The printer serves this function.

A special note on item 3. The absolute minimum function of any word processor, no matter how inexpensive or lacking in features, is the ability to record a document electronically. This central feature allows you to make the entire writing process cumulative. When you stop on one day and continue the next, you continue exactly where you left off.

6.2   A Visit with a Word Processor

The selection of word processing systems is so varied that it is difficult to compare them in a really objective or useful way. To pin down the general idea of what they can do and how you operate one, however, let us go through a sample session with one. The word processor we use is hypothetical, although its features are typical of those commercially available.

Our task is to prepare a letter with the following text:

19, Old Jewry,
London E.C.
25th October.

Dear Mr. Holmes,

re <u>Magpies</u>

Our respected client Mr. Kenneth Clark, of Watts and Armstrong, Goldsmiths of Clement's Lane, has asked our opinion on the various habits of magpies.

As we have always aimed to specialise in legal matters concerning the Probate Court, we feel we are not adequately briefed to reply to Mr. Clark. We have therefore suggested that he might arrange a mutually convenient date to meet you and to discuss more fully his exact requirements.

I am sure your professional views would be of considerable assistance.

Yours sincerely,

Clutterbuck, Rackham, and Chamberlain
per E. G. C.

We assume that you have prepared a cup of coffee and are ready to use your word processor.

Your first task is to find a proper floppy disk on which to record your letter. You have a rather large collection of disks, one of which is used for correspondence. You take it from its box, and turn on the power switch of the word processor. After a short pause, the screen comes to life. The sterile message

```
INSERT SOFTWARE RELEASE
```

is displayed. You reach for another box of floppy disks and, being careful not to spill your coffee, pull out the latest software release, Number 2.6. You insert the software disk and press the RETURN key. The red light comes on, you wait 30 seconds, and then the machine prints another message:

```
INSERT STORAGE DISK
```

Now you remove the software disk, take your disk for storing letters, insert it, press the RETURN key, and finally see the message you were waiting for:

```
READY
```

A few notes are in order here. First, the RETURN key. This key is similar to a carriage return key on a conventional typewriter. Unfortunately, on most computers this key serves a variety of purposes, some of them unclear. In the above case, the RETURN key means "do it," i.e. read the contents of the disk. In other cases, the key may mean advance to the next line, or continue reading data on the next line, or even nothing. This overloading of meaning in keys is a frequent source of confusion.

Second, the *software* disk. This disk contains all of the data and programs needed to make the word processor behave like a word processor. Without it, you would have a helpless piece of hardware.

Software is issued in periodic new releases. The vendors sell this idea with the theme of promoting advances. "Upgrade," they say, "to release 2.6." All too often, the reasons for the new release are cloudy. There may have been errors in the previous release, or mistakes in design, or they may have added features you have no use for. And, watch out, some of the features of the previous release may have been altered, including a feature you use every day. Oh well, let's get on with release 2.6.

Your first thought is to give a file name to the letter to Holmes. You press a key marked NEW. The message

ENTER NEW FILE NAME:

appears at the top of the screen. You now type the name

HOLMES

and to your surprise, you see the message

FILE ALREADY EXISTS

Ah yes, you had entered another similar letter several weeks ago, and had named it HOLMES. You hit the NEW key again, get the message

ENTER NEW FILE NAME:

and cautiously enter the file name

HOLMES.1

The screen is cleared, all is well.

You now start typing in your letter. As you type the first line,

19, Old Jewry,

the characters nicely appear on the screen with a small arrow, called a *cursor,* immediately under the last character typed. The second line you type contains a little spelling error:

Londin E.C.

No problem. You move the cursor directly under the "i" in "Londin," then type the correct letter. Your mistake is corrected!

You now press the RETURN key, enter the third line, and see:

19, Old Jewry,
London   E.C.
25th October.

You notice that the third line should be indented three more spaces to the right. So you move the cursor under the "2" in "25th." Caution. You want to add three spaces, but if you just type the three spaces, the original characters will disappear. What you must do is press HOLD key (which puts the characters to the right of the cursor on "hold"), type the three spaces, press the HOLD key again (which takes you off "hold"), and then RETURN. It works.

We pause again. With the HOLD key we venture a bit deeper into the mysterious conventions of computers. Its use here is to insert rather than overstrike the text with spaces. The assorted use of special purpose keys often puzzles the imagination.

As for moving the cursor, four keys on the terminal serve this purpose, marked with left, right, up, and down arrows. They perform exactly as you expect, moving the cursor in the indicated direction. They have the wonderful role of allowing you to move to any position in your text and then to modify the text at the indicated position as needed. This kind of roaming through text and making corrections is the essence of word processing.

The body of the letter is now entered. You decide to ignore any mistakes and correct them when you are done. You notice how the word processor senses the end of a line and automatically advances to the next line. When you have finished, the screen contains a complete copy of what you have typed. You notice that a couple of characters are mistyped, move the cursor, and correct them.

You now observe a serious error, the omission of two words "legal matters." This is serious in the sense that if you add the two words, the line will overspill the right margin. Now for a bit of electronic wizardry. You insert the two words, allowing the line to spill over. You now press the CONTROL key, the letter P, and RETURN. Before your eyes, the full paragraph is readjusted to fit within the required margins. A strange set of keys to press, but it works.

You are now satisfied with what you see on the screen. It's time to print out the letter to Holmes. This is not as simple as it appears. You press the PRINT key and immediately get the message:

```
PRINTER NOT IN SERVICE.
```

You remember that the printer is switched off. You rise from your chair, turn the printer on, and insert a sheet of paper. In doing so, you realize that you do not want to use the standard printing options supplied by the computer; for instance, you wish an indentation of 15 and not 10. So you press the keys CONTROL and PRINT. The screen responds with:

```
LINES PER INCH =   4  6  8  12
```

This is the first of a series of questions, indicated by the fact that the given numbers are blinking. You respond by positioning the cursor over (not under) the answer, and pressing RETURN. You want single spacing and fortunately you remember this means 6 lines per inch. Heaven knows why you would use 12 line per inch, one of the possible answers. So you move the cursor under the 6 and press RETURN.

Now it says,

```
PAGE  =    66
```

meaning 66 lines per page. This looks fine, and although you can type a new number, say 60 or 72, over the 66, you take what is offered by simply pressing RETURN.

Now the computer says,

```
LEFT MARGIN =    10
```

you change the 10 to 15, and press RETURN. Now it says:

```
RIGHT MARGIN =    JUSTIFIED  UNJUSTIFIED
```

Justified text has an even right edge, just as in the pages of a book. The computer does this by inserting extra spaces between words so that each line has the same width. The letter to Holmes should be justified, so you move the cursor under JUSTIFIED and press RETURN.

You now see the message,

```
PRINT?
```

You press RETURN, and the printer starts typing. You are delighted, wait a few moments for the typing to be completed, and pull out the page. The result is shown in Figure 6.1.

The output is disappointing. The computer justified every line, even lines in the heading of the letter. To get around this you must type a special symbol after each line that should not be justified. This symbol is called a "fixed return," and is entered by pressing the CONTROL key followed by the RETURN key. So back to the word processor to add the fixed returns. In a couple of minutes you have finished the minor, but annoying changes.

You insert a new sheet of paper, press the PRINT key again, the printer takes over, and now the result is that of Figure 6.2. Just what you want.

You are not quite done yet. If you shut off the word processor now, your file will be lost, and you will get *no* warning. What do you do? You press the OUT key, the following message is displayed,

```
FILE HOLMES1 SAVED
```

and the text of the letter disappears from the screen. Do not fear. The letter is now recorded on your floppy disk. So you remove the disk, put it back in its box, and turn off the word processor. Total elapsed time— a half hour.

19,   Old   Jewry,
London   E.C.
25th   October.

Dear   Mr.   Holmes,

re   Magpies

Our respected client Mr. Kenneth Clark, of Watts and Armstrong,
Goldsmiths of Clement's Lane, has asked our opinion on the various habits of
magpies.

As we have always aimed to specialise in legal matters concerning the
Probate Court, we feel we are not adequately briefed to reply to Mr. Clark.
We have therefore suggested that he might arrange a mutually convenient
date to meet you and to discuss more fully his exact requirements.

I am sure your professional views would be of considerable assistance.

Yours   sincerely,

Clutterbuck,   Rackham,   and   Chamberlain
per   E.   G.   C.

Figure 6.1   *First Printed Version of a Letter to Holmes*

19, Old Jewry,
London E.C.
25th October.

Dear Mr. Holmes,

re Magpies

Our respected client Mr. Kenneth Clark, of Watts and Armstrong,
Goldsmiths of Clement's Lane, has asked our opinion on the various habits of
magpies.

As we have always aimed to specialise in legal matters concerning the
Probate Court, we feel we are not adequately briefed to reply to Mr. Clark.
We have therefore suggested that he might arrange a mutually convenient
date to meet you and to discuss more fully his exact requirements.

I am sure your professional views would be of considerable assistance.

Yours sincerely,

Clutterbuck, Rackham, and Chamberlain
per E. G. C.

Figure 6.2   *Final Version of a Letter to Holmes*

6.3   The Dazzling Marketplace

When it comes to buying a word processor, the array of choices and options is dazzling. You can spend several hundred dollars on word processing software for a small home computer, or spend tens of thousands of dollars to buy a fancy one. And for any price range, there are a number of vendors who will be happy to sell you their product.

Probably the most important fact to keep in mind in selecting a word processor, or any computer for that matter, is the deep commitment once the choice is made. This commitment holds even if you rent one or use someone else's computer. You have to install it, learn its conventions, find out how to read the manuals, become familiar with the technical terms that go with it, develop procedures for using it, and live with its output. Most important, you will record documents on its external storage. These recordings are unlikely to be compatible with those of any other manufacturer.

To illustrate, suppose you had a word processor for a year and, for one reason or another, wanted to change to a different one. You may find the screen too glaring, have trouble training people to use it, need more storage, want fancier printed copy, discover you need proportional spacing, or want a more efficient way of preparing mailing labels.

Changing at this point is very difficult. You probably have hundreds of pages of recorded text and a rather heavy investment in adapting to the conventions of your own machine. In other words, you cannot think of a computer as you do a washing machine, a copying machine, a television set, or an automobile. Once you start down a path with a given computer, it is hard to turn back.

But of all the issues, the major one is how easy you find it to use. We shall take up this matter on its own in Chapter IX. All machines may appear easy when demonstrated by an expert, but *you* have to use it. Try to get hold of the manual that goes with it and see if you can read it. Take a look at what is printed on the screen during operation, and ask if it makes sense to you. Look at the keys as well. For the moment, all we say is that you cannot look closely enough.

Aside from these issues, there are myriad other details, some of which may matter greatly to an individual application. Table 6.1 itemizes some of the features of typical word processing systems. If you are about to enter the marketplace of word processing, be cautious of the dazzling lights.

Table 6.1
Some Word Processing Features

Screen Size — Many word processors come with a full (page-sized) screen, many with a half-page screen, and some with only a one-line window display. Others may have no screen but interact through the typewriter. A full screen is immediately attractive, but the drawbacks to the other options may not be serious.

Automatic Paging — With this feature the word processor automatically prints the text in a specified page layout with page numbers. It is truly useful.

Automatic Hyphenation — This feature varies from system to system, but generally lets the computer make some decisions about hyphenating words at the right margin. An over-rated feature.

Global Search and Replace — Suppose you wanted to change all mentions of "analytical engine" to "Analytical Engine." With a global search and replace, one command would do the trick. This is a much promoted feature, but it is surprising how little most people use it.

Screen Tones — Screens come in all kinds of tones, from conventional black letters on a white background to white-on-green, white-on-black, white-on-blue, and other shades. The conventional white-on-black can be glaring, and dark screens can cause eye strain. The final word on this matter is not in.

Printing Speed — Obviously the faster the printing, the better, but faster means more expensive. Many word processing systems are set up for 45 characters per second, or about a page every 2 minutes. For many uses this is fast enough.

Print Quality — This is a sticky area. If you look at some less expensive models, the quality of print may become tiresome to read and produce poor photocopies. It's probably a good idea to go for the highest quality you can afford. Whether you need boldface type, proportional spacing, or multiple typing styles is really dictated by your application.

Work Stations — Many commercial applications have several work stations that share access to common files.

Keyboard — If the keyboard looks mysterious, and many do, watch out. A good keyboard is easy to understand, and the keys are properly placed for efficient use.

Physical Characteristics — Back and neck complaints are quite high among users of computer terminals. Can you alter the tilt of the screen? Can you adjust its height? Can you put the keyboard on your lap? If long hours of use are planned, this can be a major issue.

CHAPTER VII

‡

The Adventure of the Toy Train

(Part I)

 N EMERGENCY summons one evening last winter drew me away from my comfortable chair beside our hearth to the Manchester Street home of one of my patients. When my services were no longer needed and the patient was sleeping quietly, I took my leave. On an impulse I decided to go round to Baker Street and call upon my friend Sherlock Holmes, as I had not seen him in upwards of a month. Rather than disturb Mrs. Hudson, his housekeeper, I decided to announce myself and accordingly ascended the stairs.

I opened the door to find Holmes sitting cross-legged on the floor in a blue dressing-gown, surrounded by mounds of yellowed newspapers and his many scrapbooks. A long cherry-wood pipe and a box of matches, as well as a lens, all lay within easy reach.

"You are busy, I see. Perhaps this is a bad hour for social calls," said I.

"Oh, no, Watson," he muttered, hardly aware of my presence. "You are always a welcome guest. Take a seat and I will be with you presently."

He had been deeply involved with a scrapbook, the pages of which bulged with newspaper cuttings that had not yet been pasted in.

"You are working on a case?" I ventured.

"No, things are quiet for the moment," he replied.

Taking the basket-chair to his left, as usual, I glanced around our old chambers. His homely untidiness had gone unchecked by Mrs. Hudson, with most of the familiar landmarks gathering dust. But there was a new addition to the congenial surroundings. Pinned to the mantel-piece, to the walls, and even to the sofa, were hundreds of news clippings, pieces of paper, and an occasional lengthy document. He had a horror of destroying papers, especially those that were connected with his cases.

"You have a grand gift of silence, Watson. Such an invaluable companion," he remarked, taking up a glowing cinder with the tongs and casually lighting it in his pipe. "So you still smoke the Arcadia mixture of your bachelor days. Help yourself, if you care to."

"Of course," I said, brushing away the evidence on my trouser-leg. I took out my pouch and smoked for some time in silence, waiting patiently until he should choose to bring up the subject of his studies.

"No doubt you are wondering about my unique filing system," he said at last, gesturing about his head towards the memorabilia that surrounded us.

"I take great pleasure attempting to unravel the mysteries that hang about you, Holmes, but I must confess this system, if you can call it that, is beyond my comprehension."

"TAKING UP A GLOWING CINDER WITH THE TONGS."

"Oh, there's no mystery about it, actually. I'm experimenting with a new idea for filing the minutiae that clutter my bookshelves as well as my mind."

"What, by posting them to the walls?"

"Yes, what do you think of it? Clever, is it not?"

"Absurd!" I protested.

Suddenly his eyes kindled and a slight flush sprang to his thin face. He was laughing aloud and once again at my expense.

"Forgive me, Watson. You are such a wonderful confidant, what with your perpetual surprise at each new development and the future such a closed book."

"Well, what's your explanation, then?" I demanded.

"One which should find enormous favor with you, dear fellow, since it should effectively eliminate this mildly disorganized state of affairs," my friend replied. "You've already recorded my remarks that a man should keep the attic of his brain stocked only with the furnishings he will put to use, with the remainder tucked away in the cupboard of his library, where he can reach it when needed. I think you put it even more eloquently in one of your earlier accounts. Nevertheless, I now have in mind some thoughts about storing all of these data." He waved his hand about his head, cutting through the thin veil of blue smoke that surrounded him. "Our cupboard shall be that wonderful device we often have had occasion to call upon."

"The Analytical Engine?"

"I expect Mycroft to arrive here any minute. He is as anxious as I to put the Engine to some personal use. If this trifling experiment with my own papers works, it could be adopted at Whitehall and Scotland Yard."

"But Holmes, you would have to take digs at Whitehall and surely your hours at the Engine would be restricted."

"On the contrary, Watson. I thought I'd put your old room to good use. It does not get much airing since you resumed general practice."

I was deeply hurt, and it must have registered on my countenance for Holmes quickly added, "And of course there's the box-room. I could shift some of my impedimenta into the back hallway, and perhaps the curtained recess would make a suitable location for the Engine."

"It will certainly require sizeable lodgings," said I, regaining my composure. "You may be right about my old room."

"The Engine could never replace you as a constant companion, my dear Watson," he replied, rising from his seat. He advanced to the draperies which screened the alcove of his bow window and drew them aside. Sunlight splashed across his strong-set aquiline features and revealed the cloud of dust he had dislodged from the curtain's folds.

"I have in mind a smaller version of the Engine, Watson, one that could fill this gap nicely. Imagine if I had at my disposal only the mechanisms for entering and receiving data with the huge mill and all its other appendages sitting in Whitehall."

"You would need some sort of connection between them."

"A telegraph cable. What do you think?"

"What, you'd run a cable out this window and across half of London? Mrs. Hudson would surely give you notice to quit."

"Mrs. Hudson has already endured the vagaries of my disposition; one more peculiarity should not be too burdensome. Besides, the cable would run only to the nearest telegraph office, which is just down Baker Street at number Sixty-six."

Upon the stairs came the sound of a slow and heavy step which paused in the passage immediately outside the door.

"That will be Mycroft now," said Holmes. "Come in!" he cried.

Like a hay-cart coming down a country lane, the portly figure of Mycroft Holmes moved into the sitting-room, which seemed smaller for his presence. He greeted us and sank his bulk into the chair I had lately occupied.

"I am afraid we shall have to defer discussion of the Analytical Engine," said Mycroft in a brisk, business-like manner. "There are more pressing concerns that bring me here."

"Nothing that cannot be resolved, I trust," said Sherlock Holmes.

"A minor affair, but in need of some attention."

"To a great mind, nothing is minor. Now tell me, what would bring a man

"MYCROFT HOLMES."

such a distance when his only exercise from one year to the next is a short stroll round the corner from his lodgings in Pall Mall to his office in Whitehall? Sounds rather serious to me."

"I'll come straight to the point. You have heard of Sir Harold Chesterfield?"

"I have read his reports for *The Times* from the Sudan. He is somewhere in the Balkans now, isn't he?"

"He is, at this moment, on the Orient Express just outside Paris. I expect him in London tomorrow morning."

"So, he has filed correspondence for the Foreign Office as well. Is he in some danger?"

"I expect he will arrive with his left arm in a sling: an untidy, unprofessional attempt in Istanbul."

"This is to my liking. Watson, would you hand me that volume to your right, marked 'C'?" Sherlock Holmes began to flip through the pages of the formidable looking scrap-book. "Hmm, Cantlemere, Charpentier, Cowesworthy—no, Chesterfield. Now this is strange, indeed, for I am absolutely certain that I recently clipped a number of items for filing under his name. They must be buried in with all these other cuttings."

"Perhaps they are filed under 'T' for *Times*," I suggested, "or on the wall to the left of the chiffonier."

"Well, this certainly proves my point about the potential of the Analytical Engine," said Holmes, turning back to his brother. "Now how are my services to be engaged?"

"Sir Harold will refuse a bodyguard, I'm sure, but he will need better protection than Scotland Yard can provide."

"How long is he to be in London?"

"Less than a week."

"Can you get Sir Harold safely to Whitehall and then bring him here while there is still sunlight to-morrow? Say, four o'clock?"

"I will do so," replied his brother, rising and turning for the door. "Meanwhile, I have left word that you are to receive full cooperation on any plans you may have for the Engine, no matter how far-fetched they may sound."

The next morning I paid an early visit to a patient on Marylebone Road and, being in the vicinity of Baker Street, decided to drop in on Holmes. I was keen to know what plans he had for handling this delicate and dangerous assignment.

When I entered the flat, my first impression was that a fire had broken out. The smoke was so thick that the light from the gas lamp above the table was blurred. Through this haze I could vaguely see Holmes in his dressing-gown pacing the floor. An unusual whirring noise accompanied by a low-pitched hum was audible, but from whence it came I could not tell.

"Making your rounds, I see," remarked Holmes, as I walked passed him to open the windows.

"And lucky that I am. Your brother would have found you asphyxiated when he returned this afternoon!"

"Yes, it is pretty thick, I suppose."

"And how can you tell that I have been on a call?"

Holmes chuckled and tapped his pipe out against the grate of the hearth. "A man whom I know to be of the medical profession walks into my quarters at such an early hour with the black mark of nitrate of silver upon his right forefinger and his stethoscope secreted in his top-hat. Now what other deduction am I to make?"

I glanced down at my right hand and to the tubing protruding from my hat, which I held in the other, and smiled broadly. The smoke was beginning to clear, and my attention again turned to the gentle whirring that seemed to emanate from behind the curtained recess.

"What the devil is that sound?" I asked.

"The Orient Express, Watson, carrying Sir Harold Chesterfield to Baker Street." Holmes drew back the curtain. I strolled across the room and in the alcove saw a tiny battery-powered model train moving round a metal track. Holmes operated a switch and it came to an abrupt halt. "Wonderful thing, electricity."

"What is this? A plaything from Hamleys?"

"Hours of entertainment," he replied, setting the little train going again. "I suppose you are wondering about Sir Harold Chesterfield."

"I don't mean to be meddlesome," I said.

"Oh, no, Watson. Actually I'm hoping that you will help us out. It may even provide material for your chronicles."

"Then count me in, dear fellow. Business is slow these days."

"So, married life has not harnessed your ambitions. You bear every sign of the busy practitioner with calls for his service each hour. But what I have in mind should not interrupt your professional responsibilities."

"I have an accommodating neighbour and should be glad to assist you."

"Splendid! Here it is then," he said, rubbing his hands together. "I plan to have Sir Harold stay here with me when he is not at Whitehall under Mycroft's care. If your way could lead you down Baker Street once each night, say, around nine o'clock, I shall signal from the window that all is well. Should you spot any variation upon my signal, report at once to Inspector Gregson. Do you follow me?"

"Simple enough. But what signal will you use?"

"Something that will not serve to alert anyone else who may be watching the house. Suppose I have the blind down with the light against it to carry my silhouette? I'll pass by, stopping in front of the window a few times, to show that nothing is amiss."

We agreed upon our signal, and that night I walked past the building at the prescribed hour. Holmes's quarters were brilliantly lit. I could see his tall, spare figure, with his head sunk upon his chest and his hands clasped behind him. The dark silhouetted figure passed twice across the window frame. The next two nights we again played out our roles without incident, but on the third I noticed a rough-looking fellow standing in the doorway of Camden House, immediately across from Holmes's quarters. I observed him for a while from the corner. He never once looked up at the window and after a short spell moved on.

I decided that should this ruffian make another appearance I would put in a word to Gregson. As an added precaution, I planned to carry my service revolver beneath my coat for the remainder of the assignment.

Late in the afternoon of the next day I returned to my home, weary from my rounds. We were seated at our dinner table, my wife and I, when the maid brought in a telegram. It was an urgent request from an old colleague of my days at Netley. He was living now in Essex and I would have to leave at once to be of any assistance to him.

"What will you do, John?" asked my wife. "Will you go?"

"I must," I said. "But I will have to get word to Holmes somehow."

"Mr. Gregson!" she exclaimed.

"Yes, he'll know what to do."

I was a prompt and ready traveller and was soon out the door and in a cab, on my way to that great baronial structure on the Embankment. But on my arrival I found that Gregson as well as the sergeant working with him were out. I engaged another cab and headed for Baker Street, which seemed to be my only alternative.

I rang the bell. There was no answer. Worried, I ran across the street and, looking up to the window, saw the silhouette of my old companion pass by the blind. Again I went to the door, rang the bell, and hammered loudly. Still no answer. I crossed back to the front of Camden House. I watched his figure pass by several times and wondered if I should shout up to him.

I cupped my hands around my mouth, about to cry out, but suddenly there came the report of a rifle followed by the sound of splintering glass. I stood dazed for a moment but guessed at once what had happened. Sherlock Holmes had been shot.

7.1   Personal Computers

Holmes's possession of his own Analytical Engine for use with his personal files brings up an issue almost unthinkable twenty or thirty years ago: personal computers for home use. More than anything else, the existence and the dramatic rise in the popularity of personal computers is the result of the technology of the silicon chip, a wafer-sized device with layers of electronic elements. The elements in each layer can be fabricated to form complex electronic circuits, often with millions of components. This is exactly what is needed to fabricate the insides of a computer. These chips are at once small, reliable, fast, and inexpensive.

What is a "personal" computer? Of course it's a computer, and personal computers vary just as ordinary computers do. The key difference, quite simply, is that personal computers are *affordable*. They sell for as low as a few hundred dollars, up to, say, five or ten thousand dollars, well within the budget of many consumers. Normally a personal computer has a keyboard for entering data, a screen or typewriter for displaying results, and some means of recording data and programs (usually a floppy disk or a tape cassette). The fancier personal computers also have a printer whose speed and print quality vary according to price.

Many claims are made about personal computers. It is said that they can control your heating system, tell you when to water your garden, or provide you with medical advice; that they can keep track of your Christmas list, home diary, and recipes; that you can type letters on them, prepare legal documents, handle your inventory, or keep tabs on your finances; that they can help students learn geometry or English. And of course, they do play games.

Some qualifications are in order here. A computer is useless without the appropriate software. To do something useful, the computer must be programmed to do it. Unless you have the time and knowledge to do your own programming, this means you have to buy the appropriate software.

As you might guess, there are many vendors who sell software, and their numbers grow every day. But getting truly usable software is not easy. Consider something simple like keeping an updated list of your personal telephone numbers. You may type in someone's name incorrectly and want the computer to second-guess the spelling and give you the person's number; or you may want to see the names and numbers of all people whose names begin with "L"; or you may want the computer to let you enter only a person's initials and return the correct number. Building or buying such software may not even be possible—it may not exist.

One point few people mention is the considerable overhead in using a computer. You have to power-up the machine, set up the initial software, find the programs and data you need, and maintain all your

The EDSAC Computer Developed at University of Cambridge, 1950. Less powerful than today's personal computers.

A Selection of Personal Computers

personal files. Unlike keeping a handwritten telephone directory or shopping list, in which you can jot down an entry in a minute or less, the use of a computer requires a substantial block of time. You may find this so inconvenient that you do it by hand anyway.

Although, as mentioned earlier, a personal computer is simply a computer scaled to the needs and means of an individual, the world of personal computers is markedly different from that of commercial uses or university computer science programs. Personal computers have brought the technology of computers to our doorstep, and with it many new concerns.

7.2 Three Interviews

While it's always risky trying to divide the world into two parts, there are basically two kinds of people who own personal computers. First is the person who gets one for casual use: a student who likes to program or play computer games, a curious parent who takes up computers as a hobby, or someone who just wants to learn about computers. Second is a business person who has a task that could be automated. Such a person might want better control over customer billing, more reliable accounting of sales and inventory, or an easier means of producing mailing lists.

To appreciate the phenomenon of personal computers and to understand some of the related issues, let us recreate three interviews. Each interview was with a different owner of a personal computer: a sixth grade student, a high school senior, and a professional business person. The questions were posed in the order given; the responses have been slightly edited.

1. *What prompted you to buy your first computer?*

Sixth grader: Well, when my father was in college he got some experience on computers, and he sent away for a small one—it was called a Sinclair. We didn't think it was very good, so we sent it back. Then he bought a VIC, and I was getting excited about it. So we decided for my birthday, I would get a VIC, and I would take all the money I got for Christmas and all those things and put them straight into the VIC.

High school student: My father was getting into the business of designing computer systems and bought one for our home. I started to get into it and had a lot of fun with it. I decided I wanted one for my own.

Business person: I had some computer experience about ten years ago. The idea of being able to have something inexpensive, small, and if you will, 'turn it on, there it is,' was attractive. I have a strong aversion to doing repetitive tasks, like bookkeeping and such things. When it became possible to buy a machine to handle those jobs, I couldn't resist.

2.   *How much did it cost?*

Sixth grader: The computer itself was $299, and with the other things it was about $400. This is pretty good because if we had decided to get, say, an Apple, it would have cost much more.

High school student: At the time, four years ago, about $1000. The price has since gone down.

Business person: About $1500.

3.   *What did you think you were buying it for?*

Sixth grader: I decided I wanted to take up programming.

High school student: Fun—the fun of writing a program to play a game, and then playing the game.

Business person: I had three things in mind. The first was to get my kids to some level of computer literacy. The second was to put it to use in my business. The third was the possibility to develop for my own use (and for potential resale) a low-cost computer system for very small businesses.

4.   *When you bought it, did you anticipate that you might need to add to it?*

Sixth grader: Yes, because I knew the first thing I would have to get was a tape cassette recorder, at least. Because, if I ever wanted to write a program, it would take an hour to key it in each time I wanted to run it.

High school student: Yes. I immediately recognized the problem of using tape cassettes.

Business person: Yes. I had a clear idea that I would need to expand it, especially for more memory and a disk unit.

5. *How did you decide, among the many computers available, which one you wanted?*

Sixth grader: The name of the computer is a Commodore VIC-20, and it has color graphics. Right now it has 4K memory, but you can expand it up to 32K, I think.

We decided to get the VIC because there was a place where I could get it serviced right nearby. My father has one, and my grandfather has one, so we could set it up with modems (telephone connections) and talk to each other on it.

High school student: Well, I have an older Radio Shack TRS-80. But if I bought one today, I'd really go into graphics and drawing pictures and get an Apple.

Business person: I really applied a kind of inverse logic. I want a machine with the least software available at the moment. With the Apple, for instance, there are thousands of programs available and the market for new software is saturated. With a really low cost system such as my own, I would have a chance to enter the computer market with my own products and compete favorably.

6. *Do you think the computer is easy to learn?*

Sixth grader: Yes I do, but not very easy.

High school student: I found it easy.

Business person: Yes and no. The problem is that there really is no good documentation on how to use it. Getting started is very difficult, but once you get it, it's easy to go on.

7. *Do you think a person should know something about computers before buying one for the home?*

Sixth grader: Definitely. They should know what the thing does, and a little bit about programming. At the least they should know Basic.

High school student: Yes, definitely. They should read some books and get familiar with the terms people use.

Business person: It depends on your financial strength. For the average person, it should be treated like any major purchase. I've heard horror stories of people spending several thousands of dollars only to find they didn't have the right setup.

8. *Do you think a person who gets one ought to learn how to write programs?*

Sixth grader: Yes. If they want to go out and buy a computer and don't learn how to program, they will just have to play games all day.

High school student: Of course. That's the fun of it. That's where it's all at.

Business person: Yes, most definitely.

9. *Did you learn how to program your computer?*

Sixth grader: Yes, of course. My father taught me how to program in VIC Basic.

High school student: Yes, in Basic.

Business person: Yes, in Basic.

10. *What feature, for example a game or a document editor, do you use most?*

Sixth grader: The PRINT statement, which is how you get output from it when you write a program. I do play games on it a lot, I have to admit that.

High school student: I use the line editor for writing programs.

Business person: The interactive editor for writing programs.

11. *Do you have a printer?*

Sixth grader: No.

High school student: No.

Business person: Not yet, but one is on order.

12. *Do you do anything practical with your computer like balancing your checkbook or keeping a diary? That is, anything someone would normally do without using a computer.*

Sixth grader: Well, every now and then, if my teacher will allow it, I do my homework on the computer. This sounds like cheating, but it isn't, because you have to tell the computer how to do it.

High school student: No. Very rarely, maybe sometimes as a calculator. For me, it's a hobby.

Business person: At this point, no. Obviously, I expect my answer to change soon. Several projects are on the edge of being operational.

13. *How many hours a week do you spend using your computer?*

Sixth grader: About 5.

High school student: A year or two ago I was spending 10 hours a week, a lot of time. Now, not very much.

Business person: 3 or 4.

14. *What fascinates you most about it?*

Sixth grader: Teaching it how to do things. It's just like a teacher who teaches you how to work with numbers. When my teacher teaches me something, I try to teach the computer how to do it, which I can't do all the time.

High school student: Well, I've had a computer for four years and much of the fascination is now gone. But at first, it was the ability of making it do whatever you wanted it to do.

Business person: The discipline it imposes on your thinking, the necessity to reduce any idea to a firm algorithm. The machine is always there as a control on your wandering thoughts.

15. *What don't you like about it?*

Sixth grader: Having to key in the program, because it takes a lot of time and is boring.

High school student: On this computer, using the tapes. Disks would be much better, but I've learned to live with the tapes.

Business person: Presently, the lack of sufficient memory. Of a more general nature, it is the lack of good documentation. This particular computer's manual says: "for further information refer to the programmer's handbook." The handbook has not been published yet.

16. *Have you ever been annoyed at it?*

Sixth grader: Yes, very. Trying to debug programs. You have to keep changing your program, and things keep going wrong.

High school student: No, not really. It's a challenge when it doesn't work correctly.

Business person: Yes. There are times you wish it would meet you a little more than half way.

17. *Do you think people learn something from having one?*

Sixth grader: Yes, and if you use it a lot, you learn a lot.

High school student: Yes, no question about it. You learn to organize things and think logically.

Business person: Absolutely. The necessity to clarify your thinking is so important.

18. *Do you wish you had a better one?*

Sixth grader: No, not really. But I'd love to have a floppy disk drive, because the tape player is so slow and you have to wait so long for it.

High school student: Yes, I do. Especially a better graphics facility and a disk.

Business person: Well, that is true of anything you buy, like a more comfortable car or a bigger house. But, all in all, price considered, I am happy with what I've got.

19. *How much would it cost for a good one?*

Sixth grader: Well, that depends on what your needs are. I really can't answer that.

High school student: With everything I want? $3,000.

Business person: To get the best, where the machine would not be a limiting function, I'd say $5,000.

20. *Do you think that eventually, say in 10 or 20 years, every home will have a personal computer?*

Sixth grader: I think so. Computers are coming everywhere, and will take over the world. You know, cars are even being made using robots.

High school student: No, but I'm not really sure. They will become much more popular.

Business person: No. If it becomes possible to get voice-operated input, and if it becomes possible to develop systems that program themselves, then they would become universal.

21. *This is the last question. If you could give one piece of advice to someone who was thinking about buying a personal computer, what would it be?*

Sixth grader: To think about what your needs are going to be. For instance, if you are running a business you'll need a lot of memory and special programs. If you just want to play games and do a little programming, then you could probably get a TRS-80 color computer and just buy cartridges for the games.

High school student: Get one with a very comprehensive language. If not, and you use it for any length of time, you will outgrow it. If you get a language with many, many commands, you can keep growing with it.

Business person: Treat it like any major purchase—know what you want—and do comparison shopping. I might add, think about whether you can afford it; it is all too easy to spend more and more.

Notes on the Interviews

Conducting interviews can bring a surprise or two, and such is the case here. When computer professionals think about computers, it is serious business. This is not always so with owners of personal computers. There tends to be a lightness about buying a computer and what to expect from one. All that can change if the owner comes to depend on it, but by and large the lightness remains.

There appears to be no common aim motivating people to decide to buy one or choose which one to buy. It is hard for a layperson to assess the marketplace and what it offers. Most owners, including those interviewed, quickly see the need for storage devices better than tape cassettes. With the continuing decline in costs, it is likely that this will become less of a problem.

The three persons interviewed suggest that learning to use the computer is not too difficult. Generally speaking, we disagree. A large number of new conventions must be learned to operate one with confidence. This difficulty is surely one of the reasons why more people do not own a personal computer. It's deceptively simple for the expert to press the magic keys and claim how easy it is, but you are the one who will have to learn which keys will do what. When you're on your own, you will quickly see the snags.

Perhaps of most significance is the value of owning your own computer. For each of the three interviewed, the educational value was very high.

7.3   Video Games

By far the most popular use of computers in the home is through video computer games. A video game is a special form of personal computer designed to play the many action "arcade" games that are available today. The games are pre-programmed and come on tape cassettes.

Some of the larger makers of these machines are the same people who make the video games for the arcade people. They rely on the games that prove popular on the big machines to sell their home video games. You can get almost any good game you find in the arcade, and often the home version is made by the same people who put it in the arcade. Similar games are often available on similar machines, but there are a number of court cases about copyright infringement, so a given game may not be supported on your machine forever if your manufacturer loses his court battle.

Some home video computers can be used as stand-alone computers, with "language cartridges" instead of game cartridges and a cassette tape recorder for storage. Some even offer conversions to full computer status. When purchasing these devices with the idea of using them for a computer later, some thought must be given to the storage available as an add-on. Cassette tape recorders work, some better than others, but they are a poor solution. Their main advantage is that they are very cheap. Storage format is also an important consideration if you want to exchange tapes with anyone. Floppy disks are a much better solution as far as capacity, speed and reliability go, but there are as many formats for storing data as there are manufacturers of floppies.

The first thing to remember about home video games is that they are inexpensive. They almost always use a TV set for the video display. This not only cuts down the cost but allows color graphics. Most sets use channels 3 or 4, but they can be customized to run anywhere on the television band within reason and your pocketbook. There is no reason to change them, however, as most have a TV-game switch that prevents the television from picking up channel signals when they are being used with the video game and vice-versa. Some of the machines that specialize in high-quality graphics offer a video monitor, a very high quality, high-cost picture tube, in either color or black and white. When it is used, the blurrings and smudging often associated with a television video display disappear. These units are often used in television studios to obtain the best possible picture.

There are some obvious differences between video game computers and computers designed to do general or business work. One is that the video display functions on the game computers are quite sophisticated. People enjoy lots of movement and animation in their games. The control of animation takes up much of the memory and processing time in the video computer.

Along this line, the video games often have sophisticated methods of making sounds. Game players like snappy graphics with action sounds to round out the play. The sound-making abilities range from a simple beep (available on most professional terminals) to polyphonic synthesis and voice "creation." Programs to compose music and an amazing host of other features are available. They are impressive and are one of the ways in which video game computers can be really useful to professional or hobbiest alike. The voice creation equipment is getting more sophisticated and less expensive. Such features are finding their way into the home, while business machines are not usually equipped to do this sort of thing, except for the ever-present beep.

The video game computers usually come with strange, non-standard keyboards. This is not the handicap that it would be for a business computer. The strange keyboards are often spill-proof and rugged, a plus for the intended market. And their low cost increases their attractiveness to the recreational consumer. For those who also use the machines as a computer, a "number pad" is provided to enter numbers, a tedious task on a "shifted number" keyboard. The keypads are not very expensive, and they mollify the computer user. Professional typewriter-type keyboards can usually be added to the ones with the cheaper kind of keyboard.

A video game computer often has at least a connector for a "game paddle" somewhere on it, and most come with the paddles included. These are the little knobs and buttons that are attached to the computer by a wire a couple of yards long. They allow the players to communicate directly with the brain of the machine, telling it where to move the spaceship or when to fire the weapons.

Some video game computers have a device known as a "light-pen." This is a small rod, much like a ballpoint pen, with a wire connecting it to the computer. A light detector on its tip indicates where the pen is when it is touched to the display screen. In games it can be used to make a choice of something or tell the computer where you want to be. These light pens are finding their way into business computers to reduce the amount of typing and to make interaction with a computer easier. They are also used in sophisticated drawing, drafting, and graphic design programs for making and deleting lines on the screen. They are great fun to watch and operate. As they become cheaper they will probably appear, at least as an option, on more machines.

In general, most video game computers and most personal computers have all sorts of optional attachments. Some of these machines can now help operate your house with a computer-controlled switching network. They use the power lines to shut things off and on and to detect whether a sensor has been activated. Some are used in a heat sensor or a master control in burglar-alarm systems. A few can even dial the phone if the alarm is set off. Some of the more expensive ones can connect to a weather station on the roof and record or act on data it receives.

The more successful of these machines have very fanatical fans. Some have started "user groups" to help each other, sponsor competitions, maintain newsletters, and plan meetings. These aficionados discuss new releases of games and try out new products. There are experts on any particular machine. So if you are planning to buy, perhaps you could locate such a group and find out if what you think you're going to get is really the way it is. Some of these "clubs" can be reached only by computer, using a device called a "modem." A modem connects a computer to the phone lines. It can be used for sending and receiving data and exists only in the computer. Several enterprising individuals are making this a business, an "arcade" with no arcade.

Several magazines are now dedicated to games and the machines that run them. They usually have a list of high scorers of currently popular games and a "Top 10" list of best-selling games. For those of you who might wish to make a living at writing game programs, there is usually an article on someone who has done just that. You can read and learn whether you really have what it takes to do so. They are usually 20 to 25 years old, but some of them are much younger. Several have made hundreds of thousands of dollars, with an odd millionaire or two. Interesting reading.

As video game computers are being developed, they are being given more and more abilities to do things not possible even a few years ago. Just as personal computers are becoming capable business machines, so the video games are slowly expanding their power toward those of a personal computer. And prices are dropping.

CHAPTER VIII

The Adventure of the Toy Train

(Part II)

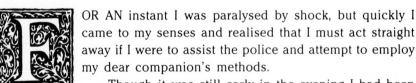OR AN instant I was paralysed by shock, but quickly I came to my senses and realised that I must act straight away if I were to assist the police and attempt to employ my dear companion's methods.

Though it was still early in the evening I had been the only person standing on Baker Street when the shot was fired. Doubtless the smell of ozone and massing clouds that portended thunder kept everyone indoors. I surmised that the assailant had been positioned above me in Camden House, which has been vacant for quite some time. I ran into the middle of the street and, looking up at the house, saw a window open on the first story. The door was locked and I rapidly made my way round to Blandford Street where I could see the rear of the building. Down a narrow passage, through a wooden gate and into the deserted yard I ran and there found the back door of the house ajar. I hesitated but a moment. Drawing my revolver, I entered into the shadowy house.

I crept down a long hall and found the stairs. With a deep breath I began to ascend them. Once at the top I could feel a gentle draught and knew that it came from the open window over Baker Street.

Cautiously, need I say, I moved in the direction of the breeze and into a large, square room. It, too, seemed empty, but in the darkness something beneath the window caught the faint light from the street and glinted. I stood motionless until my eyes had adjusted to the gloom. I was alone. Walking to the window, I looked out across Baker Street to the brightly lit apartment that had been the beginning of so many adventures and struck a match. The sudden flare revealed a small carbine on the floor, which I pushed with my foot. Suddenly there came the clatter of feet ascending the stairs, and I quickly shook out the match and crouched down and away from the light of the window, my revolver pointed towards the door.

The steps came to an abrupt halt just outside the door. I heard the creak of a very slow and careful move into the room. I could vaguely make out the silhouette of a man against the darkness of the hallway. The odour of sulphur hung in the air from my match, and he must have suddenly noticed it, for he quickly stepped back through the door and disappeared.

Neither of us made another sound and it seemed as though several minutes went by while I held my breath. I thought of Holmes across the street, that he might be wounded and in need of medical attention. I could wait no longer.

"I have a gun," I said, "and your rifle!"

"You will not leave this room," came the voice. "The house is surrounded."

"Gregson!" I exclaimed at the familiar voice. "Is that you?"

"Who is there?"

"Watson."

"Strike a match and hold it before you then," he said. I rummaged through my pocket and was about to do this when it occurred to me that he might not be the Scotland Yard official after all.

"How do I know it is you?" I asked.

"I received your message at the Yard and came at once."

Again I thought of Holmes and the attention he needed. I struck the match and the shadow entered the room.

"How is it that you are here, Doctor?" said the Inspector, as he knelt down beside me and peered out of the window.

"I was outside when the shot was fired and rushed in here when I realized what had happened."

Gregson had picked up the small, light-weight rifle from the floor and was examining it. "You were to be in Essex."

"How did you know?"

"It was Mr. Holmes's idea," he replied, "to keep you out of danger."

"We're wasting time," I said. "We've got to break into his flat."

"My sergeant is there now."

I looked across and saw a dark figure passing against the blind.

"Can you come down to the office, Doctor?" Gregson asked.

I acknowledged that I could, and he helped me to my feet. Outside two uniformed constables were waiting. A few loiterers had begun to assemble in the street.

"Is there anything I can do? I am a physician," I said to the sergeant when he emerged from the door of 221B.

"I am afraid not, sir," he answered.

In vain, I begged him to tell me more.

"Let's get you home and rested a bit, sir," said Inspector Gregson. "Our business at the Yard can wait until morning."

I accepted his suggestion with great reluctance, and a constable saw me to my door. The next day, as I made my way over to the C.I.D. for my appointment with Gregson, I passed several news-vendors displaying the morning papers. There, black upon yellow, were the terrible news-sheets proclaiming the death of Sherlock Holmes.

We sat, Gregson and I, for an hour or more in his office discussing the details of the previous evening. More than once he asked me if I were certain that I had seen no one as I entered from the rear of the house. I was reminded of the ruffian who had waited in the door-way of Camden House the night before, and I gave as accurate a description of him as I could.

As we were talking a young, plain-clothes detective entered the office and handed Gregson a cable. He quickly read it.

"Dover?" he said, looking up from the paper. "Well, Doctor, we may have them. Could we continue this at Baker Street to-night? I may have some very comforting news to report."

"Baker Street? Of course," I said. "Is there anything you can tell me now, Inspector?"

"No. I am afraid it must wait."

And so, I took my leave and spent the remainder of the day at home. The events of the last twenty-four hours were only now just beginning to weigh upon me. Wearily, I made my way over to Baker Street as the sun was setting. I think I could point to the very paving-stone upon which I stood when my eyes caught sight of the hard, black outline of a man behind the luminous screen of the window at Number 221B. A gasp of amazement escaped me. There was no mistaking the squareness of his shoulders, the poise of his head, and the sharpness of his features. The shadow moved away from the window, and I hurriedly advanced to the door.

It was unlocked and I did not bother to knock. I took the seventeen steps three at a time. In an instant I stood before my old companion's door. I hesitated, raised my fist to rap, and then, without knocking, burst into the sitting-room.

Sherlock Holmes was lounging on a kind of Eastern divan he had constructed with pillows and cushions from the sofa and arm-chairs. In the dim light I saw him sitting there, his eyes fixed vacantly upon the corner of the ceiling, a pipe-rack within his reach, and a lens and forceps lying beside him.

"Watson. Good of you to come," he greeted me warmly.

I was stunned. "Good heavens! This is marvelous!" I managed to blurt out.

"Yes, quite, but much of the credit must go to your American illustrator, Frederic Dorr Steele," he replied, shaking with laughter.

It was then that my attention was drawn to the window by the gentle whirring sound of his electric train. Atop the model engine was a perfect black silhouette, much like those which our grand-parents loved to frame. It was an astonishing likeness of Sherlock Holmes. As the train passed by the window, the lights from within the room projected the portrait of its unusual passenger onto the blind.

"I've had to patch it up a bit," said the real Holmes as he rose and stepped to the window. He interrupted the flow of current and the toy train stopped. "You know that I can never resist a dramatic situation, Watson. I do owe you an apology for all this."

"My dear fellow, this is wonderful," is all that I recollect being able to say.

"Now if you can endure the draught from my broken window, you'll find the gasogene and cigars in their old place. A half-hour here may provide you with some profitable amusement. Have you been keeping notes on this case?"

"Naturally," I answered.

"Then you will have to write a sequel."

"It is a chapter I shall write with great pleasure," I said.

"Yes, and with enough material to appease even your fertile imagination!" cried he with a laugh as he inspected the silhouette and poked his right forefinger into the small patch covering the bullet's hole. I noticed that the bullet had passed straight through the paper brain and flattened itself on the opposite wall.

A shiver ran through me. "What of Sir Harold?" I asked.

"Quite safe. He was only here for an instant that first night. I ushered him straight out the back entrance. We shared quarters in Chatham, where he gave Mycroft a full account of what he has learned in Serbia."

"Chatham? Why, that's miles from here. Who managed the train set for you?"

"I did, myself."

"SHERLOCK HOLMES WAS LOUNGING UPON
A KIND OF EASTERN DIVAN."

"But how?"

"I am pleased to report that my little experiment with the Analytical Engine has worked remarkably well. A telegraph wire runs directly behind Mrs. Hudson's house. So I was able to have the Engine's sending and receiving parts installed in the box-room with a cable stretching that short distance. With Mycroft's help I connected a lamp and the switching mechanism for the toy train to the Engine. After that it was simply a matter of cabling my instructions directly to the Engine, which I did from the nearest Post and Telegraph Office."

"Remarkable!" I interjected.

"Ah! But we haven't even begun to grasp the dizzying advances which this Engine can bring! I had my doubts, and I still do. However, I am beginning to think my reservations are ill-founded. I paid a visit one night to make certain that all was working as planned. We met in the street, do you recall?"

"What? No! Did you speak to me?"

"No, but you gave me a severe glance and later reported my loafing about to Gregson."

"So, you were that rough-looking fellow in the door of Camden House! Why didn't you identify yourself to me, Holmes?"

"I couldn't, my dear fellow. The house was being watched, even then as you grimaced at me. However, it was imperative that certain persons believed Sir Harold and I were here when we were actually miles away."

"This is astonishing."

"We believed that, with our trap set, these agents would make their move soon. Gregson and com-

"YOU WERE THAT ROUGH LOOKING FELLOW."

pany kept a watchful eye on Camden House. When the assault was made I was there, watching the rear entrance. We knew that the assassin did not work alone and so I followed him. He met his confederates, two of them, at Victoria Station. They were soon on the Dover Coach, bound for the safety of the Continent. I cabled Gregson and took the same train. The police came on board when we reached Dover. My dear Watson, if only you could have seen their faces when they were taken!"

Such was the remarkable narrative to which I listened that night—a narrative which would have been utterly incredible had it not been confirmed by the actual sight of this Engine and my own witness to the duties it executed at my companion's command. We related it once again a few nights later for the benefit of Mycroft Holmes in the Strangers' Room at the Diogenes Club, Mycroft's habitual evening retreat. Holmes had brought me with him on this visit, the purpose of which was to have that discussion with his elder brother which had been postponed due to the more pressing matter of Sir Harold Chesterfield. I learned as we talked that Mycroft was serious indeed about investigating other possible uses of the Analytical Engine.

"Not only are we anxious to make use of it at Whitehall," said Mycroft as we sipped some excellent port, "but I understand that Scotland Yard has been contacted by officials of the French police. It seems that they are interested in acquiring not only their own Engine but in establishing a communications link with ours."

"Such a move would be beneficial for both, I would say," Holmes observed. "I am sure you are well aware of the recent rise in international crime."

"The link would also be of enormous value for diplomatic correspondence," added Mycroft.

Later that evening, as we sat in the comfortable surroundings of Baker Street, I commented to Holmes on the rapid spread of interest in the Analytical Engine's capabilities.

"I think, Watson, you can begin an entirely new chapter in the history of criminal investigation," he concluded with a whimsical smile. His hand made a languid gesture as he threw the switch and set the train in motion. Once again the noble profile of the keen-witted logician of Baker Street moved across the drawn shade, and the city was better for his presence.

‡ ‡

8.1 Many Users, One Computer

Although Sherlock Holmes admitted to a strong taste for the dramatic, he had an equally strong preference for expanding his methods of deduction. We now turn to a number of issues which, taken together, expand the simple concept of one user, one computer. Most often, these issues concern large computers and access to them by many, often hundreds or thousands, of individuals. We begin with a concept generally known as *time-sharing*.

The concept of time-sharing is so important that even some of the small micro and personal computers are equipped this way. More people are using computers than ever before. Time-sharing essentially multiplies the number of computers available. This is achieved at minimal extra cost by making efficient use of the power and speed of even a small computer.

Let's say you have an hour of work to do in order to modify and run a program on your computer. You initiate a dialogue with the machine, respond to a few questions, and name the appropriate files of data. The program is displayed on the screen. You make a few corrections and re-examine it. After some thought, you make a major modification to the program. Each new line is carefully entered and proofed. When completed, the program is displayed again and re-checked.

Now you execute the program, giving it some sample data. The first run works as expected. A second and third set of data are tried, and all work well except for a minor flaw. This is corrected, the program is tested again, and the files are saved. The session is completed.

If you consider your behavior during the session, you will see that during a good percentage of the time (well over half) the computer is idle. You may be thinking, reading the information on the screen, or even daydreaming. If you look carefully at the dialogue between you and the computer, you can also see that most of the computer's actions are accomplished in a matter of seconds.

Contemporary computers are incredibly fast. If you ask the computer to replace a line of text, it may take you a couple of minutes to enter and check the line, but the computer does its share of the work in an instant. In short, for at least 95 percent of your hour's session the computer itself was idle!

Time-sharing

One of the most remarkable developments in computer technology was that of a time-sharing system, first brought into operation at MIT in 1961. The system was popular almost instantly.

In a time-sharing system a single computer works with many users at individual terminals, as illustrated in Figure 8.1. The basic principle is that of switching the computer's attention from one user to another. As a very simple illustration, suppose a tenth of a second is allocated for each burst of attention. If there are five users, the first will get a tenth of a second of the computer's time, then a tenth of a second for the next user, and so on in a round robin fashion. Thus every second each user gets two short bursts of attention.

The key to this scheme is simply the computer's remarkable speed at processing the user requests. If a user happens to be idle, the computer can get right to the next user. If a user happens to request more work than can be accomplished in one burst, the computer can continue the next time around. On average, the computer need be only fast enough to keep each user satisfied. In all cases, the computer must record the status of the user's work and, if necessary, save the user's programs and data for the next burst.

Normally a time-sharing system is built around a large computer with rapid work speed and a great capacity to save information. Such a computer can often handle hundreds of users. Quite remarkably, each user has the *illusion* that the entire computer is dedicated to the task at hand.

Nothing is free, however, and as the number of users on a system passes a certain critical, system-dependent number, the time to respond to a user gets longer, and the wait for processing time becomes more and more noticeable.

The spinoffs of the time-sharing concept are much more than simply keeping the computer busy. With a time-shared system it is reasonable to offer a variety of computer services that would simply not be cost effective otherwise. A user can be charged for only that portion of the computer's resources actually used. As there are many users, the cost of the system is thus distributed. Both the small and the large user are accommodated.

If you like, you can get a terminal in your home, pay for a connection to a time-sharing service, and have at your disposal the facilities of a large computer installation—you pay only for what you use.

The Great Telegraph Room at the Offices of the Electric and International Telegraph Company, Moorgate Street, 1860

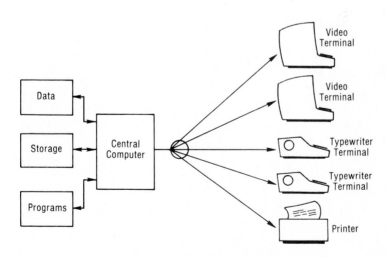

Figure 8.1   *Time-Sharing*

Time-sharing saves not only money, but resources. Many users, for instance, can share access to a single collection of data. Airline reservation clerks share access to plane reservation information and seat bookings. Ticket sales personnel can record each sale in a central data base. Credit card bureaus can share access to a repository of data on all valid accounts. Even police records are being centralized, with access to the data available in an instant.

However, when data are shared, there can be a problem in protecting certain data from those not authorized to use them, for instance, medical, tax, and social security data. This is a complex issue, and there is much debate over how much protection is enough. Current systems handle the problem fairly well, but you may have read a story in a local newspaper about some smart computer person changing bank account balances and getting caught. You might wonder how many people with the necessary skill do not get caught.

8.2 Communication with Remote Users

The concept of time-sharing implicitly brings up an important related issue—the user need not be physically near the central computer. Normally the central computer contains the programs, data, files and storage needed by the user. Often the resources offered by the computer will be quite vast. The user, as long as access is provided, doesn't need to visit the computer room. The user may be in an adjacent building, on the other side of town, or hundreds of miles away. With satellite communication, the user can even be across the ocean from the computer. Expensive? Yes. But not as uncommon as you might think.

The desire for communication over long distances has brought with it a related computer technology, some of which existed before computers, but much of which is new.

A somewhat simplistic view of a communication link is shown in Figure 8.2. Here all communication between the computer and a terminal is by means of a sequence of characters. The characters can comprise a short message from the computer, a response by the user, an entire computer program, or files of data.

The sequence of characters actually transmitted will contain "control" characters that enable proper communication. In the ASCII character set of Appendix A, some of these control characters are:

STX   Start of text—used at the beginning of a sequence of characters.

ETX   End of text—used at the end of a sequence of characters.

EOT   End of transmission— used to terminate an entire transmission.

ACK   Acknowledgment—used as a response to the sender that the sequence sent was understood.

NAK   Negative Acknowledgment—used as a response to the sender that the sequence sent contains errors.

The user at the terminal never sees these control characters, but they allow the computer to carry on its own private communication correctly.

One of the key issues in communication is the handling of transmission errors. In a telephone call or a television program, faulty transmission is observed as a lessening of quality, which can be tolerated by the listener or viewer. The computer, however, needs much more reliable transmission. The loss of even one bit of information can be crucial. Suppose, for instance, the computer put the decimal point in your paycheck one position off to the left or right. One way would make you complain; the other would cause difficult problems.

To handle errors, transmission of computer data is accompanied by additional (redundant) information used to spot errors. The data received are checked for missing or erroneous codes. If the message is received correctly, the receiver sends an acknowledgment code back to the sender; if not, a negative acknowledgment is sent back and usually the sequence is retransmitted. This underground communication takes place so rapidly that the user is seldom aware of it, except perhaps for an occasional delay in the terminal's behavior.

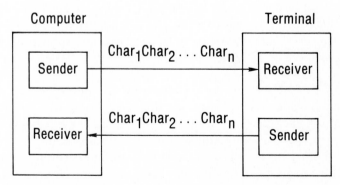

Figure 8.2   *A Simple Two-Way Communication*

Transmission of computer data is usually handled over the conventional telephone lines or specialized communication lines. If you use a remote terminal, this means you have to pay for use of the line and may need special equipment. The competition to develop this use of computers is strong, since this technology is probably the most promising aspect of the modern computer. It means that very costly resources and devices can be shared, lowering the cost to the consumer of advanced computing abilities and methods, while allowing the "personal" computer market to flourish.

The use of remote terminals brings up yet another technology—the so-called *intelligent* terminal. An intelligent terminal has a small computer in the terminal itself. The purpose of the local computer is to handle routine tasks, such as editing a line of text or displaying a document, on site. This spares the larger computer at the other end from a lot of busy work and gives very quick response time for routine tasks.

With or without an intelligent terminal, the potential impact of remote communication is enormous. The services of a large computer, with all of its programs and data, can be brought into the home. Even more than "stand-alone" personal computers, this technology is likely to enter our lives over the next few decades.

8.3 Computer Networks

Side by side with time-sharing and remote communication with a computer is the technology of *computer networks*. The possibilities offered by this technology are sweeping, and its impact on society is already significant.

A computer network already in common use is sketched in Figure 8.3. This network is called the *ARPANET*, which stands for *A*dvanced *R*esearch *P*rojects *A*gency *Net*work. It was originally sponsored by the U.S. Department of Defense and is managed by the Defense Communications Agency.

The ARPANET links a wide variety of computers in the United States and Europe. The network is intended to support only projects related to official U.S. Government business, but the hosting computers in the network are individually owned or sponsored.

A computer network is a collection of computers connected to one another for the purpose of sharing resources. Communication can be through a direct link, telephone lines, microwave, or satellite. The

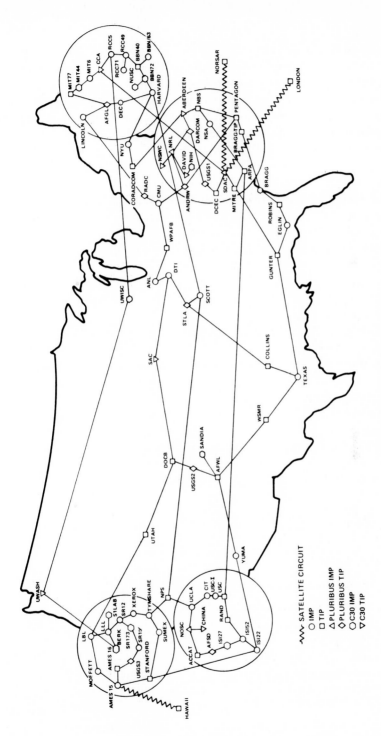

Figure 8.3 *The ARPA Network*

computers in a network are often time-sharing systems, but this need not be the case. A computer may offer a specialized service such as satellite tracking or access to a single data base.

A sketch of a simple network with only two computers is shown in Figure 8.4. Each of the two has its own users, data, and programs. The essential ingredient is the communication link. By means of this link, data, programs, or messages can be transferred from one computer to another.

Suppose, for example, user A is using one computer and user B is using the other, each interlinked as in Figure 8.4. User A is preparing a document on the computer and wishes to have the final copy typeset, that is, printed with proportional spacing, italic typing fonts, boldface headers, and the like. B's computer has the specialized hardware and software to produce typeset documents. A, provided he has the necessary information, can prepare the document on his own computer. When it is ready, A can send the document to B's computer for the final typeset copy.

We see here the major advantage to the networking of computers— sharing of resources. The user of any one computer has, theoretically, access to the equipment, programs, and data of any computer in the network. This means that the size and capability of any one computer can be extended arbitrarily.

In the sketch of Figure 8.4, notice that user A can have a message sent to the other computer. This message, if appropriately addressed, can be sent to user B. Conversely, user B can transmit a message to user A. This simple setup gives rise to another phenomenon of the age of time-sharing and computer networks—*electronic mail.*

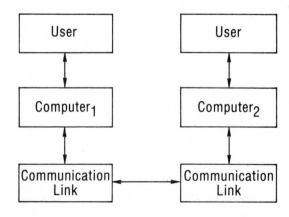

Figure 8.4   *Sketch of a Two-Computer Network*

The conventions for sending mail with computers goes something like this. The sender prepares a letter (or, for that matter, any kind of document) using his own computer; the letter may be edited and revised as needed. The sender also enters information about the person or terminal to which the document is to be sent. This little step may require looking up some mysterious codes. When everything is set up, the sender issues an instruction to forward the letter. Normally, the letter is immediately sent to the recipient's computer. The next time the recipient uses his own computer, the computer will type out a message indicating that mail has been received, at which time the recipient may ask that the letter be displayed.

With the computer's speed in both processing and sending data, electronic mail can be sent and received in a matter of seconds. Moreover, if two users are both at a terminal, messages can be exchanged directly. John can send a message to Mary, Mary can reply immediately, and a conversation can begin. If she likes, Mary can send John a copy of an entry from her diary or a clipping from her electronic newspaper.

It doesn't take long to imagine all kinds of uses for computer networks—the possibilities are almost boundless. The practicalities, however, are another matter. We now turn to some of the difficulties in realizing this technology.

Limitations

One of the greatest obstacles to using a computer network is the difficulty learning to use what is available. Learning to operate even a single computer is time-consuming and difficult. When we place several computers in a network, the difficulty escalates. For one, we must learn the protocols and conventions of the network itself. For another, we must learn how to use a second, probably totally unfamiliar computer.

Side by side with learning is the question of documentation. Computer systems have traditionally been plagued with manuals that are often almost impossible to read. Some systems require shelves of documentation. When a network is introduced, this problem is compounded by the practical difficulty of even obtaining documents about some remote computer system.

The technology itself poses problems. Communication failures are not uncommon, and the lack of standardized procedures is confusing. The operating hours of another computer might be different from those of your own computer. When difficulties arise, getting assistance on the network or the remote computer may be very frustrating. It is also possible to intercept messages, which raises matters of security.

All of these issues bring up the question of whether standards should be adopted that would help alleviate most of the problem. The level of co-operation needed makes this solution unlikely, even when its merits are obvious.

All of this means that the full impact of computer networks may be slow in coming. The day when you, your neighbors, your bank, and your mail are all comfortably linked on your own terminal may be quite distant.

CHAPTER IX

---‡---

Upon the Various Shortcomings of the Analytical Engine

 DITOR'S note: The following monograph is the abstract of a chapter intended for Mr. Holmes's unfinished work *The Whole Art of Detection*. It was found among some papers stored in the library at Trinity College, Cambridge. The papers were filed under "Sigerson, H.," with the general heading Mathematics.

Mr. Holmes is the author of *Upon the Distinction Between the Ashes of the Various Tobaccos; the Dating of Documents; Applications of the Analytical Engine to the Writing of Ciphers; Use of the Analytical Engine in the Work of the Criminal Investigator; Reflections on the Mathematical Genius of Ada, Countess of Lovelace; Upon the Polyphonic Motets of Lassus;* &c, &c.

An Examination of some Questions respecting the Various Applications of the Analytical Engine; With an Attempt to Address Some Common Shortcomings of Mr. Babbage's Calculating Machine and Its System of Conventions

by

Sherlock Holmes, Esq., OM

Intellectual enquiry gains by mutual support. With Mr. Babbage's research on the calculation of mathematical tables, we are led to such extended prospects as to place the whole of arithmetic within the grasp of a machine. As a result all the sciences receive fresh stimulation. So too does every educated man who understands the forces at work in our society as he views the advantages the Engine promises to bestow upon science. Mr. Babbage's remarkable invention will assuredly play an ever larger role in mathematical calculation, deductive reasoning, and, in the not-too-distant future, the halls of commerce and the daily life of the common man.

Having some acquaintance with several branches of science, most notably chemistry, I have eagerly embraced the possibilities of the Engine in my chosen field of study, namely, the Science of Deduction and Analysis. If we review the progress of science, following the success of any new invention there have always been a great many claims for its benefit to mankind and a corresponding volume of efforts to prove, or disprove, its worth.

In earlier writings I have discussed the phenomenal operations which the Analytical Engine is able to perform with great speed and supreme accuracy. On this occasion I shall concentrate my attention on its *human operator*. The human adjunct to the Analytical Engine has been given little attention. This is an oversight to which I take personal exception, for the Engine would not have been able to solve a single case without my contribution.

Although the principles upon which the Analytical Engine rests are themselves elementary, any man who acts as the Engine's operator will know that its system of conventions is so complicated as to baffle the most tenacious mind. Already the amount of precise intellectual food the Engine requires is so vast that no length of mortal years could enable one's imagination to grasp its limits. The human brain is rather like an attic of limited capacity. The walls of this attic refuse to stretch like India rubber; as we store more information, some of the old is jostled out to make room for the new.

Allow me to illustrate my point. Soon after my colleague, John H. Watson, M.D., and I had commenced work on the application of the Analytical Engine to my own endeavours (and those of Scotland Yard), my attention fastened on the imperfection of the various means for stating precisely how the Engine was to aid my investigations. A remarkable number of instructions are necessary to operate the Engine.

These must slavishly follow some very peculiar rules of grammar and punctuation. I was greatly disappointed when further research into this matter forced me to deduce that this system of grammar and punctuation does not remain constant. I have trained my mind to be systematic and find it most perplexing that simple human logic does not suggest any uniform approach to the Engine's own language of operation, one based on common notation.

I first broached this subject in my paper, "Statement of the Circumstances respecting the Analytical Engine," which was read to the Royal Society last spring. In the ensuing discussion some members of the Society attempted to maintain the proposition that all the information needed for operating the Engine is to be found in the Documents of Operation. These are: *An Introduction to the Principles of Operation; Practical Handbook for the Analytical Engine* (of which my own "Observations on the Methodology of Operations" played a small part); and *Operator's Instructions and Reference Handbook.* With due respect to the rarefied minds of the Royal Society, I would suggest that the opinions of those members were based more on reasonable expectation than on solid personal experience.

How well I recall the confusion arising when I wished to determine the specific instructions to change the coding mechanism for a cipher I had designed for the Home Office. The organization of the Documents of Operation is far from logical, and, from the point of view of the average man at Scotland Yard, the vocabulary is singularly unfamiliar.

Let me now proceed to summarize briefly the shortcomings of the Analytical Engine and the system of conventions provided for its operation.

1.   The collected documentation of instructions, features, and equipment is much too extensive and thus is confusing.

2.   Frequently, either too much or too little information is provided to guide the operator through a single operation.

3.   The few examples of operation provided in these documents are often of an obscure or highly specialised nature and do not serve the practical needs of the operator.

4.   The vocabulary describing the Engine's behavior is foreign to the class of educated men most apt to make use of the Engine in years to come.

5. Several alternative sets of instructions, often with minute differences, are provided for carrying out the same task.

6. The information supplied by the Engine is often confusing to the operator.

7. Assistance in understanding the Engine's behavior is seldom provided by the machine itself.

8. The exact sequence of key-strokes for each operation is a tax on the most retentive memory.

9. The precise meaning of each key is not made clear.

10. Characters symbolising special functions are employed in unusual and misleading ways.

11. There is no uniform set of rules governing the grammar and punctuation of the Engine's special language of operation.

12. It is much too easy for the operator to make an error.

13. It can be exceedingly difficult to locate and correct an error.

14. The Engine offers little explanation when it has detected an error.

15. Parts of an operator's library of data can easily be erased during operation.

16. It is not possible to shut down the Engine during a particular operation and later resume that same task without having to return to the first step.

Each of these issues deserves a full paper; I shall not undertake the task of addressing them here.

Lest the reader argue that these issues are matters of detail rather than of substance and so diminish their importance, let me remind him that these minutiae are exactly what the operator confronts on every occasion when the Engine is put to use. In this respect, they may have a *greater* impact on the ultimate success of the Engine than those larger issues (such as speed of operation or capacity for data storage) with which mathematicians and engineers have concerned themselves.

Evidence on the Costs of Poorly Designed Arrangements

The improvements I would like to see made on the Analytical Engine cannot be carried out without considerable expenditure, especially given the fluctuations in the demand and supply of our most skillful draftsmen. However, rising costs of operation will surely result if we fail to make such improvements. While the costs of an arrangement poorly designed for the Engine's human operator may not make themselves immediately obvious, they are likely to prove exorbitant over the years. The man in the street, the majority of those in the commercial world, and indeed many of our mathematicians find the Analytical Engine so complex that they elect to ignore it. This is a hidden cost— the cost of wastefulness of a marvel of invention and engineering.

In terms of actual monies, the costs I refer to can be measured as those directly associated with use of the Engine and those on the periphery of common operations.

I shall begin with direct costs, as they are easiest to identify and address. The poor design of any machinery ultimately leads to wasted human time and, in turn, wasted machine time. It is not unusual for the operator to receive a baffling message from the Analytical Engine and spend several hours attempting to decipher it. He may, for example, repeat the complete sequence of instructions in hope of avoiding the message entirely and so waste several cards punched with data.

Too much time is consumed correcting errors. It would be a great advantage to be forewarned of certain pitfalls in the course of an operation.

There are numerous unnecessary costs associated with direct use of the Engine and the day-to-day problems that arise. I shall only mention a few, all of which could be avoided by improved arrangements :—

1. The time required to understand the vocabulary of a particular arrangement.

2. The cost of publishing excessive Documents of Operation.

3. The amount of time that must be spent attempting to understand these documents.

4. The time spent learning special abbreviations.

5. The time spent comprehending specific instructions.

6. The delays in a particular project because the operator has had to deal with said difficulties.

7. The failure among the Engine's diverse users to communicate ideas and problems to one another.

8. The time wasted understanding errors.

9. The mental effort to remember repetitious and confusing instructions.

10. The costs of arrangements that could have been carried out by the Engine itself instead of by its operator.

Now I direct any reader who has had cause to use the Analytical Engine to the frustrations likely suffered because of a recurring error he has encountered, not in his work but in the unreasonable demands of the Engine. Or the anxiety he may undergo when an arrangement behaves erratically. Or even the fatigue caused by demanding irregularities and unnecessary repetition.

We will only be able to estimate the importance and the scope of these issues when we have concluded a series of applications of the Analytical Engine to science and industry. For the present, we must look beyond the narrow confines of our laboratories in assessing all the foregoing. I can only conclude that many possible applications will not be made. Half a century may elapse before any man will be able to appreciate the nature of my efforts and, mindful of the history of the Engine and its applications, realize what could have been done but was not.

If we continue to focus our attention on the Engine itself and the problems it presents, ignoring its human operator, then we shall surely lose sight of the basic problems that first stimulated its invention. It is the users of any new device who ultimately determine its success or failure.

The limited use of the Analytical Engine is, I fear, the major price we will pay for poorly designed arrangements. In light of the issues outlined here, we may safely predict that there are many who *could,* perhaps should, but will *not* put this remarkable invention to practical use.

9.1 Behind the Glossy Brochure

People buy computer systems with great expectations. They have every reason to do so. As the ads say,

FLEXIBILITY AND PERFORMANCE ARE YOURS
Gives You More Features Than Any Other Machine
Streamline Your Paper Flow
Cut Your Shopping Time in Half
Learn at Home in Your Spare Time
THE SYSTEM OF THE FUTURE
Balance Your Books in Seconds

As you open the glossy, color brochure it is hard not to be convinced.

The promise of computers is almost endless. Computers *can* be used to balance your books and order your groceries. They can reduce the seemingly unlimited need for paper copy (although usually they generate an enormous amount of paper). And they can be used to write books, prepare letter-perfect copy, issue paychecks, keep the inventory in a warehouse, compute insurance statistics, and control your household lights.

Implicit in all this is the assumption that computers are entirely suited for human use. In practice this means that people must be able to operate the computer and to correct matters if something goes wrong. Knowing an airplane can take you from Boston to Chicago is one thing, but for almost all of us, flying the airplane ourselves is an entirely different matter.

How well do computers match the needs and capabilities of the human user? In particular, how simple are the language and conventions needed to operate a computer? What kind of treatment does the computer give to the user? How helpful are the documents describing the computer's operation? These considerations are variously called *ease of use, human engineering,* or *human factors.*

Generally, the poor human engineering of computers is one of the worst features of computer technology. Concern for the human user has been quite unnecessarily neglected. With rare exceptions — notably the popular video computer games — it is difficult to think of one major computer system or product that could not be vastly improved in this respect.

With the power of computers at their fingertips, designers have concentrated on more and more capabilities — more memory, more speed, more features, more applications, and, always, on lower cost. Little effort has been spent to make things really simple. Imagine trying to justify the extra cost of providing a superbly written user's guide. Or designing an UNDO key so a mistake by the user can be undone by simply pressing the key. Or spending the time to redesign a set of commands so only half the original number are required. Such efforts add no additional power, no additional speed, no additional applications. They contribute only to ease of use.

If you are about to make a purchase or meet someone with years of experience with a given system, you will hear quite a different story. It is true that persons believe their system *is* well human engineered. They can point to several nice features or show how some particular task is easy to do. Watch out. Good intentions are common, and you may be lulled by the "feature syndrome." All systems have some good features, or they wouldn't have been built in the first place.

To understand what it is like to use a computer and to get an idea of the various human shortcomings, we draw upon a few examples.

Let us start with a simple and common task, making corrections to a program or other piece of text, as described in a handbook for the computer's operation. The following excerpt, although hypothetical, is typical:

3.6 Making Deletions

Certain features of EASY ED allow correction of errors and replacement of text without affecting other portions of the text. If needed, entire sections may be erased. In version 2.4 of EASY ED, additional features are provided (see Appendix J).

3.6.1 Deleting Characters. Characters that are incorrectly entered can be corrected immediately with the DELETE key, or on some terminals the RUBOUT key. If there is no character, an advance to a new line is made. The DELETE (or RUBOUT) key only affects the last character on a line.

3.6.2 Deleting Lines. An entire line may be deleted by pressing the CONTROL key followed by the DELETE (or RUBOUT) key. Alternatively, the ESCAPE key may be pressed.

In Extended EASY ED available on disk versions, typing SHIFT C will bring in the commands available with the EASY ED editor, which can be applied to the current line.

3.6.3 Deleting Entire Files. Moving the entire text below the typing line allows the entire text to be deleted. To bring the text down, press PAGE and DOWN. To delete the entire file, press SAVE. The text will then disappear from the screen.

At first glance the excerpt above appears harmless. It is written in English, it is concise, and the features described are useful. However, notice the reference to "version 2.4." This version, not a standard feature, is presumably available to users with additional software. Notice also, in section 3.6.2, the reference to "Extended EASY ED," which is available to users with disk storage. Such enhancements are commonplace. But there are serious drawbacks. As illustrated above, the information about such features is often spread through various documents or appendices. Moreover, we can expect that other, similar enhancements exist. An average user may have some but not all of them. Trying to understand exactly what is available and what is not may lead to a chase through the manual. This illustrates a first common annoyance—the failure to provide a *single* set of features whose description can be found in a single place.

Next, notice that two different keys can be used to delete a character, and two methods to delete a line. Why two? Should you use the DELETE key or the RUBOUT key to delete a character. To delete a line, should you use the single ESCAPE key, or use the CONTROL key followed by DELETE or RUBOUT? Most users are confused by such trivial options. Some will even search for probably nonexistent differences. This leads us to another point—the failure to provide a *single* method for accomplishing work.

Third, notice the actual keys pressed. For deleting characters, a DELETE or RUBOUT key correctly suggests the intended action. But pressing the CONTROL key for deleting lines is unexpected. This step has to be memorized and is all too easy to forget, even a few minutes later. If, perchance, the system is unused for a few weeks, these and other similar conventions become very difficult to recall. This problem is compounded by the completely different convention for deleting entire files. Here the text is moved below the typing line and SAVE is pressed. For deletions the word SAVE has the wrong connotation entirely. The justification presumably is that "saving nothing" is the same as "deleting everything." A reverse logic, to say the least.

Computers often come with thirty, fifty, or even hundreds of pages of such conventions. All of this indicates a failure to set simple conventions for operation.

The game is not over. Interacting with a computer is a demanding task in itself, made more so when good human engineering is lost. It is easy to get confused and make a mistake. All too often, the assistance offered is meager. On one widely available computer (a word processor), if you type too many lines of text into a file—and five pages of this book are too many—the computer "locks up." All you can do is shut off the power switch and start over. An hour or two of work can be lost in an instant.

Most people limit, often drastically, the operations they perform to those they consider comfortable and safe. Sometimes as much as 90 percent of the available features are never used. This reluctance to explore the limits of the machine's capability is a clear consequence of the widespread failure to meet human needs.

Using a computer requires the computer itself to respond. The picture here is just as bleak. All kinds of messages are printed by the computer. The computer may tell you it is ready to receive your request by printing

    ?

or by using a sterile message like

    ENTER COMMAND:

It may say nothing. Normally you must figure out what to say next.

If you make a typing error and the computer cannot interpret your erroneous request, the machine will complain with justification. You might hope the message about the error would be courteous and helpful. This is rare. Rather more common are messages like those in the following list:

    NO COLUMN   -- Which one?

    ERROR IN LINE 25   -- Most often the error is in line 25,
                              but not always

    ILLEGAL DATA   -- Illegal? Who committed the crime?

    UNDEFINED FIELD   -- Almost hostile
    *** COMMAND REJECTED

    FATAL ERROR, ABORTED -- Sounds gruesome

Computerese also brings with it a new vocabulary, much of it unnecessary and distracting. Every system requires that you learn this vocabulary not only to read the manuals, but even to know which keys to press or what the computer's messages mean. When you see something like:

    FILEMODE INCORRECT

or

`SUBCOMMAND CONTAINS ILLEGAL IDENTIFIER`

you won't get very far if you don't know the meaning of "filemode," "subcommand," and "identifier." And some systems employ hundreds of such terms. Small wonder that many people who might benefit simply don't use computers at all.

Beyond these computer-jargon terms, most systems use a number of everyday words whose computer meaning may come as a surprise. Do you know what a "menu" is? A "page"? A "directory"? Or, just for fun, "garbage collection"? It's hard to complain about such terms—at least they're friendly and give you some clue as to their meaning. But you do, at least, have to learn them.

As our last example, we refer to the subject of computer-generated output—the forms, tables, bills, and summaries printed every day. Even if you never use a computer, your bank statement, paycheck, or insurance may be handled by one. And you must face what is sent to you. The minimal care given to the human reader may produce lines like

```
07   08   JOURNAL ENTRY     -100 CENTS SAVINGS    POSN
```

or

```
BALANCE     $0.02 CR
```

as is common. How long does it take to figure out that 07 08 means July 8 and not August 7? What does -100 CENTS mean? Or the code POSN. And how did you ever get a balance of two cents?

Unfortunately, most people take the computer-generated forms for granted. Computed data, special codes, and all kinds of information can be turned out all too easily. The idea that more is better generally prevails, but the result is overwhelming. The next time a computer printout baffles you, you might consider making a complaint.

9.2   Taming the Beast

Many would argue with our view that computers could be dramatically easier to use. We believe, for example, that it is possible to develop a word processor requiring no user manual. Imagine for the moment a computerized word processor you can plug in, turn on, and start using immediately—with no training and no documentation to read.

Such a feat would involve major changes of design and engineering. But the gains would be equally great. If computers were truly easy to use, even friendly and fun, their popularity would surge, and a great deal more productive work could be accomplished. The long range benefit would be enormous.

Regretfully, the widespread lack of attention to human needs and preferences has compromised the computer's utility. What can we do? If you have had a computer for some years, you may have learned to tolerate the computer's shortcomings; immune to its behavior, you may be quite satisfied. But if you are just now considering buying a computer, or at least have some influence, you can do something.

As a starter, ask for a copy of the user's guide to operation. Do not make any decision until you see the *complete* documentation and try to read it. If the vendor tells you that the manuals are not available unless you purchase, be wary. If you can get only a synopsis of what's available, be just as wary. Never make a judgment on a brochure and a demonstration.

You might want to check the options and features for all the things the computer is supposed to do. Fewer options and features mean less to learn and to comprehend. Unless you really need them, choose fewer, not more.

Although it may be intimidating, you should use the computer yourself before buying it. Pick a simple task, like creating a file containing only your name and printing the result. Look at the sequence of keys needed for the task. Does what you press make sense? Aside from the letters of your name, you may have to press as many as thirty keys. When you are at the terminal make a mistake, a big one, and see what happens.

Look at the keyboard. If you see a key marked PAGE, ask what it does. If you see keys marked ESCAPE or CODE, or if the keyboard looks technical, be very wary.

Try to adjust the tilt of the screen. If you can't, bear in mind it may become uncomfortable to look at during prolonged use. Check the height of the keyboard, the glare on the screen, and the size of the entire unit. Some terminals are much more comfortable to use than others.

There are a few things that, if they exist, are very good signs. Suppose you issue a command with a typing error and then want to correct and reissue the command. Is there a facility for doing this without entering the entire command again? A few systems offer an

UNDO key to rectify a mistaken command. This is a superb feature. It means that if you accidently erase a line, move some data to the wrong place, or even delete the wrong file, you can hit the UNDO key and all will be well.

But most importantly, be aware of the issues. Don't be misled by claims about power and versatility. These are surely valuable. But so is the ability to learn easily and work without frustration. Next time you are at McDonald's, take a look at one of the cash registers. That's human engineering.

Horizons

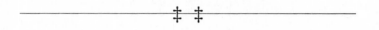

CHAPTER X

✝

The Affair at the Golden Eagle

CHANCED one day to be in the vicinity of Baker Street, on a call to one of my patients, and decided to take the opportunity to look up my old friend, Sherlock Holmes. My wife, Mary, was away visiting relatives and I was in no hurry to return home to a solitary meal and a silent evening.

I climbed the steps of Number 221 and was about to ring the bell when the door swung open and Holmes emerged, rather more briskly than was his wont.

"Upon my word, Holmes, is it battle, murder, or sudden death?" I exclaimed.

"None of those, I hope," he responded. "Why don't you come along and we'll find out? I'll explain as we go." He hailed a passing cab and instructed the driver to take us to the Golden Eagle Printing Office on Brook Street.

"Watson, I shall always maintain that your nose for a promising case is as infallible as Toby the hound's is for creosote," he began when we were on our way.

"Why, have I arrived in time to be dragged into yet another of your insufferably mysterious cases?" I feigned to grumble, all the while unable to repress a smile at my good fortune in finding something in the wind.

"Tut, tut! I seem to recall your having had little objection to being 'dragged into' the situation involving the engineer Hatherley's thumb," came my friend's sally. "But, yes, Watson, I am about to dabble in another insufferably mysterious affair, if this telegram from my brother portends anything."

Holmes handed me the telegram which was dated that very day, only a few hours previously :—

> *Leaving at once for Siam. Need your assistance in vital matter here.*
> *My man Brough at Golden Eagle Printing Office has details. —*
> *MYCROFT*

"So we are on our way to keep an appointment with Brough, I take it," I ventured.

"Dear Watson, your powers of deduction astound me," my friend drawled.

As we approached Brook Street our nostrils were assailed by an acrid smell. A uniformed policeman stopped our cab at the end of the street.

"Sorry, sir, can't go down there now. Been a nasty fire and the police and the firemen got a job to do."

"Well, we can proceed on foot," said Holmes calmly.

We alighted from the cab and Holmes tossed the fare to the driver without so much as a glance, instead scanning the scene up the street. The Golden Eagle, or rather its charred remains, lay in the middle of the block.

"I'M BROUGH."

"Has any one been hurt?" Holmes asked conversationally, as he turned to us.

"One gentleman got 'imself badly singed. Dead 'e is, in fact," returned the policeman soberly.

"I am sorry to hear that. In which building was the fire?"

"Golden Eagle Printing Office, sir."

I stifled an exclamation of horror as Holmes shot me a warning glance, and we proceeded in grim silence over the firemen's hoses and through rivulets of water to our destination. The firemen were preparing to leave, having extinguished the blaze. As we neared the shop a man detached himself from a group of spectators and approached us.

"I'm Brough," he introduced himself. "I've been watching for you, Mr. Holmes, and I was told that Dr. Watson might be with you. This fire is a nasty business, sir. I was on my way to post a watch on Frensham's movements. He is—was—the owner of the establishment. I could see the smoke as I turned onto Bond Street. That would be about an hour ago, and the fire engines were rushing here then."

"What was your interest in Frensham?"

"This," replied Brough, producing from his inside coat pocket a buff envelope which he handed to my friend. From it Holmes drew forth two sheets of paper which he scrutinised closely.

"*Most* interesting," Holmes commented, with a faint edge of excitement in his voice, well controlled but evident to one who knew him as well as I.

He passed both sheets to me. The uppermost was a carbon copy of a typewritten note which, if not in code, was the work of a singularly incompetent typist. The second note—not, this time, a carbon copy, read thus :—

> This is one of the documents which I have encoded and passed along to be sold to foreign governments. I will turn over all the documents I have sent and the key to the code. This will enable you to detect the traitor in your ranks. My price is a set of forged credentials to provide me a new identity, guaranteed safe passage to Canada, and the sum of 2,000 guineas. Direct your answer to J.F. at the Bow Street Post Office.

"J.F., I surmise, has been established as the late Mr. Frensham?" Holmes quizzed Brough.

"That is correct. The timing of the fire seems extremely suspicious to me, sir."

"Is Frensham's body still in the offices, and have you any idea who his contact was in the Foreign Office?" Holmes asked.

"Yes, to the first part of your question, Mr. Holmes. And 'maybe' to the second. At least there are several suspects—your brother, Mr. Holmes, is very anxious that you pursue an investigation of the case immediately. He would be even more anxious if he knew of this morning's development."

"Rest assured, Mr. Brough," said Holmes soothingly, "that I shall proceed as expeditiously as possible."

To that end, the three of us approached the door of the printing offices. The fire had burned with appalling fierceness in the area surrounding the large main press, which was completely ruined. Beside the press lay the charred form of the proprietor. Two constables were draping a sheet over the remains. The remainder of the offices were damaged by smoke and water but noticeably less by the extreme heat.

"Watson, would you be so good as to take a quick look at Mr. Frensham's remains, while we make a tour of the building?" my friend enquired.

I approached the body with little enthusiasm, for no good doctor likes to arrive too late to be of help. As expected, I found Frensham so badly burned that it was a mercy he didn't survive. I was unwilling to disturb the body in order to make a complete examination—that dismal duty best served by the District Coroner. Holmes and his companion returned from their inspection as I was again covering the remains.

"Did you find anything of import?" I asked. Holmes held up an empty bottle.

"Methylbenzene," he said, "a solvent commonly used for cleaning printing-presses. It is my belief that Frensham died in a flash fire caused by the explosion of a volatile substance."

"Then perhaps this was simply an accident?" I suggested.

"No, Watson. It is possible that we shall never know exactly how Frensham's death was engineered. But there is more to learn of his life. Let us go upstairs to see what we can discover."

On the upper story we discovered a door fastened on the inner side. Holmes threw himself against it with all his strength. One hinge snapped, then the other, and down came the door with a crash. Beyond it was an open garret, used for storage of supplies. The only potential hiding place was a door in the west wall.

"Now, that is interesting," remarked Holmes as he stared at it. "This printing office is in the middle of a row of terraced shops. Why would there be a door through a dividing wall? Open it, Watson, like a good fellow, and we shall see what we find."

"It's probably locked," I muttered. But it was not, and I cried out in astonishment.

"Coats—a whole row of coats. It is nothing but a clothes cupboard!"

"And beyond the coats?" queried Holmes.

"Why, my goodness, another door."

Holmes turned to Brough, who had been examining a bit of discarded printing equipment atop a desk. "What is adjacent this side of the printing office?"

"A dressmaker's shop on the ground floor and, on this story, the meeting rooms of——" Here he mentioned a fraternal order which, to save them embarrassment, I shall not name.

"BEYOND WAS AN OPEN GARRET."

"Ah, this must be their coat closet. I wonder why there are so many coats here this time of day," Holmes pondered.

"It is my understanding, sir," said Brough, "that this is a day on which they have a luncheon, with committee meetings following. They are involved in a number of benevolent efforts to which they give a great deal of time."

"I see," said Holmes. "I question whether these benevolent gentlemen could have enjoyed their lunch today.

"Now, then, what of this curious machine here?" he went on, turning his attention to the mechanical device on the old desk.

"A ruined typewriting machine, by the looks of it," I ventured.

"Possibly, and yet——" Holmes pried the top of the machine loose and inspected the interior. "I for one, gentlemen, have never encountered such a typewriting machine as this. See, Watson, the keys connect not to the hammers directly, but rather to these gears here; and they in turn——"

Holmes continued to scrutinize the inner workings of the device. "This is assuredly no ordinary typewriting device. I believe, in fact, that it is an encoding machine. By means of this device Frensham was able to encode the documents supplied him by his contact. If I can successfully restore it to working order——"

"Holmes, are you mad? The machine is almost in ruins!"

"Indeed, Watson, and deliberately so. The murderer sabotaged this machine purposely, for it is a remarkably clever apparatus. But our murderer was not so clever, or else he would have given more attention to destroying it properly.

"I need some time to complete my investigation of this machine," Holmes said after peering into its inner parts for several minutes. "While I continue here, perhaps you would be good enough, Watson, to go next door to the lodge above the dress shop. See if you can find out from their commissionaire whether any members of the Foreign Office are of this fraternity. Take Brough with you in case you have any difficulties, but try to rely on your own supreme tact, if possible."

It was not easy to obtain the information Holmes desired, and Brough's credentials had to be flourished before the commissionaire would divulge the identity of two Foreign Office staff who belonged to the lodge. Brough and I returned to find Holmes slipping a disk-like part of the coding machine into his overcoat pocket.

"Any luck?" asked Holmes, turning to us with the demeanour of the cat that swallowed the canary. I deduced that he was well pleased by his encounter with the converted typewriter.

"Two Foreign Office men," Brough replied, "are members of the lodge—Sir Thomas Nettleton and Nigel Barringer. Both attended the luncheon meeting. Sir Thomas excused himself before the meal ended but was unable to leave because the police detained all the members while the enquiry proceeded. Now we know why the closet is so full of coats. Robinson—that's the commissionaire—suggested delicately that Mr. Barringer seems to be three sheets to the wind, and I formed the impression he doesn't care for Barringer."

"Well, at least the suspects are narrowed to two, but we have more work to do before we establish the identity of Frensham's contact and, I suspect, killer. There's nothing more for us here, Watson. I suggest we adjourn to Simpson's for tea."

"Now, Holmes? In the midst of an investigation such as this?" I was astounded until I realised the direction in which Simpson's lay and the purpose behind my friend's apparently preposterous suggestion. "Ah, you propose to make use of the Analytical Engine at Whitehall!"

"Bravo, Watson! I really must remember not to underrate your deductive ability," Holmes replied. "Yes, I have need of the Engine's capabilities once again. The murderer was thorough enough in destroying Frensham, but he ought to have given more attention to the encoding device. It will take me some time but, with the help of the Analytical Engine, I believe I shall be able to unlock the code and discover the traitor."

While we were talking, the District Coroner had arrived and was in conversation with Brough, whom Holmes now drew aside with an apology.

"Dr. Watson and I are leaving for Whitehall, where we shall continue the investigation. I would like you to have some enquiries made into the backgrounds of Sir Thomas Nettleton and Nigel Barringer. We will meet you later in my brother's office, when I hope you will have some useful information and I may be able to close the case. Meanwhile I would also like you to have these two gentlemen discreetly watched and their movements documented."

It was a relief to emerge once again into fresh air, and we decided to walk to Simpson's to clear our lungs and our brains.

While we awaited our tea and its accompanying sandwiches, scones and biscuits, Holmes produced his note-book and a pencil. "If I am to crack this code, Watson, I had best begin to work. You will excuse me if I am not overly responsive for a while."

"Are you devising an algorithm for a programme to use in the Analytical Engine?" I asked.

"That I am, Watson. It will take a bit of doing."

He fell to work, and I meanwhile pondered the gravity of its eventual outcome. Should either Sir Thomas or Nigel Barringer prove to be a traitor, the scandal which might arise could prove devastating to Britain's foreign relations. We were both abstracted as we consumed our afternoon tea and remained so as we continued our walk to Whitehall.

Within a very short time after our arrival at Mycroft Holmes's office, my friend had completed his algorithm. He turned the next phase of the investigation over to the Analytical Engine and its capable attendant. Now we awaited the results, comfortably sitting in club chairs with our pipes going. While we smoked Holmes explained what he had been able to determine about the encoding machine's mode of operation.

"The machine's function, so far as I can ascertain, is not unlike that of the Analytical Engine. As you saw, it had a keyboard very much like a standard typewriting machine. The operator would type in the information to be encoded, letter by letter. The coding machine would start out in one of a number of predetermined 'states.' As each letter of the document was read, the machine's state would change according to the letter being read and the prescribed instructions contained in its control unit. In its new state the machine would type a specified code letter for the original letter. Its instructions would then direct it to read and encode the next letter, and to proceed thus until it reached the end."

"Holmes, I fear I can make neither head nor tail of your explanation," I confessed.

"Let me see if I can clarify it somewhat," said my friend, sketching a diagram in his note-book. I have reproduced this sketch below.

"We will begin with a hypothetical set of letter equivalences. As you can see from the disks"—hereupon he took the disks from the table and handed them to me—"that the inner disk is able to rotate clockwise. On the inner disk the alphabet is arranged in its customary order, while it is scrambled randomly on the outer disk. I have filled in the five letters which were destroyed on the outer disk, though I will not know their proper arrangement until I have broken the code.

"These disks determine the state in which the machine is set; I have arbitrarily set them to the state 'A equals V,' which I shall represent thus :—

$$S_A = V$$

"The symbols which the machine uses are the twenty-six letters of the alphabet, and correspondingly there are twenty-six possible states in which the machine can operate. We will indicate this information so :—

Symbols: A, B, C, . . . Z

States: S_A=A, S_A=B, S_A=C, . . . S_A=Z

Initial State: S_A=V

"Now let us assume we wish to encode your name. We would type JOHN H WATSON into the machine, disregarding spaces and punctuation for the time being. The machine is set to the state S_A=V initially, and in this state it reads the first letter, J. This next part may prove somewhat confusing, Watson, so pay careful heed.

"As I said, the machine contains a control unit. In this control unit are specific directions on what letter the machine is to produce, depending on its current state and the letter it is to encode. Since we have twenty-six possible states and twenty-six available letters to be read, there are twenty-six squared, or six hundred and seventy-six, possible state-plus-letter combinations."

"Good heavens, Holmes, that is an unwieldy number!" I exclaimed.

"So it is, my dear Watson. You can see now why I must resort to the Analytical Engine to assist me.

"To continue, in initial state S_A=V the letter J is encoded as A. At this point the control unit commands the machine to advance the inner disk clockwise by one letter. The machine is now in the state S_A=R. Can you determine, then, what letter will be used to encode the O?"

I studied his sketch for a moment, trying to rotate the inner disk mentally. "It would be H, I think," I conjectured finally.

"Excellent! You understand the procedure," Holmes said. "Would you care to try your hand at determining what the machine does next?"

"Let me see," I said, thinking. "According to the pattern we have established, the machine should receive the command to advance the disk one letter, setting it into the state of S_A=W. The machine then reads the next letter, H, and encodes it as—why, Holmes, it encodes it as A again! But earlier it encoded J as A! How is that possible?"

"Remember that when the machine rendered J as A, it was operating in the state S_A=V, Watson," Holmes explained patiently. "Here, let me finish encoding your name according to the pattern we have set up." He took the notebook and slowly wrote down each letter as he mentally encoded it, then showed me the result.

"So my name becomes AHAJ E RZVVOO then? My word, Holmes. This would be a poser indeed for anyone trying to crack the code without the key. There are so many different things one would have to know. It will take you forever to decode the document!" I cried.

"It would indeed, Watson, had the murderer succeeded in destroying the coding machine. For some reason, however, he failed to complete his task. The machine's disks were sufficiently undamaged that I needed to determine the location of relatively few letters in order to cut my way through this Gordian knot. Moreover, this cipher, though clever, is relatively simple. I dare say we'll have our answer fairly soon."

"Exactly what have you requested the Engine to do, Holmes?"

"It is a relatively simple process really, Watson," he answered. "You see, five letters were destroyed beyond recognition on the outer disk of the coding machine. This means that the five letters could be arranged in any one of 120 possible permutations. I have simply directed the Engine to run through the code utilizing every possible permutation. The one producing an intelligible result is the correct arrangement. It will take some time. I expect we shall be hearing from Brough by the time the programme is finished."

We waited for nearly an hour while the Analytical Engine completed its work. Holmes lit his pipe, then drew out his note-book. He sat there puffing away, deep in thought, pausing now and again to make some notation. I waited patiently, knowing his great dislike of interruptions, and secure in the knowledge that I would receive a full account when he had satisfied himself.

"Do you know, Watson," he said at length, "today's little problem has set me thinking about this curious encoding machine and its relation to the Analytical Engine. While their external mechanisms are different, they follow the same basic principle. I mean, of course, the predetermined nature of each machine's operation. From this I have indulged in something of a Platonic fancy, if you will."

"Indeed!" said I. "Pray tell me about it."

"You are familiar, of course, with Plato's theory of ideas—that there exist in the higher plane of reality ideas of every conceivable abstract notion, from Truth and Beauty and Justice to more mundane concepts such as a Chair, a Table, and a Lamp. I have conceived of an idea for what I shall call an Ideal Machine. My specific examples are, of course, the coding device and the Analytical Engine.

"By comparing the common elements involved in the function of each, I have extrapolated the fundamental requirements for this Ideal Machine. I am sure that experimentation would prove that any humanly constructed machine similar to the Analytical Engine would employ these fundamental requirements.

"The first is a means by which data are presented and by which the machine may issue its results. I envision this as a long paper tape with the data written upon it, and upon which the new data may be written.

"Second, the machine has the ability to read the data fed into it and to write its response. For this I see a section of the machine through which the data tape passes. This mechanism reads whatever is on the tape and has the ability to write out a response.

"Third, there is a control section to the machine which can be set to any one of a finite number of 'states' or 'conditions.' Each particular state causes the machine to respond in a certain predefined way based upon the data fed into it."

"That's quite a charming fancy you've constructed, Holmes," I chuckled. "I suppose it will find its way into yet another of your never-ending list of monographs."

"Hardly, Watson," he replied, pulling out the page from his notebook, crumpling it into a ball, and tossing it aside. "An amusing bit of idle speculation, nothing more. I far prefer to devote my meagre writing abilities to more useful topics."

Shortly thereafter the Engine's attendant appeared with a sheaf of paper in hand. No sooner had the attendant delivered the results than the door opened, and Brough entered the room.

Holmes waved him to a seat while he perused the sheets the machine had produced. Once done, he nodded in satisfaction and addressed Brough.

"You have the information I requested, I trust," Holmes stated.

"I have, but there is little in it to reveal either man as a traitor," answered Brough. "Sir Thomas Nettleton's credentials appear impeccable. Robinson says that his only idiosyncrasy is a steadfast refusal to drink anything but Lapsang Soochong tea.

"Nigel Barringer is a bachelor, and Robinson reports him as rather more fond of his cards and liquor than befits a gentleman in his position. Aside from that, Barringer's main personal quirk appears to be an extraordinary attachment to his overcoat. According to Robinson, Barringer behaves very oddly about the coat. It seems he will allow no one to handle the garment and insists on hanging it in the closet himself."

"Brough, you have done a superb job," said Holmes excitedly. "I have, with the aid of the Analytical Engine, cracked the code, and this tells me how the documents were transmitted to Frensham."

"Well, for heaven's sake, Holmes, out with it!" I insisted. "Which one is the traitor and murderer?"

"Think, Watson. Apply the rules of scientific deduction. Which of the two is more likely to have been in a position in which it would be advantageous to him to sell governmental secrets? The financially secure man with no bad habits to sustain, tea being a fairly frugal tipple—even Lapsang Soochong? Or the card-player whose gambling and drinking cannot fail to be costly?"

"Then—Barringer!" I gasped. "What a disgrace to the Foreign Office—a high-ranking official turning traitor to pay off his gambling debts! And then, fearing betrayal, he resorts to murder, setting the fire to make Frensham's death appear an accident!"

"Yes, I fear it is so, as this proves only too clearly." Holmes handed me the papers he had been studying. "This first is the encoded document which Frensham sent to Mycroft's agents."

I took the paper, which read as follows:

WDWMKAKVJIR:
    D DWQD JCBSTFF XMFD WH QBHSICCUIM CJOAKCV WQ IVBRDMD
EVQ OJFHUIM UXLFNUNEPW QJ LYNWNQ OBEOVH ZG VGDBPIZ UJWL
GUPBODQ ECDAEH NGEXMP ATZMCI WHHTGNVEV WQ EIPLK LH EVQ
IHXIKERPENNQ SGW HSUZP OU CSO QDHRENY HB HHCTGAOS. RVFEH
AFZQWJ, PRPIGWGKAZM; WKVQ OOWKXPWW QA XBI KVJ JNLHHA VYJOCG
SP FLXH CRD H PDTO RPAV.

    RRKMGNGES

"Now read this," said Holmes, handing me the decoded form. Appalled, I read:

```
CHARPENTIER:
    I HAVE LEARNED THAT MY GOVERNMENT INTENDS TO COUNTER
THE CURRENT DEPLOYMENT OF FRENCH FORCES IN ALGERIA WITH
BRITISH TROOPS UNLESS FRANCE CONTINUES TO ABIDE BY THE
STIPULATIONS SET FORTH IN THE ENTENTE OF POITIERS. TREAD
WARILY, CHARPENTIER; YOUR POSITION IS NOT YET STRONG ENOUGH
TO GIVE YOU A FREE HAND.

                    BARRINGER
```

"Holmes," I asked, nearly choking on my words, "what are we to do?"

"We must call upon Brough again," my friend stated firmly. To Brough he said, "You must obtain Barringer's overcoat and deliver it, along with a copy of this message to Charpentier. Take this note from myself to Sir George Smyth-Atkins. The Foreign Secretary will know how to deal with Barringer without creating a scandal. It will be simple for you to acquire the coat by the same means Frensham removed secret documents. Little did our two conspirators think that it would prove to be their undoing when they cut that door."

"But will Barringer not realise something is up when the police release the lodge members?" I asked.

"Of course. But I trust that he will be quietly apprehended before that happens. As I see it, Brough will have a word with the officers on duty when he collects the coat, asking them to detain everyone until he returns. When he does, he will bring Barringer's coat and will be accompanied by Sir George."

"Masterly!" I breathed.

"Thanks to the Analytical Engine," said my friend, modestly. "Now I suggest we dine together—Mary, I believe, is away from home—and I will tell you about the subject for my next monograph. The idea has just come to me."

"And what may that be?" I responded. "Coding machines, perhaps?"

"Why no, Watson," was Holmes's rejoinder. "Gentlemen's overcoats, of course."

10.1   Turing Machines

Over a decade before the development of computer technology, Alan Turing began investigating the properties of a simple idealized machine. This hypothetical, but remarkable, machine has had a profound effect on the study of the theoretical properties of computers and programming. In particular, the study of this idealized machine gives us some insight into the primitive requirements for a computer and its theoretical limitations. These topics will be taken up later in this chapter. Without much fanfare, we start with the device itself.

Although hypothetical, a Turing machine has components analogous to a computer. First, it has a tape, upon which data can be read and written. The symbols on the tape can be digits, letters, blanks, punctuation marks, or anything you please. The tape can be infinite; if need be you can read or write data forever. Normally the tape will have some initial sequence of symbols and will end up with some new sequence of symbols. A general sketch of a Turing machine is shown in Figure 10.1. Here the asterisk symbol (*) denotes a blank.

The second component of a Turing machine is its "read-write head." This gadget can read the symbol over which it is positioned, write a new symbol over the existing symbol, and then move one square left or right. The read-write head is thus very limited in its behavior.

The third component of a Turing machine is a finite number of "states." At a particular time, the machine is said to be in one of these states. Generally, each state represents some state of knowledge. Figure 10.2 depicts an example Turing machine. Here we have three possible states, named S_{odd}, S_{even}, and S_{halt}.

The final component of a Turing machine is its "control unit." This contains a "program" that directs the operation of the machine. A program consists of a sequence of instructions in a form described below. Consider the instruction

$$S_{odd}, 1 \rightarrow S_{even}, 1, \text{Move\_Right}$$

taken from the Turing Machine of Figure 10.2. This instruction means:

If the machine is in state S_{odd} and a 1 is over the head, then set the state to S_{even}, write a 1 over the head, and move the head one square to the right.

Notice here that writing a 1 over the existing 1 effectively leaves the 1 in place.

In general, each instruction has the form:

state, symbol → *new-state, new-symbol, direction*

The full program must be such that no two *state, symbol* pairs are identical. This guarantees that only one instruction can be applied at a given time. The Turing machine, however, is not required to apply the instructions in any written order. The machine obeys whichever command applies, depending on the state it is in and the symbol it is reading on its tape.

To start a Turing machine we simply set up the tape with some initial sequence of symbols, position the head at one of them, and define the initial state. In the machine of Figure 10.2 we put a sequence of 1's on the tape, position the head at the leftmost 1, and start in state S_{even}. To run the Turing machine we apply the instructions in the given program.

The machine of Figure 10.2 runs as follows. The initial state is S_{even} and the head is initially over a 1. Applying the second instruction, the state changes to S_{odd}, the head writes a 1 and moves to the right. This gives

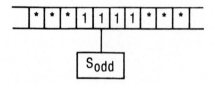

Now the first instruction applies,

S_{odd}, 1 → S_{even}, 1, Move_Right

which changes the state to S_{even} and again moves the head right, giving

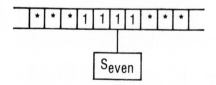

In a similar fashion, applying the third and first instructions again, we come to the situation

Tape (data)

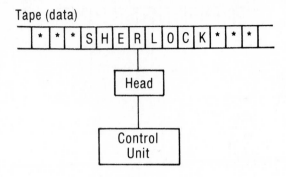

Figure 10.1   *Sketch of a Turing Machine*

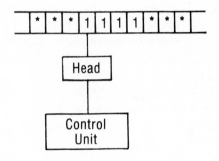

Tape symbols: * 1 D E

States: S_{odd}, S_{even}, S_{halt}

Initial state: S_{even}

Program: S_{odd}, 1 → S_{even}, 1, Move_Right

S_{even}, 1 → S_{odd}, 1, Move_Right

S_{odd}, * → S_{halt}, D, Move_Right

S_{even}, * → S_{halt}, E, Move_Right

Figure 10.2   *A Simple Turing Machine and its Program*

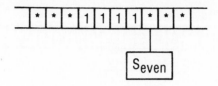

Here we apply the fourth instruction, giving finally:

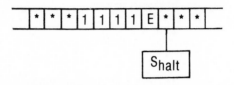

Now no instruction applies, and our little machine terminates its execution. Notice the letter E has been written at the end of the sequence of 1's. With some elementary Holmesian deduction, we conclude that our given Turing machine simply determines whether the sequence of 1's is odd or even. If odd, the letter D is printed; if even, the letter E. In both cases the final state is S_{halt}.

Two key features should be noted. First, within the limits of the instruction format, a program of arbitrary length and purpose may be written. Second, a program terminates when the current machine state and symbol over the head are such that no *state, symbol* pair in the program gives a match. We now turn to two examples, each illustrating an important property of both computers and Turing machines.

An Infinite Loop

The first example is given in Figure 10.3. The tape contains the single letter A and the machine starts in state S_1. It runs as follows:

a. Apply the first instruction: a B is printed over the A, the state is kept at S_1, and the head moves right.

b. Next apply the second instruction: the * is left alone, the state changes to S_2, and the head moves left.

c. Next apply the third instruction: since the head is now over the B; the B is replaced by an A, state S_2 is kept, and the head moves left.

d. Next apply the fourth instruction: the * is left alone, the state becomes S_1, and the head moves right.

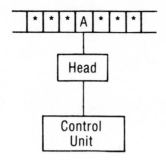

Tape symbols: *   A   B

States: S_1, S_2

Initial state: S_1

Program: S_1, A   → S_1, B, Move_Right

          S_1, *   → S_2, *, Move_Left

          S_2, B   → S_2, A, Move_Left

          S_2, *   → S_1, *, Move_Right

Figure 10.3   *An Infinite Loop*

This configuration is exactly the same as when the machine started, i.e. the head is over an A and the state is S_1. So we cycle through the instructions again, and again, and again, forever. The A's and B's keep switching, but nothing else happens to stop the machine. In computer parlance, we have a case of the *infinite loop*.

The infinite loop is a possibility on all computers. That is, it is possible to write a program that never terminates. This can happen in Basic, Pascal, Fortran, or any other programming language. Obviously, programmers usually don't intend to write such programs. Rather, they are a result of error or misunderstanding. Even in our earlier program of Figure 10.2, a simple error can lead to an infinite loop. For example, if we replace the fourth instruction

S_{even}, * → S_{halt}, E, Move_Right

with

$$S_{even}, * \to S_{even}, E, Move\_Right$$

the Turing machine of Figure 10.2 will keep writing E's forever. The computer is indeed an obedient servant.

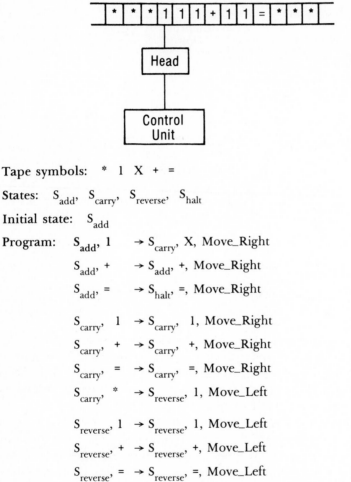

Tape symbols: * 1 X + =

States: S_{add}, S_{carry}, $S_{reverse}$, S_{halt}

Initial state: S_{add}

Program:

S_{add}, 1 → S_{carry}, X, Move_Right

S_{add}, + → S_{add}, +, Move_Right

S_{add}, = → S_{halt}, =, Move_Right

S_{carry}, 1 → S_{carry}, 1, Move_Right

S_{carry}, + → S_{carry}, +, Move_Right

S_{carry}, = → S_{carry}, =, Move_Right

S_{carry}, * → $S_{reverse}$, 1, Move_Left

$S_{reverse}$, 1 → $S_{reverse}$, 1, Move_Left

$S_{reverse}$, + → $S_{reverse}$, +, Move_Left

$S_{reverse}$, = → $S_{reverse}$, =, Move_Left

$S_{reverse}$, X → S_{add}, 1, Move_Right

Figure 10.4 *A Unary Adder*

A Unary Adder

Our second example is more typical of ordinary computers. We consider the problem of building a unary adder. In unary arithmetic there is only one digit. For example, 111 + 11 is 11111, and 1111 + 111 is 1111111. Such a machine is shown in Figure 10.4.

The machine starts with two unary numbers on its tape, in the form

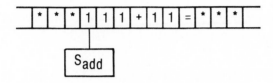

The starting state is S_{add}. To begin execution the first instruction applies, giving:

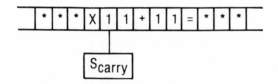

Notice that the first 1 has been marked with an X. Next, the fourth instruction applies, giving:

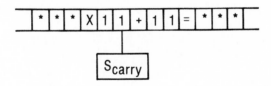

Appropriately applying the fourth, fifth, and sixth instructions, the head continues to move right, arriving at

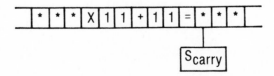

Now the seventh instruction applies, which records the first digit of our result, changes the state to $S_{reverse}$, and moves the head left:

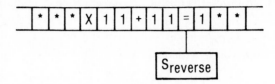

Next we continue in $S_{reverse}$ as the head moves left (applying the eighth, ninth, and tenth instructions) until we arrive at:

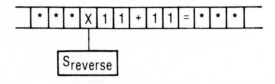

Now we apply the last instruction to give

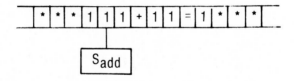

all of which sets us up to add the second digit and start the process anew.

The entire process terminates with the configuration

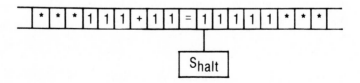

exactly the desired result.

10.2 The Nature of Mechanical Computation

Our interest in Turing machines lies in a single proposition, often called *Turing's thesis:*

> *Any* processes that intuitively can be written as an algorithm (and thus any process that could be programmed on a computer) can be realized by a Turing machine.

The implications of this proposition are broad, for it treats a number of issues fundamental to computation. What can a machine do? Precisely those calculations that can be performed on a Turing machine. What basic properties does a machine need to be classified as a computer? At least those needed to mimic a Turing machine. What does it mean to say you can write an algorithm for a process? It means your statements could, if needed, be stated in the form of a Turing machine program. Probably most importantly, the proposition states that there is a simple idealized machine that we can use for studying the nature of computation.

Turing's thesis cannot be proved. It is, if you will, an assertion requiring support. Although there now is a formidable mathematical case supporting Turing's thesis, we turn to Turing's own arguments in its favor.

We start with the observation that computations are normally done on ordinary paper. The two-dimensional aspect of paper is not essential, although in practice unbelievably convenient. We may assume then that any computation can be carried out on one-dimensional paper, in particular on a tape where the symbols are printed on individual positions.

The tape itself is presumed to be infinitely long. This should not be troublesome—we can initially install a tape of some fixed length, attaching more tape if necessary. Theoretically we may even need a paper mill to supply the machine, but since our machine and our paper tape are hypothetical, an equally hypothetical paper mill will strain only the imagination, not the bank account.

The behavior of a computer, or of a person doing a computation by hand, is characterized by the symbol being observed. While a person may observe several symbols at once, we can limit the computer's observation to a single symbol. More symbols can be obtained by further observations.

The behavior of a computer, or a person, is also characterized by a "state" of knowledge. The number of possible states is finite, since any computer or person will have some limit to the amount of information that can be kept in mind.

Finally, the operations performed by a computer (or a person) are ultimately based on some number of primitive operations that are so elementary they cannot be further divided. A new symbol may be written, the next symbol may be observed, or the state of mind may be changed. In essence, Turing's claim is that each primitive operation can be stated in the form of an instruction for a Turing machine.

The jump from Turing machines to contemporary computers is not hard to make. Obviously, programming languages like Basic or Pascal are far more expressive than the instruction format for a Turing machine. Moreover, the devices for reading or writing data are much more varied, and the control units are vastly more powerful. But the parallel remains. To qualify as a machine for performing calculations of any kind, we need supply only (a) devices for reading and writing data, (b) a control unit for keeping track of the states of computation, and (c) a set of instructions (i.e. program) whose form is at least as powerful as the instruction format for a Turing machine.

There are other formulations of Turing's thesis, each of them equivalent. All lead to the same basic proposition—the concept of an algorithm, with all of its intuitive meanings, can be precisely captured in a fixed notation, be it as primitive as a Turing machine or as sophisticated as a shiny new computer.

10.3   Unsolvable Problems

It may come as a surprise that there are computer problems for which there are no solutions. We do not mean problems like predicting the price of gold twenty years from now or calculating the number of grains of sand on the earth. Rather, there are well-defined problems for which one can write an algorithm and for which, on the surface at least, there appear to be solutions. The subject of unsolvable problems has various mathematical formulations, one of which was posed by Alan Turing.

The Halting Problem

Recall the program of Figure 10.2, where the given Turing machine decides whether a sequence of 1's is odd or even. As soon as the sequence is scanned, the machine comes to a halt. Recall also the program of Figure 10.3, where the machine keeps switching states and never halts.

In general, a given Turing machine is started in some initial state, with some initial input tape. The program is then executed. The question may be asked "Will the machine eventually halt?" More precisely, is it possible to write an algorithm to determine (yes or no) whether a given machine with its given program and input tape will halt? This is called the *halting problem.*

In some particular cases, for example those in Figure 10.2 and Figure 10.3, we can answer the question. The particular machine of Figure 10.2 halts, the machine of Figure 10.3 never halts. The halting problem, however, asks if we can write an algorithm that can *always* determine the answer.

Notice that simply running the machine is not an acceptable solution. A given machine may never halt, and even after running it for a very long time we cannot safely conclude that it is in an infinite loop.

The halting problem is *not* solvable. To show this, the method of contradiction is used. That is, we first assume a solution exists, and then show an intrinsic contradiction in making this assumption. This line of reasoning is presented in Appendix H. For those of you who have not seen this kind of argument before, be prepared for some fancy footwork in order to understand it. The conclusion, however, is simple: there cannot exist a universal program that can determine if another Turing machine will halt or not.

Implications

This kind of result and others like it deserve a brief review. In computers there are a variety of problems that can never be solved, at least not in the general sense. For example, it is not possible to write programs to do the following:

- determine if a computer is in an infinite loop.

- determine if a given answer is printed by another program.

- determine if all available memory storage will be used by another program.

- determine if another program is free of errors.

- determine if a program performs what it is said to perform.

Such results can be sobering, for they place ultimate limits on what we can expect to accomplish with computers.

On the other hand, it may be argued that these limits are really of only passing or theoretical interest. Writing a general purpose program to solve the halting problem or to determine if another program is error-free would be so difficult, it is barely imaginable that anyone would try.

Nevertheless, there are some absolute limits to the power of computers. At the very least, Turing's result should put to rest the belief that "computers can do anything."

CHAPTER XI

---‡---

The Adventure of
the Red Queen's Race

(Part I)

A! CHECKMATE!" cried Sherlock Holmes.

His exclamation was so unexpected that it startled me into dropping the morning *Telegraph,* which I had been quietly reading in our sitting room while partaking of the breakfast Mrs. Hudson had fetched up. Holmes had been reading the mail which had accumulated while he was in Rome investigating the death of Cardinal Tosca. My attention had, meanwhile, been stolen by yet another in the never-ceasing stream of inflammatory letters which Mrs. Ruby Queensley visited upon the local newspaper editors. I suspect that they saw the lady's outraged though articulate epistles as an opportunity to enlarge their readership, since Mrs. Queensley had only recently created a minor scandal with a public announcement of her separation from her husband. This letter was, as always, on her special subject—the singular lack of conscience and social responsibility on the part of anyone who favored the rapid development of modern technology.

Holmes, upon opening one of the envelopes in his stack, immediately read through its contents carefully, and turned to the chess-board which had occupied one of the room's stuffed chairs throughout his absence in Rome. He consulted the letter again, moved one of the pieces, then sat staring at the board for some time. At length he let out the aforementioned ejaculation which had so jolted me, and made a counter-move.

"Holmes, do you think you might manage to annihilate your opponent a bit less noisily?" I asked rather snappishly as I attempted to rescue my toast from the carpet, where it had fallen marmalade-side down.

"My apologies, Watson," Holmes replied. "It is just that I have only now determined the winning stroke in my game with Queensley. I must dash off a note to him at once." Hastily scrawling on a card from his desk, he added, "Do you know, Watson, I am delivering the *coup de grace* far sooner than it would normally fall. My opponent is definitely not playing his usual sharp game. 'Mechanical' would be the appropriate adjective, I should think." Holmes chuckled to himself. "Chess master Queensley has become quite an automaton of late."

"Is this Queensley fellow of whom you speak any relation to the piously indignant Mrs. Ruby Queensley of this morning's letter column?" I asked.

"Professor Alfred Queensley has the dubious distinction of being the lady's estranged husband," replied Holmes. "The Professor is a scholar in mathematics at Trinity College. He is also one of the scientists who constructed the University's more advanced version of the Analytic—why, hullo! Here is yet another envelope from the man. He has invited me to a demonstration involving the Engine tomorrow afternoon."

"For what purpose?" I inquired.

"He does not let on," said Holmes with a knowing smile, "but I believe I have some idea. Yes, I shall certainly attend his demonstration— it should be most interesting."

"Well, at present, I find our good landlady's toast and marmalade far more enticing," I answered, heaping another slice with the tangy orange compote.

After breakfast Holmes and I went about our various errands, myself to call upon my patients, and Holmes to post his winning move to Professor Queensley. We returned just before lunch and were on the point of sitting down to it when the bell rang. Soon the tread of feet upon the stairs informed us of the arrival of a caller.

"Pardon me, Mr. Holmes, sir," Mrs. Hudson said as she appeared in the doorway followed by a man with a veritable lion's mane of greying hair, "but this gentleman—"

"Why, Queensley!" exclaimed Holmes. "Only something truly urgent could bring you here at this time. It concerns your new chess-playing programme for the Analytical Engine, perhaps?"

Queensley's mouth dropped open. "How on earth did you know, Mr. Holmes? There are only two people who know of its existence!"

"Come now, Professor," Holmes replied. "When you make the unusual request to play a match by mail, then proceed to play that match in a mechanical style—hardly your customary manner—and throughout the game you continue to refer in an oblique fashion to some major project which is occupying most of your thoughts, what else could possibly be concluded?"

"Good heavens, what is this?" I interposed. "Have you taught the Engine how to think? How can a machine play chess?"

"My astonished friend is Dr. Watson," Holmes said with a smile in my direction. "He frequently assists me in my investigations."

"How do you do, Doctor Watson?" said the Professor.

"Professor Queensley, may I repeat my question?" I asked. "Have you indeed made the Analytical Engine capable of reason?"

"Oh, dear me, no, not at all. I have simply written a programme which enables the Engine to play chess."

"But surely if the Engine can play chess, it must think about how to move in order to devise its strategy," I protested.

"Not at all, Watson," said Holmes. "Consider the mathematical nature of the game. The Professor has simply found a new way to express the moves and strategy of chess in mathematical terms understandable to the Engine."

"Precisely, Mr. Holmes," agreed Professor Queensley. "You see, Doctor, I have been attempting to study the Engine's function and to see if it were able to learn in some method analogous to the process of learning in humans. I chanced upon the game of chess because it is not unlike other complex situations which humans are apt to encounter."

"But it can take a human being years to master the game," I objected. "Surely not even your programme can enable the Engine to become an instant master of the game."

"No, I fear the poor machine has some way to go yet before it will be able to play a truly challenging game. Its memory is quite limited, and it requires some highly complex maneuvering on my part to create a programme to teach it what for a human would be a relatively simple idea."

"I had, for instance, to invent a method of representing the board and the pieces in a form that is intelligible to the Engine. Then there are the formulas describing each piece's move. These have been difficult enough, but when compared with teaching the Engine even some very simple strategy, they were remarkably easy. Fortunately, for the purposes of my experiment I was able to reduce some of the goals and strategies of the game to precise mathematical terms, giving the Engine the ability to calculate in numbers the best move in a given situation."

"A prodigious undertaking, Professor," said I. "But you say that your purpose was to determine whether the Analytical Engine could learn in the same manner as a human?"

"Not quite," said Queensley. "My programme directs the Engine to calculate all possible moves and their respective values. For this purpose the programme looks ahead a number of moves to estimate the outcome of each. It then selects the best move based on the pre-established criteria that I have devised. In addition, the value of each move, and the corresponding choice that resulted, are recorded and stored in the Engine's memory.

"Essentially, the Engine is capable of remembering a situation in one game and applying this knowledge in another. However, this is hardly practical. It can take the Engine longer to run through its memory to find a parallel situation than to choose a move by simply recalculating existing criteria. Because of this, I am beginning to consider other methods more suited to specific situations."

"I'm sorry," I said, "I fear you have lost me."

"Let me see if I can give you an example," said Queensley, running his fingers absent-mindedly through his hair. "Let us consider driving a carriage. After acquiring the basic skills required, you then apply them as the situation demands. You drive a skittish horse one way, a steady one another; you accommodate such factors as hills, corners, or twilight; and you must also adapt for two horses, or a dogcart as opposed to a hansom."

"Ah, now I take your meaning," I said. "But to have mastered all this, Professor, the Engine's ability must be sophisticated indeed. Have you also taught the Engine to speak, then?"

A wistful look came into Professor Queensley's eyes. "Oh, dear me, no, Doctor. I am certain that no one in our lifetime will succeed at that—it's far, far too complicated. For one thing, it is all but impossible to express the richness of human conversation in mathematical terms. No, we can only hope that someday, perhaps—— Ah, but I'm forgetting the reason for my visit."

Queensley's face turned sober.

"It must be a serious matter," observed my friend, "that has brought you to London to visit me today, knowing you would see me to-morrow at the demonstration."

"Mr. Holmes, it *is* serious," said Queensley severely. "They want to destroy the Engine!" He searched his jacket pocket and produced a wrinkled envelope. "Just today this note arrived for me in the mail. I cannot make sense of most of it, but it is most definitely a threat against the Analytical Engine. You must help me prevent something terrible from happening!"

Holmes glanced at the letter. "Common stationer's envelope, Cambridge postmark, addressed by a typewriting machine. Someone obviously did not wish you to recognise the handwriting."

"What a strange message!" I exclaimed, for the note contained what appeared to be only a bit of doggerel verse :—

"MR. HOLMES, IT IS SERIOUS."

BEWARE THE METAL JABBERWOCK, THE BEAST WITHOUT A
SOUL!
ON DAY OF BLOOD AT BRILLIG, VORPAL BLADE SHALL FIND ITS
GOAL,
FOR THE VILE MACHINE MUST BE DESTROYED TO END ITS
WICKEDNESS,
ERE MORE MEN'S LIVES ARE RUINED THROUGH ITS TREACH'ROUS
GAME OF CHESS.
WHILE LION PROUD EATS WHITE BREAD, UNICORN EATS BROWN
IN SHAME:
BUT A RUDDY SCEPTRE'S VENGEFUL FIRE SHALL SINGE THE LION'S
MANE!

"It must be the work of some harmless crack-brain," I declared.

"Hardly, Watson," my friend rejoined as he took the note back. "This is more than mere jibberish, and you are quite right, Professor, in concluding that it portends harm to the Engine. I'm certain the Reverend Mr. Dodgson never expected his poetry to be put to such a use as this."

"You recognise this, Holmes?" I asked in amazement.

"You may find it amusing, if not enlightening as well, Watson, to read a pair of remarkable volumes by one Charles Lutwidge Dodgson, though you will find them published under the pen-name of Lewis Carroll. They are entitled *Alice's Adventures in Wonderland* and *Through the Looking-Glass and What Alice Found There*. This verse draws upon two poems from the latter book, one dealing with the battle of the Lion and the Unicorn, and the other having the curious title of 'Jabberwocky.' There is clearly a message for us here. The 'metal Jabberwock' is of course the Analytical Engine. In Dodgson's poem, the Jabberwock is a fearsome creature which is destroyed by the vorpal sword. The term 'brillig' refers indeed to four o'clock. The 'day of blood,' however—let me see——" Holmes thought for a moment. "To-morrow, of course. Tuesday is named for the Teutonic god of war Tyr or Tiw—hence the association with blood. So to-morrow at four o'clock an attempt shall be made against the Engine."

"But—that is when my demonstration is to be held!" the Professor cried.

"To make a public attempt against the Engine can only mean that the author of this note has some strong motive, and that he or she intends to be present to-morrow," Holmes declared. "The rest of the poem should provide clues to that person's identity. The person obviously feels that the Analytical Engine was the cause of ruin to someone's life. That would be the person symbolized by the Unicorn. The Lion, if you will forgive my saying so, is clearly yourself, Professor Queensley. Moreover, I deduce from the reference to the bread that you and the person called Unicorn were involved in a contest or struggle at some time, which you won."

"How can you tell that?" I asked.

"In the original poem, the Lion and the Unicorn are fighting for the crown," my friend explained. "The next verse tells us that 'the Lion beat the Unicorn all around the town.' The Lion in our note is eating white bread, a symbol of luxury, while the Unicorn's brown bread, coarser and cheaper, symbolises poverty.

"The ruddy sceptre," he went on thoughtfully, tapping the note against the arm of his chair. "That can be a reference to either the Red Queen or the Red King. They are chess-pieces which have come to life in *Through the Looking-Glass,* Watson. The sender of this note has, for some reason, chosen to be identified with one of these characters. Tell me, Professor, have you been playing chess with anyone else by means of the Analytical Engine?"

"Indeed, yes," replied Queensley. "There have been four of you altogether, Mr. Holmes — yourself; my friend and fellow mathematician Basil Mountjoy at Oxford; another colleague of mine, *Professore* Vittorio Rosso of the *Faculta di Scienza e Matematica* in Rome; and Herr Johann Koenig, the European chess master." He chuckled quietly. "It may interest you to know, Mr. Holmes, that I, or rather the Engine, checkmated Herr Koenig two days ago. All of them will be at the demonstration tomorrow. Surely you don't believe that one of them sent this note?" he asked anxiously.

"Professor, I have found that in these situations it is best to rely solely on what the facts reveal," Holmes said. "Will there be anyone else at your demonstration besides ourselves—I take the liberty of including my friend Watson—and the gentlemen you have named?"

"Oh, my technician, Killington, of course," said the Professor. "His daughter may be there as well. That will be all."

Holmes was making notes in his notebook. "Now, Mountjoy is at Oxford, you say?"

"At the moment, no. He is here in London, at the Dorchester. I shall be meeting him after this and we will go on to Cambridge together. Herr Koenig and Professor Rosso are already there."

"Have you spoken to the police?" Holmes asked.

"Yes, I went to the Cambridge constabulary as soon as the note arrived. The inspector there simply shrugged it off."

"Then I shall do my best to enlist the aid of Scotland Yard on your behalf," said Holmes, writing out a note. "Take them this note and the message, and ask for Inspector Tobias Gregson. He and I have worked together before, and he has proved most helpful on occasion. Oh, yes— you mentioned earlier that there were two other people who know about the chess programme. I presume that your technician Killington is one. Who is the other?"

"My wife," answered Queensley, appearing quite vexed. "It was over the chess programme that she left me, in fact. She called it the final straw."

"Do you think her disdain for the Engine could be great enough to prompt this?" my friend asked.

"Do you mean, did Mrs. Queensley send this? Oh, no, Mr. Holmes," Queensley objected. "It's not her way. She would never resort to such an underhanded tactic as a cryptic note. My wife may be forceful and even violent, but she can hardly be called devious."

"I see," said Holmes, taking up his hat. "Then may I suggest, Professor, that you pay a visit to Scotland Yard while Dr. Watson and I call upon Basil Mountjoy."

We took a cab to the Dorchester Hotel and had a message delivered to Mountjoy's room, asking to see him. The porter returned a short time later. "Mr. Mountjoy is preparing to leave, sir," he reported. "He can only spare you a few minutes. He is in Room 23."

Holmes and I made our way to Mountjoy's room where we found him packing a portmanteau. Basil Mountjoy was a man in his middle years, and of average build and appearance, save that he walked with a limp and carried a cherry-wood cane. "You asked to see me, Mr. Holmes?" he began, limping to a chair. "I fear I can spare you but a few minutes. I am due to catch a train."

"To Cambridge, in fact, sir," Holmes said. "You are on your way to witness Professor Alfred Queensley's demonstration with the Analytical Engine to-morrow at Trinity College."

"Why, yes, that is so, Mr. Holmes," Mountjoy affirmed in surprise.

"You have known Queensley for some time, I take it?"

"Yes, indeed. Queensley, his technician Killington, and I were all at Oxford together. My word, to-morrow will be the first time in years that I have seen Killington. But how does the demonstration concern you, sir? Have you been invited as well?"

"I have, but my interest is somewhat more than that of an ordinary spectator. You see, a threat has been made against the Analytical Engine and Professor Queensley has asked me to investigate."

"Good heavens! A threat? Of what sort? And by whom?"

"Those are precisely the questions I wish to answer," replied Holmes. "Do you know of anyone who might have reason for wishing to destroy the Engine?"

"Apart from Queensley's wife?" Mountjoy smiled a little. "No, Mr. Holmes, I cannot imagine—but, wait," he checked himself suddenly. "I don't know. It was all so long ago."

"What is it, sir?" Holmes asked with some impatience. "Your information could preserve innocent lives and prevent the destruction of a valuable machine."

"Oh, dear me," the mathematician said anxiously. "In that case—— you see, Mr. Holmes, Queensley and Killington were originally rivals for the position now held by Queensley. Killington is an ambitious man. I cannot imagine him taking kindly to being Queensley's assistant."

"That is certainly something to bear in mind. May I ask how you fared in your chess match against Queensley?"

"I lost, Mr. Holmes," said Mountjoy, looking puzzled. "Quite an odd game, if I may so. The man was definitely not playing in his usual manner. Normally I can defeat him often enough, but this time his moves were quite difficult to play against."

"Did you think so?" asked Holmes. "I thought my mate came rather easily."

"A mate? I am impressed, sir. You must be a formidable opponent on the chess-board. I should like to engage you in a match sometime."

"Certainly, if you like." Holmes rose. "We must be leaving now, sir, but I do thank you for your time."

"You said you had a second question, Mr. Holmes, or had you forgotten?" Mountjoy reminded him.

"Oh, yes. Tell me, Professor, are you acquainted with the works of Lewis Carroll?"

Mountjoy thought for a moment. "No, I can't say that I am—though, wait, I do recall my former colleague remarking once that they were amusing. But I don't read much outside my own field these days. Well, I'm off. Good day, sir; good day, Doctor."

As we stepped out the hotel door, we discovered Queensley alighting from a hansom, followed by Inspector Lestrade. "Lestrade!" groaned Holmes to me. "I told the Professor to ask for Gregson."

"Perhaps Gregson is on another case and unavailable," I suggested.

The four of us came together on the hotel steps and Holmes and I exchanged civilities with Lestrade.

"Gregson is looking into an embezzlement case, Mr. Holmes, so I have offered my services to the Professor," Lestrade informed us, a trifle smugly, I thought.

"Ah," Holmes allowed. "May I have a word with you before you leave for Cambridge, Professor?" my friend said, turning to Queensley.

"Of course, Mr. Holmes."

"I LOST, MR. HOLMES."

"Professor Mountjoy mentioned an old rivalry between you and your assistant, David Killington. What was the nature of your rivalry?"

"Mountjoy is exaggerating if he calls it a rivalry," Queensley said with a frown. "It's simply that Killington and I both applied for my position to research the Analytical Engine when it was begun. I was chosen, as you know, but I felt that Killington's vast experience ought not to be wasted in some career for which he was unsuited. I convinced him to work as my assistant. His knowledge has been invaluable. Our work together has always been cordial. And, I might add, our relationship extends beyond the laboratory since his late wife was a cousin of my wife. We did what we could to help him raise their only child—a daughter, Lareina."

"Lareina," I remarked. "A curious name. Is it Spanish?"

"Why, yes. Luisa was very proud of her Castilian ancestry. She claimed kinship with the Spanish Royal Family," Queensley explained.

Holmes nodded. "Watson and I will follow you to Cambridge this evening, Professor. Do you think it possible for us to find rooms in the hotel where Herr Koenig and Professor Rosso are staying?"

"Oh, yes, certainly. They are at the Garden House. I will see to it personally," said Queensley as he shook hands with us. "Thank you, gentlemen. I sincerely hope you can save the Engine from harm. It represents my life's work."

"We will see to that, Mr. Queensley," Inspector Lestrade assured him. "Good day, gentlemen."

Late that day Holmes and I boarded the last train from King's Cross to Cambridge. "I begin to wonder, Watson, if I have not made an error in allowing Lestrade and the Professor to precede us to Cambridge. I cannot help but feel that he is on a scent already—a false one, of course, if our fine Inspector carries on with his usual disregard for facts. I swear that when he left he looked like a garden toad about to swallow a fly."

"Oh, come now, Holmes," I remonstrated as the train pulled out of the station, "surely even Lestrade would not go off rashly to make an arrest without some sort of grounds for it."

"Perhaps not without *some* sort of grounds. But I fear he may ignore some important possibilities. Original thinking is not our friend Lestrade's strong suit. Remember that the reference in that threatening piece of doggerel to the 'ruddy sceptre' could apply to the Red King or the Red Queen. I am more inclined to believe it to mean the Queen."

"You suspect a woman? Why is that?" I asked.

"Because His Red Majesty does little in the story but sleep under a tree."

"A Red Queen," I mused. Suddenly a thought struck me. "My word, Holmes, you don't suppose it is an allusion to the name Ruby Queensley, do you? And considering the woman's attitude toward machines——"

"Indeed, Watson, the coincidence, if it is one, has occurred to me. There seem, in fact, to be a number of such curious coincidences of names in this affair. Herr Koenig, for example, would in English become Mr. King; Professor Rosso's surname is the Italian word for red; and Professor Mountjoy's Christian name, Basil, derives from the Greek word for king, *basileus*."

"I BEGIN TO WONDER, WATSON."

"Why, true enough, Holmes!" I exclaimed. "Then any one of them could have sent the message."

"Or none," my friend pointed out. "It could be a reference to Queensley himself, though I think not, for the man's distress over the Analytical Engine seems genuine enough. The ruddy sceptre could also have some symbolic meaning which I have not yet uncovered. For instance, Watson, did you notice Mountjoy's red cherry-wood cane? No, I need more data before I settle on any conclusion. I should also like to enlist your services, my good fellow, once we arrive in Cambridge."

"What would you have me do?" I asked, eager for a chance to assist him.

"If you would be so good, I should like you to speak with both Herr Koenig and Professor Rosso. Try to determine if either of them has any motive for wishing to destroy the Engine."

"Of course, Holmes," I promised. "I should mention the books by Carroll, should I not?"

"By all means, but I have little hope there, since neither gentleman is British," Holmes said. "Still, one of them may have encountered a translation, or perhaps even read the original. In the meantime, I shall pay a visit to David Killington and have a look at the Analytical Engine. Our suspect may have already found an opportunity to tamper with it; Killington must make frequent use of it, and Koenig and Rosso have been in Cambridge long enough to have had access to it." Holmes removed a book from his Gladstone, leaned back in his seat and took out his pipe and tobacco pouch. Glancing at the title, I noticed that it was a copy of *Through the Looking-Glass*.

"A little light reading, Holmes?" I chaffed him mildly.

"I intend to refresh my memory of the work in the hope of chancing upon some clue I have overlooked," he returned, settling back into his seat. "We have a true 'Red Queen's Race' to run, Watson. We must run twice as fast as we possibly can if we are to win it."

"What the devil is that supposed to mean?" I asked.

"It is from the book again," Holmes explained. "The heroine, Alice, encounters the Red Queen in the Looking-Glass Garden. As they are talking, it becomes the Queen's turn to move; she seizes Alice by the hand, and they begin to run as fast as they can. When they stop, Alice observes that they are still where they were when they began to run. The Red Queen explains that this is part of the Looking-Glass Land order of things: to stay in one place, one has to run as fast as one can, and to make any progress at all, one must run even faster."

11.1   Artificial Intelligence

There is considerable public confusion when it comes to the subject of computers and intelligence. This confusion persists even among programmers and others who use computers every day. Will computers soon be able to communicate in English? Will computerized robots take over industrial jobs? Will machines be able to be programmed to think? Will computers be able to write music?

The confusion about the outer limits of computer behavior is confounded by beliefs of the opposite nature. For instance, many people consider a computer nothing more than a fancy calculator, a dull machine that can only obey its instructions exactly. Literally, this belief is true. But it is not often helpful. Certainly the instruction set for computers is limited. Nevertheless, the instructions are capable of producing great varieties of behavior. But what really undermines this belief is the computer's speed of execution and its memory capacity. Traveling at the rate of a pedestrian is one thing, but increasing the speed to that of an automobile or an airplane changes the picture markedly.

The general question of what machines can and cannot do will be discussed in the following chapter. Here we consider the area of computers generally known as *artificial intelligence:* that is, the technology needed to make computers perform tasks that, by human standards, require intelligence.

Consider the apparently simple problem of recognizing handwritten digits. A typewritten digit is one thing, but humans write digits in all sorts of ways. *You* may readily recognize that both

and

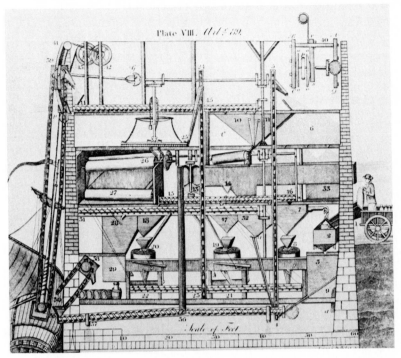

Oliver Evan's Proposed Automatic Cornmill, drawn in 1791

are simply two different ways to write the digit 5. Getting a computer to recognize this is another matter. If you look at a program to do this, you will be amazed at its complexity. Moreover, if someone explains the program to you, you will probably see ways to improve the solution or find cases that the program doesn't handle. This is characteristic of all topics within artificial intelligence. There is no "fixed" or "perfect" solution.

The topics treated under artificial intelligence are varied. They include computer understanding of natural language, speech recognition, perception of visual objects, and computerized robots. Such applications often require specialized hardware to translate factors like speech signals or spatial information into a form that can be processed by computer. In the recognition of handwritten characters, for instance, a grid can be superimposed over a character. When an optical scanner reads the character, it will encode the character as a series of zeros and ones. For example, our two 5's can be encoded as illustrated in **Figure 11.1**. You may notice that this encoding is hardly perfect. The grid of zeros and ones is not an exact replication of the handwritten 5. From the computer's point of view, however, we're directly into binary, and the computer can take over.

11.2   An "Intelligent" Program

We draw upon an early and classic work in artificial intelligence, the checker-playing program developed by Arthur Samuel [see Feigenbaum and Feldman, 1963]. This program was remarkable for the number of important issues it raised: the attempt to exhibit intelligent behavior, the representation of real-world knowledge, learning, and the tricks needed to overcome the eventual limits of a computer's finite resources. Although the methods and technology used might seem primitive by today's standards, the insight and simplicity of Samuel's work are highly illustrative.

The Game of Checkers

The American game of checkers (or "draughts," as it is known in Britain) is played on a standard 8-by-8 chessboard, as illustrated in Figure 11.2. There are two players, one with black pieces and the other with white pieces. The object of the game is to capture all of the opponent's pieces.

Play begins with the setup shown in Figure 11.2. Each player can move a piece one square forward along a diagonal or can capture an opponent's piece by "jumping" over it along a diagonal. Whenever a capture is possible, it must be made. If a player's piece reaches the opponent's back row, the piece becomes a "king." A king can move both forward and backward along a diagonal. The game ends when one player (the winner) captures all of the opponent's pieces.

Programming a computer to play against an opponent is of interest for several reasons.

■ *There is no ultimate algorithm for perfect play.* Suppose the computer could explore every possible combination of moves. Samuels estimated that there are 10^{40} (i.e. 10 multiplied by 10, 40 times) combinations. Even assuming the computer could evaluate three billion combinations a second, it would take 1,021 centuries to evaluate each combination and then choose the "perfect" move.

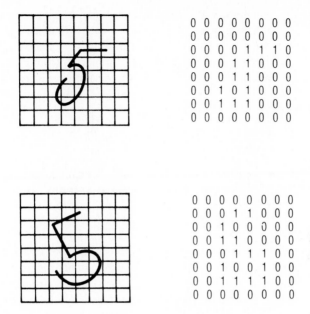

```
0 0 0 0 0 0 0 0
0 0 0 0 0 0 0 0
0 0 0 0 1 1 1 0
0 0 0 1 1 0 0 0
0 0 0 1 1 0 0 0
0 0 1 0 1 0 0 0
0 0 1 1 1 0 0 0
0 0 0 0 0 0 0 0
```

```
0 0 0 0 0 0 0 0
0 0 0 1 1 0 0 0
0 0 1 0 0 0 0 0
0 0 1 1 0 0 0 0
0 0 0 1 1 1 0 0
0 0 1 0 0 1 0 0
0 0 1 1 1 1 0 0
0 0 0 0 0 0 0 0
```

Figure 11.1 *Two Fives*

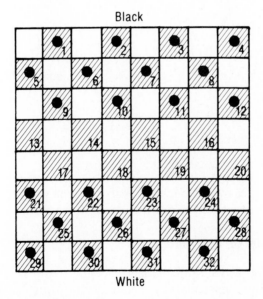

Figure 11.2 *Standard Checkerboard*

■   *The problem is well defined.* In most areas of artificial intelligence, the problem itself is so complicated that rules for determining correct performance are tenuous. In voice recognition, for instance, even humans do not understand every utterance. This makes such problems vastly more difficult for the computer.

■   *There is a reasonable way to measure success.* The game of checkers is familiar, and the performance of the program can be tested against players of various levels of skill.

■   *It raises some general issues.* The inherent difficulties in writing such a program bring up problems that are common to many areas on the edge of computer technology.

As a side note, playing such a game with a computer can be fun.

There are some more mundane parts of any checkers program: the program must ensure that the game is played according to the rules. This means the program must accept moves from its opponent and check their legality. Normally, moves are entered by giving the square numbers of a moving piece. For instance, at the start of a game where the opponent is black and the computer is white, we might have

```
Computer:    LET'S START, YOU GET THE FIRST MOVE
Opponent:    11 15
Computer:    23 19
Opponent:     8 11
Computer:    22 17
```

If the opponent enters an illegal move, for instance

```
11 12
```

or even

```
2  31
```

the computer must ask for a new entry. Programming the computer to do this is not as easy as it might appear, but well within the skill of an average programmer and is not our concern here.

Representation of Knowledge

One of the most difficult aspects of any problem in artificial intelligence is finding a suitable method for capturing knowledge about the actual world and encoding this knowledge in a form that can be processed by a computer. In computer recognition of natural language, this means finding some way of capturing the form and meaning of sentences. In computer recognition of images, this means finding some digital representation of the image and some way of representing its properties, for example, having a pattern of lines represent the roof of a house or a driveway. Resolving such issues can be extraordinarily difficult.

In checkers, the most obvious concern is the representation of the checkerboard. In Samuel's program a board configuration was represented by 32-bit positions in a word, as illustrated in Figure 11.3. A 1 in a given position represents a piece, a 0 represents its absence. With two players and the possibility of kings, four such words were actually required. A new board configuration resulting from a move can be represented by updating the pattern of bits. The squares to which a player can move can also be represented by a sequence of 32 bits, as shown in Figure 11.3.

By current standards, this method of representing the board is quite primitive. The board representation is central to the operation of the program, which must frequently calculate a new board position and derive properties from it. Modern programming techniques and languages allow a much richer set of possibilities from which clearer or more clever representations can be derived. For our purpose, the important point is that it is possible.

A more subtle and problematic issue is representing knowledge about the properties of a given board position. Intuitively, we know that certain board positions are superior to others. One player may be further advanced than another or may have better control of the center of the board. One player may have pieces in a better attacking position or may have a better defense against the opponent's pieces. It is not at all obvious how to represent such knowledge.

Samuel adopted a simple, uniform method for dealing with this problem. It goes like this. For any board position a fixed number of "parameters" is identified. The most obvious and important of these is the numerical piece advantage (or disadvantage). For instance, a player with eight pieces is usually in a far superior position to an opponent with six pieces. In such a case we say that the player has a piece advantage of +2 (or that the opponent has a negative piece advantage of -2). As for kings, the calculation of this parameter assumes that three pieces are equivalent to two kings.

Example configuration of black pieces

Black

White

Reproduction of configuration.

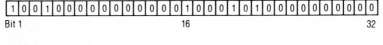

Bit 1   16   32

Potentially occupied squares.

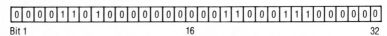

Bit 1   16   32

Figure 11.3   *Representation of Checkerboard*

Samuel had a rather large number of other parameters, for example:

Advancement: 1 point is given for each piece in the fifth and sixth rows (counting in the player's direction), and -1 for each piece in the third and fourth rows.

Mobility: 1 point is given for each square to which the player can move (ignoring possible jump moves).

Back Row Bridge: A score of 1 is given if there are no opposing kings and if the two bridge squares (1 and 3 for black, 30 and 32 for red) are occupied.

Exchange: 1 point is credited for each square to which a piece can be moved and force an exchange.

King Center Control: 1 point is given for any king occupying squares 11, 12, 15, 16, 20, 21, 24, and 25.

The choice of parameters, as well as their precise definition, is a matter of judgment. Note, however, that each parameter gives a *numeric* assessment of some property of a board position.

Having decided on the actual parameters, a total assessment of a board position is obtained by adding up the individual parameters. In this calculation each parameter is multiplied by a weighting factor or coefficient. The weighting factors give the relative importance of each parameter. In this way a total score

$$\text{Score} = W_1 P_1 + W_2 P_2 + \ldots + W_n P_n$$

where each W_i is a weight and P_i a parameter, is obtained. The total score gives an evaluation of the board position in terms of a single number.

Any scheme for reducing the intuitive properties of a situation to a number, or more generally to any rigid form required for a computer, is bound to be questioned. In checkers, several questions arise immediately. How many parameters are needed to characterize a board position? Should not the parameters vary as the game progresses? How can one ever be sure that the parameterized properties really do characterize the progress of the game? Nevertheless, the key point is that it *is* possible to characterize knowledge in some concrete way.

Basic Strategy

The basic strategy used in Samuel's program is much like that of a human player. The computer looks ahead a number of moves, evaluates the possible board situations and selects an appropriate move. The advantage of the computer (and certainly with modern, high-speed computers) is that it can look ahead a large number of moves.

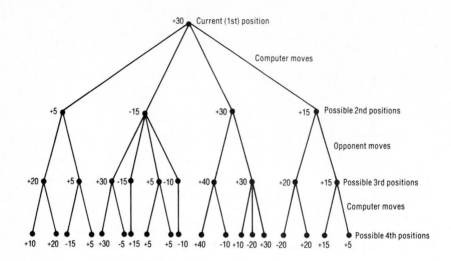

Figure 11.4   *Look-ahead for Possible Moves*

The idea of "looking ahead" also needs to be captured in a form suitable to a computer. Consider Figure 11.4. Here we assume a look-ahead of three moves, one by the program, a second by the opponent, and a third by the program. For each move ahead, the relevant player has one or more choices, as illustrated by the branching lines in Figure 11.4. At the end of each sequence of three moves, a given board position will result. Each such position can be evaluated according to the scheme outlined above, that is, by assigning a score to each position. These are shown at the leaves of the branches in Figure 11.4. Notice here that some positions have negative scores. These indicate positions that are considered disadvantageous to the computer.

Given a choice, the program will, of course, make the move that gives the best advantage. Consider, for instance, the leftmost pair of leaves where the scores are +10 and +20. The computer will choose the move corresponding to +20. This value is recorded on the node above the pair of leaves. We can do the same for the other leaves, recording the score of the best choice. The net effect is to produce a set of scores that would be obtained after two moves.

Now we have to invert the process. The second move is taken by the opponent, who presumably will select the move that is *least* advantageous to the computer. For instance, given a choice between

+20 and +5, the opponent should make the move leading to +5. Thus, all the nodes two levels above the leaves are labeled with minimum alternative scores.

This "mini-max" procedure is repeated until the top of the tree is reached. With a look-ahead of only three moves, only one more level need be evaluated. The highest recorded score (in our case, +30) dictates the computer's move.

The amount of look-ahead actually used is limited by the computer's speed and amount of available memory. Too large a look-ahead results in unacceptably slow play or exhaustion of memory. In Samuel's case, various schemes were tried in order to direct the look-ahead so that only promising alternatives were explored. In any event, memory limitations forced a maximum look-ahead of 40 moves.

The encounter with the limits of machine capabilities is characteristic of almost all applications in artificial intelligence. For instance, to achieve computer understanding of natural language input, the components of a dialogue must be processed and understood in a time period that is acceptable for normal human discourse. To use a mechanical hand in an assembly line, a great deal of sensor data must be assimilated quite rapidly. Such natural constraints pose a severe limit to any theoretical solution to a problem.

11.3   Machine Learning and Other Directions

Samuel's primary interest in his checkers-playing program was in the area of machine learning. The general topic of machine learning is especially difficult, and progress in this area has been accordingly limited. Human beings learn so many different things in so many different ways that a machine-oriented approach to learning seems barely feasible. Nevertheless, it is possible to restrict the general topic to a much narrower one—the learning of a specific task. This is just what Samuel did with the game of checkers.

Rote Learning

Probably the most elementary type of learning is *rote learning*. This kind of learning takes place when we gather data from experience and call upon the data when needed. When we are taught, for instance, that 3 times 4 is 12, we may initially count our way by 4's to 12, but once learned, the fact is stored in our memory for later recall.

In checkers, consider the following scenario. Suppose the program operates with a fixed look-ahead, say six moves. For a given board position, the program will perform its look-ahead, determine the resulting score, and select the corresponding move. This board position along with its score can be recorded for later use. Now suppose that in an ensuing game the six-move look-ahead leads to the position recorded earlier. Rather than evaluate this position again, we can obtain its score from the previous game. But wait! This score was itself obtained using a six-move look-ahead, so that the initial position has, in effect, a path with a look-ahead of 12. This situation with its look-ahead of 12 can be used for an effective look-ahead of 18. And on and on.

Tricky, no doubt, but does it work? In part, yes. Here again we face the limits of the machine. To be effective, rather than hope for the odd chance that a given board position will repeat itself, many board positions (with their scores) must be saved. The more that are saved, the longer is the time needed by the computer to test for a match. If every playing position were saved, it would not be long before the search for a match would take more computer time than a direct look-ahead itself.

Samuel studied the problem in some detail and developed a number of strategies to improve this approach to rote learning. One of these was to catalogue the various board positions into, for instance, those with and without kings, or into those where one side has a piece advantage. Other strategies included discarding positions believed to be of limited value, deleting symmetrical board positions, and breaking up the game into strategic parts.

All of this leads to two points. First, it is possible to build some form of learning, albeit limited, into a program. Second, many kinds of strategies and tricks may be needed to make even a simple idea effective.

Parameter Learning

Samuel explored another, intellectually more interesting form of learning called *parameter learning.* This is similar to that used when learning to drive a car. Initially we learn the basic mechanical movements needed to start, steer, and stop a car. These movements form a base of knowledge that can be tuned to a given situation. When we approach a curve, for instance, we adjust the steering wheel to follow a changing direction. The angle of the steering wheel is, if you will, a parameter of a learned skill.

Parameter learning invokes the popular belief about computers that there are certain key memory locations whose values can be adjusted to change the computer's behavior. Although this is not the case in general, it is precisely what can be done with Samuel's program.

Recall that the evaluation of a board position gives a score which is computed by adding the values of the various parameters. In the calculation, each parameter value is multiplied by a weighting factor. It is these weighting factors that can be adjusted by the program. To do this, histories of games need to be recorded and the actual outcomes from various board positions compared with the scores calculated. When the program's calculations do not match fit the actual outcome, the weighting factors can be altered to fit this outcome better.

More advanced and more powerful forms of machine learning, such as the learning of methods and, most importantly, the learning of concepts, do exist. Such topics are far beyond our intent here.

It is not much of a step to program a computer to play against itself. If you wish, you can think of duplicating the Samuel's program and putting both versions into the computer. One version plays black and the other white. This need not be an empty exercise. Samuel used this method to improve the learning of the program and, in general, to observe the behavior of the computer.

How well did Samuel's program play? In fact, very well. It could certainly beat its author. That should not be surprising; we build machines that can lift heavier objects than humans and planes that can fly. In fact, the program's play was at the expert level.

Samuel's checker-playing program was certainly a remarkable early achievement. Written in the 1950's, it helped create great expectations for computer technology. During the following decade, interest spread to many areas: computers that could understand English, computers that could perceive images, robotic devices that could perform mechanical tasks, and computers that could prove theorems and solve problems.

Natural Language

Perhaps the issue of greatest public interest is that of natural language. The languages used for programming a computer should not be confused with English and other natural languages. Programming languages are highly contrived, with rigid rules of grammar and very limited meaning. A great deal of work was been spent on computer understanding of natural language, and with some success. Much of this work has centered on the problem of capturing the meaning. In

```
John ate the apple.
```

the meaning is fairly clear. But in

```
He saw the pretty little girls' camp.
```

the meaning is not. Who is he? Is it a pretty-little girls' camp? Or a pretty little-girls' camp? Or even a pretty-little-girls' camp? The meaning in such cases is dependent on the global context in which the sentence is given.

Most of the progress in understanding natural language has come with systems whose vocabulary is restricted in some way. This gives the system builder a much better chance to make assumptions that follow those of the user. The first step in understanding meaning is a grammatical parse of a sentence: the identification of nouns, verbs, objects, and phrases. The meaning of each component is then attempted. When a sensible meaning cannot be described, further analysis is required, as well as some logical deduction and appeal to context. This process is repeated until some reasonable understanding is achieved.

The crucial issue in all this is the representation of knowledge. Recall that in Samuel's checkers program the board was represented by a pattern of bits, whereas the property of effectiveness of a board position was expressed as a sum of terms. In general, such "passive" representations are not nearly sufficient to depict the knowledge embodied in an English sentence. A better method is the representation of meaning in the form of an algorithm. For instance, if you were asked to define the meaning of "multiplication" of two numbers, you might just give the algorithm needed to do it.

Robotics

Another aspect of computers that has captured public interest is that of robotics. Whether it be a fear that computerized robots will eventually take over the world, a natural curiosity about mechanical "creatures," or a general interest in the technology of the space age, the subject is often a lively one. Unfortunately, the enormous complexities of this field are little understood, and the public perception of what is possible is often far from what has actually been achieved.

Robotic Systems

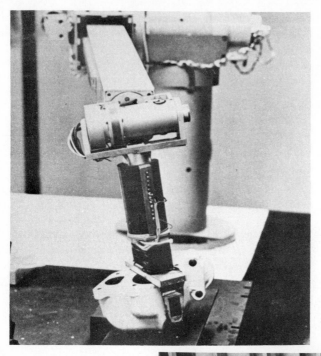

Robotic Systems

A robotic device generally contains three basic components:

1.   One or more *sensor* devices. These devices, for example a television camera or touch-sensitive equipment, can receive data about the surrounding environment.

2.   A *computer*. The computer must analyze the sensor data as well as perform the normal computing functions.

3.   One or more *motor* devices. These devices carry out the mechanical actions of the robots.

From a technical viewpoint, the most difficult aspect of designing a robotic device is developing acceptable sensor devices. Human beings take for granted the interplay of sight, sound, balance, and touch needed to perform simple mechanical tasks. Picking up a ball, turning a corner, or avoiding an object involve many intricate physical functions. Computerizing them is not easy.

Most computerized robots in actual use perform a somewhat limited set of tasks. Although limited, the performance of even simple mechanical chores is one of the extraordinary achievements of computer technology.

CHAPTER XII

‡

The Adventure of the Red Queen's Race

(PART II)

OLMES and I arrived in Cambridge late after spending a comfortable night in rooms at The Garden House Hotel, which had become almost as familiar as 221B Baker Street. On the following morning, having reduced to bare bones some fresh Yarmouth herring, I set off to execute my mission of sounding out Professor Rosso and Herr Koenig.

I found the two gentlemen in the smoking room engaged in earnest conversation. The Professor appeared to be trying to calm the German chess master, who was visibly upset. I introduced myself and explained that I, with Holmes, looked forward to attending Professor Queensley's demonstration later in the day. At mention of the demonstration, Herr Koenig rose.

"Excuse me, please, Herr Doctor, Herr Professor. I am in need of fresh air and will explore this beautiful town for an hour. *Auf wiedersehen,*" and he moved swiftly to the lobby.

I occupied the chair he had just vacated and remarked to my companion, "Herr Koenig seems troubled. May I ask the nature of the problem?"

"It will be a relief to tell you," Professor Rosso replied. "Herr Koenig was unaware of the nature of Professor Queensley's demonstration. He has been under the impression that he was being invited to attend a match of *gli scacchi*—chess. When I explained to him about the Analytical Engine he—what is it you say—jumped to a strange conclusion. He thinks that the game he just lost to Professor Queensley was a deception; that he was playing against a machine. I could not convince him that this was impossible."

"How unfortunate," I murmured, unable to bring myself to break the truth to the Italian mathematician. "Had Herr Koenig never heard of the Analytical Engine, then?"

"No. He lives for *gli scacchi*."

"No doubt, as a mathematician, you are eager to see this demonstration."

"Yes, indeed, Doctor Watson, particularly because I have been working on a programme of computations much like Professor Queensley's. He won the race, thanks to the Analytical Engine, and published his work before me, but it was almost a stalemate, shall we say!"

My ears pricked up at the words *race* and *stalemate,* but I am not a physician for nothing and masked my interest. I rose to take leave of the Professor, saying "It is my turn, I think, for some fresh air. I look forward to seeing you this afternoon, Professor. By the way, are you familiar with the works of your English colleague Charles Lutwidge Dodgson— or Lewis Carroll, as he is better known?"

"EXCUSE ME, HERR DOCTOR."

"Why yes. I read his books, in translation, to my children. Why do you ask?"

"Oh, my mind just made a connection between mathematics, chess, and a race. No special reason, really," I replied airily, said "Good morning," and left him looking slightly baffled.

I enjoyed a pleasant stroll along the Backs then returned to our rooms, eager to share my suspicions. When I arrived, Holmes's face wore a decidedly nettled look.

"Confound Lestrade," he sputtered. "What a simpleton the man can be sometimes, Watson."

"What folly has he committed now?" I asked, startled by his mood.

"The idiot has arrested David Killington," Holmes fumed. "I went over to Trinity College while you went about your business, expecting to find Killington with the Engine, checking that everything was in readiness for this afternoon. Lestrade and Queensley joined me *en route*. We arrived to find Killington standing by the Engine holding a small flask between his hands. A homemade bomb."

"A bomb!" I exclaimed. "It *was* Killington, then, who made the threat!"

"No, Watson! On the contrary, Killington is absolved completely. You see, he was not planting the bomb in the Engine, but rather removing it."

"How in the name of heaven do you know that?" I demanded.

"Watson, a man who intends to plant a bomb does not stand staring at it in horror while disregarding the presence of others. But the main reason I am convinced of Killington's innocence is that this bomb was intended as a ruse—a mere red herring. It was not intended to destroy the Analytical Engine at all."

Holmes withdrew something from his pocket and set it down upon the table. "As you can see, it is far too small to destroy the Engine, although it would cause some minor damage. The chemistry flask is filled with——" He pried out the cork and removed the twist of rag which served for a fuse. "Yes, I was quite right. This is ordinary gunpowder. Not the most sophisticated device, but effective enough to blow some minor parts to smithereens."

"This, a red herring?" I stared at the bomb in amazement. "This affair grows more mysterious by the hour, Holmes! Why the devil would someone go to the trouble of planting an inadequate bomb in the Engine merely to serve as a ruse?"

"Perhaps to allay our suspicions, Watson," replied Holmes, "by causing us to think that the bomb had been found, so that we would be off guard at the demonstration. Yes, this decoy is most puzzling, Watson. So was Killington's behavior just now."

"In what way?"

"When Lestrade put him under arrest, he was about to protest, then looked at the bomb again, shuddered, and said nothing. Something frightened him, Watson. Lestrade attempted to question him, but Killington only said dejectedly that since he had found his suspect, he should take him off to gaol and be done with it. Queensley promised to go to his daughter and tell her what had happened, and Killington begged him, 'For heaven's sake, say nothing about the bomb!'"

"Killington's behavior is certainly most peculiar for an innocent man," I agreed. "Let me tell you about my interview with Professor Rosso. At least he has cleared Herr Koenig from suspicion for he told me that the German had never heard of the Analytical Engine before today. But the Professor himself could be the culprit." I told Holmes about the references to a race and a stalemate and Rosso's familiarity with the works of Lewis Carroll.

"I think he may be our man," I concluded, "though I can't see what he could possibly gain from destroying the Engine. Maybe his pique at Queensley's publishing first has turned his head."

Holmes's eyebrows arched upward and a smile played upon his lips as he spoke. "Dear me, Watson, in future, I must remember to keep your contact with Inspector Lestrade to a minimum. The man is having a bad influence upon you."

"Whatever do you mean by that?" I demanded with some irritation at my friend's casual dismissal of my theory.

"I meant no offence, Watson. It is merely that in this instance you have fallen into the same error to which poor Lestrade is so susceptible, namely, fixing on a faulty conclusion because you have not thoroughly examined all the data. You overlooked one highly significant factor in your reasoning just now by neglecting to consider whether the *signor professore* has had opportunity to carry out the threat. Killington and Queensley use the Analytical Engine daily. They would surely have discovered the decoy bomb had it been planted before this morning. Ah, here we are," he added as a knock sounded at our door. "You will soon learn, if my reasoning is correct, why Rosso is not the man we seek."

Holmes rose and opened the door. A waiter held out a sealed envelope. "Excuse me, Mr. Holmes, but this message just arrived for you while I was at the desk. The clerk asked me to bring it to you at once. It seems quite urgent, sir."

Holmes opened the note. "It is from Queensley, Watson," he stated. "He wants us to see Miss Killington as soon as possible in regard to her father; she is apparently quite upset. Shall we go?"

Despite my mild protest, we were soon on our way to Killington's home, a stone cottage perhaps a mile from the University. On arriving we were shown into a sitting room. Queensley rose to greet us. "Lareina has gone to freshen herself and change," he told us. "When I told her about her father, she was dreadfully upset. So much so that she knocked over her ink bottle. The poor girl has always been rather nervous, and this news about Killington has disturbed her deeply."

Holmes said nothing, for he had immediately begun to examine the room's furnishings. I directed my attention to him as he was gazing at several pictures on the wall, and at a number of sketches which lay spread upon a desk by the window. A large black stain on the blotter testified to Miss Killington's recent mishap.

Holmes was examining the contents of the bookcase when a young woman with striking reddish hair entered the room. She was followed by an older woman whose night-black hair and sharp features reminded me of a raven. The young lady turned her eyes upon us and implored, "Oh, Mr. Holmes, Dr. Watson, please help my father! He is innocent—I know he is!"

She sank down upon the sofa and pressed an embroidered handkerchief to her eyes. "There, there, Lareina dear," the dark-haired woman comforted her. "Everything will be fine." She turned on Queensley with a glare, and he involuntarily stepped back from her. "No thanks to *you,* Alfred," she snapped.

Holmes had taken in the whole scene, and he directed a measured look at the dark-haired woman. "I take it, madam, that we have the honor of meeting Mrs. Ruby Queensley." He bowed curtly. "I am Sherlock Holmes, and this is my associate, Dr. Watson. The professor asked us to come so that we might reassure Miss Killington that we are working to vindicate her father."

"And how do you propose to do that, sir?" Mrs. Queensley demanded.

"By an investigation of the facts, Madam," Holmes retorted as he took a seat in the basket chair by the mantel. More gently to Miss Killington he said, "I shall begin by telling you, Miss Killington, that I am convinced of your father's innocence. But there are questions I must resolve in order to prove it. Are you calm enough now to help me?"

Miss Killington's face was pale as she rose and looked keenly down at Holmes. She nodded, holding herself erect.

"Now, then," Holmes commenced, "can you think of anyone who might wish your father ill, so that they would attempt to incriminate him?"

She shook her head. "No," she murmured. "Not Papa. No one could hate Papa." She turned in appeal to Mrs. Queensley. "Could they, Aunt Ruby?"

"One of his colleagues in his work, perhaps, desiring to discredit him and cause him to lose his position?" Holmes asked.

Miss Killington moaned and twisted her handkerchief. Mrs. Queensley glanced at her husband.

"SHE LOOKED KEENLY DOWN AT HOLMES."

Professor Queensley cleared his throat. "I'm afraid, Mr. Holmes, that Killington's only colleague is myself. Nor did he have many friends. He has kept very much to himself and has ever since Lareina's mother died. So there is no one who would have any reason to throw suspicion upon him like this." He sighed and shook his head. "Dear me, what a spot Killington is in! I should have told him at once about the threat instead of waiting until I sent that wire."

"What wire?" asked Holmes quickly.

"And what threat?" demanded Mrs. Queensley.

"Before Mountjoy and I left London," Queensley replied to Holmes, "I sent a wire to Killington, telling him about the threat against the Analytical Engine, and that I'd asked you and Inspector Lestrade to look into the situation. He must have gone to examine the Engine himself without waiting for your arrival."

"Yes, that is to be expected," Holmes replied. "You may as well know, ladies, that someone has threatened to destroy the Analytical Engine. I tell you this because everyone connected with this affair has been under suspicion—even your father, Miss Killington."

Miss Killington blanched paler still.

"Calm yourself, Miss Killington," I reassured her, for she seemed about to faint. "My friend has eliminated your father from his list of suspects. You may rest assured he will be released as soon as the one responsible is caught."

"But I am not eliminated from that list, I suppose?" Mrs. Queensley enquired. "Well, sir, I can only tell you that I wish it *had* been I who threatened Alfred's precious monster-machine."

"I understand, madam, that it was in connection with the Analytical Engine that you left your husband," Holmes said.

"It certainly was. It was bad enough that Alfred was spending all of his time with that beast of an Engine, but when he informed me of his latest project, I determined to have nothing more to do with him."

"Are you referring to your husband's chess-playing programme, Mrs. Queensley?" I asked. "It seems harmless enough."

"Oh, does it indeed, Doctor?" replied Mrs. Queensley. "I suppose you are one of my husband's sort—one of those people who sees the rapid development of our technology as something marvelous that ought to be encouraged."

"Why, madam, I——" I tried to protest, but Mrs. Queensley had warmed to her topic and was not to be deterred.

"A machine that plays chess is only the beginning, Doctor, and I shudder to contemplate the end. Oh, yes, I've heard Alfred's claims that eventually machines will become an indispensable part of civilized life. But the worst part is that it is no longer only the fools like my husband who believe this, but even people such as yourself, who would normally be sane, sensible individuals. If we keep developing more and more machines to do our work and run our lives, we'll face no end of problems, believe me! Alfred keeps boasting that some day machines like his Abominable Engine will be used to store all sorts of personal information, and that it will require only the flick of a switch to know all the intimate details about the life of anyone you choose. Privacy will become a thing of the past—one will be labelled, catalogued, and pigeon-holed for life. And probably libelled too, in the process! We'll no longer be individual human beings as the good Lord intended; why, we'll be reduced to mere ciphers in a machine, with numbers instead of names! Machines will know so much about us and do so much for us that human beings will become utterly dependent upon the fiendish creatures. The process is at work even now, Doctor. People keep clamouring for more machines and tools and devices because they think they will, somehow, improve their lives. All they are really doing is beginning to speed the dehumanisation that is creeping into our society. Just the other day I read an article which actually encouraged the development of more and better mechanical devices because it will lead to a much-needed overturning of our current moral values!

"JUST THE OTHER DAY I READ AN ARTICLE."

"Oh, yes, Doctor, I fully believe that technology is a great evil, one which leads people to depend on machines rather than on themselves to solve their problems, an evil which leads to questioning and doubting the need for morality and social responsibility. So I propose to do everything in my power to fight it."

"Including destruction of the Analytical Engine?" Holmes asked quietly.

Mrs. Queensley stared calmly back. "Yes, Mr. Holmes, I believe I might. But I'd send no threat first— I'd simply take an axe and smash the wicked thing to bits."

"Yes, Mrs. Queensley, I believe you would," Holmes responded.

"But if you're looking for persons at whom to point fingers, Mr. Holmes," Mrs. Queensley went on, "who better than Professor Vittorio Rosso? Alfred here has given Professor Rosso very good reason to be counted among your suspects."

"In what way, Mrs. Queensley?" asked my friend.

"Well, I am no mathematician, sir—thank heaven—but I recall Alfred telling me that Professor Rosso had been working on some project for months and was nearly ready to publish the results. By chance, *he* says, Alfred began to work on the same material, and he made use of his mechanical Magog to achieve his results in a mere fraction of the time it had taken Professor Rosso. Before the Professor had finished his computations, Alfred had written a paper on the work and submitted it for publication. The Italian, of course, was furious; he maintained that Alfred had somehow stolen his work."

"But, Ruby, Professor Rosso and I resolved the dispute shortly thereafter," Queensley responded. "He assured me that he was convinced of my complete lack of intent to misappropriate his work for myself. He even came to England to see the Analytical Engine when I explained how I had achieved my results, and was most impressed with them. I cannot believe that he would still harbour a grudge against me after all this time."

"Professor Rosso is innocent in this affair," Holmes asserted. "I have already established that." Holmes turned to Miss Killington. "Is your father's laboratory on the premises, Miss Killington?"

"Why, yes," she replied in surprise. "It is in the shed behind the house. Papa has always been interested in chemistry as a hobby. But how did you know, Mr. Holmes?"

"There are a number of chemistry books as well as mathematical ones in your bookshelves, and more than one of the volumes bears traces of various chemical stains in a pattern which corresponds to a human hand."

Holmes rose to leave, bowing to the ladies. "Thank you, Miss Killington, for your help. Rest assured that I shall exonerate your father before the day is out." He turned back from the door for a moment. "By the way, Miss Killington, your copies of the illustrations by Mr. John Tenniel are really very good. Watson and I will see you at the demonstration."

On our way back to the Garden House, I asked, "What now, Holmes?"

"A pipe in the smoking room over which to think for a bit before we return to the demonstration," said he. I wish to arrive by thirty minutes past three, Watson, to have one last check of the Engine before the others arrive. Please inform the good Inspector Lestrade that I should like him to be present with us then."

"Very well," I said.

Holmes sighed and shook his head.

"Some new problem to worry you, Holmes?"

"A problem, yes," he replied. "But one which is neither new, nor so much a worry to me as to Queensley. I refer to his redoubtable wife."

"Ah, indeed," I agreed. "I confess it amazed me to be set upon as a target for the lady's fury. I understand now, I think, how a man not so much older than ourselves has come to acquire such a grizzled mane as his."

"Had we not been there for a more important purpose, I do not think I could have vouched for my equanimity of temper," Holmes brooded.

"Mrs. Queensley's nature is a most flinty one indeed," I concurred. "She does seem to have a knack for touching off sparks with little effort. Yet do you not think that there may have been some validity to the lady's arguments?"

"There is, my dear Watson, but not so much as the lady has chosen to believe. I fear Mrs. Queensley's crusade will come to naught, for the temper of the times is against her. If you will pardon yet another reference to Carroll, Watson, ours is a time as full of invention as the White Knight's brain, and Mrs. Queensley has had the misfortune to have been born in the midst of it."

"You predict, then, an ever-greater influx of technology into our lives," I stated. "Do you feel that machines may in fact come to dominate us, as Mrs. Queensley maintains?"

"Dominate? Hardly, Watson. After all, are not *we* the makers and the masters of our machines? Let us take the one example which comes most readily to mind, the Analytical Engine. Professor Queensley obviously foresees that Analytical Engines will one day be as numerous and common as typewriting machines or steam locomotives.

"As for Mrs. Queensley's fear that mankind will become dependent upon machines such as the Engine, I rather believe that they will free men to extend their minds in areas where machines have no such capabilities. The Analytical Engine will not limit a man's thought, Watson, but rather expand it—perhaps into areas which we cannot even begin to predict. Certainly the Engine can extend the memory of the human mind far beyond its native capacity, with perfect recall of whatever information it holds, provided it is given data in terms which it can comprehend. Consider this bridge which we are now crossing," he went on. "With the help of the Analytical Engine to calculate such factors as stress points, degrees of arc, the strength of the river's current, and so forth, I dare say an engineer could design a bridge twice as strong as this for half the cost! And I hardly need remind you of what an assistance the Analytical Engine has been to me. How many times has the vital clue to determine a man's guilt or innocence come to light with its help?"

"But what of Mrs. Queensley's concerns about dehumanisation and a breakdown of morality?" I asked, curious to hear Holmes's opinion now that he was as deeply engaged in the subject as Ruby Queensley had been earlier.

"My own belief in this matter, Watson, is rather less bleak," said my friend. "True, I have often despaired at man's ingenuity in devising wickedness, but his ability to scale the heights of mortal existence impresses me no less. No matter how complex, how wonderful, how nearly life-like a machine may become, there will always be that gulf between man and machine, that chasm across which we shall gaze in wonder as we realize what an awesome creation is a human being."

I remained silent for the rest of our journey. Whose words, I wondered, foretold the future? Should I trust in those of Holmes, proclaimer of hope, or those of Ruby Queensley, prophetess of doom? Or did the truth lie somewhere in between?

I ached for a glimpse at what life would be like a hundred years hence. Only the sight of Lestrade in the hotel lobby brought my thoughts back abruptly to the present. I remembered that we had very little time in which to prevent a possible tragedy.

We arrived at Trinity College in the company of Inspector Lestrade at half past three. "It may interest you to know, Mr. Holmes, that you'll have one less suspect to keep an eye on at this demonstration," Lestrade informed Holmes. "Herr Koenig told me that he will not deign to honor us with his presence."

"You have directed him not to leave, I trust," said Holmes. "Now, then, we shall have to be most vigilant, lest the culprit somehow elude us and succeed in his pernicious intent despite our efforts. Everyone must be searched. It would take no time at all for the room to fill with smoke or noxious gas. I trust you have your bag with you, Watson."

"We'll have no need for your services here today, Doctor," Lestrade interjected confidently. "I've seen to that, despite what Mr. Holmes believes."

"Even though the bomb was nothing but a decoy, and though Killington capitulated far too readily, you find no cause to question his guilt, Inspector?" Holmes queried.

"Not in the least," Lestrade replied smugly. "Killington intended to plant the bomb and then 'discover' it in our presence as a ruse to provide himself an alibi so that we should no longer suspect him, leaving him free to plant a real bomb later. When I caught him in the act of planting the bomb, he realized his game was up. You might even believe me after the demonstration has taken place without any trouble whatsoever."

"It is very kind of you, Lestrade, to humour me this way," Holmes said dryly.

Queensley had given us a key to the laboratory, which we now entered. "Watson, Inspector, kindly have a look at the tables, the shelves, or anything else which might provide a hiding place for a bomb or weapon," Holmes directed us. "I shall have one last look at the Engine to ensure that no one has tampered with it."

I turned my attention to the tables, examining the drawers, legs and undersides of each carefully, while Lestrade checked the shelves and the rest of the room. "No, Holmes, I can find nothing which could serve as a weapon against the Engine," I said finally. "Nothing seems amiss here."

"I've found nothing either," added Lestrade, wiping a pencil with his handkerchief. "I even pushed my pencil into the cigar urn by the door to check for a concealed weapon, but all that it contains are ordinary cigar stubs."

"Nor can I find evidence of sabotage to the Engine itself," Holmes announced. "As I said before, Watson, we are in a true Red Queen's Race indeed. So far we have run as fast as we could, and done no better than to remain exactly where we are."

"And who will win, I wonder, ourselves or the Red Queen?" I mused. "And who is our would-be 'avenging angel'?"

As I spoke, the laboratory door opened, and Professor Queensley and Miss Killington entered the room. We went to the door to meet them. "You will excuse me, Professor," Holmes said to Queensley, "but I must ask you to permit Inspector Lestrade to inspect your pockets and your hat. You, Miss Killington, will be good enough to permit the Inspector a view of the contents of your reticule."

"Not my hat, Mr. Holmes?" she asked, smiling slightly.

Holmes bowed. "With all due respect, my dear lady, it seems hardly large enough to conceal anything dangerous."

"Professor Mountjoy and Professor Rosso will be in shortly," Queensley told us as the Inspector went through his pockets. "They're finishing their cigars outside." After Lestrade had completed his search, the Professor immediately hastened to the Engine as if to assure himself that his beloved machine was undamaged.

Miss Killington's reticule likewise proved empty of anything harmful, and she took a seat in one of the chairs which had been placed in a semi-circle before the Engine. Holmes watched her intently as the remaining guests entered the room.

"Let me just extinguish this, sir," Mountjoy told Lestrade as he reached to tamp out his cigar in the large sand-filled urn which stood by the door.

As the stub touched the sand, a blinding flash of light blazed up. Mountjoy staggered backwards and fell heavily, while Rosso, who had also been near the urn, was doubled over coughing. A thick grey smoke was filling the room. Lestrade and I ran to assist them, stumbling past the laboratory tables as we groped our way out. Wheezing and coughing, we pulled them outside, with Queensley behind us, frantically mopping at his eyes. I deposited Mountjoy, whom I had been all but carrying, on the lawn, then looked round to see if the others were out safely.

"Holmes! and Miss Killington! They're still inside!" I shouted.

The Inspector nodded even as he coughed, and started back to the laboratory while I looked after the others. Mountjoy was dazed from his fall, and both he and Rosso had had sand blown in their eyes by the explosion. As Lestrade reached the door, he was all but knocked down by Miss Killington, who darted out, holding her handkerchief up to her eyes. I went to her at once and guided her to the grass, where she collapsed, overcome by the smoke. My heart pounded in my throat as I anxiously awaited Holmes's emergence from the laboratory. Had the author of the threat somehow eluded all our precautions, I wondered desperately, and managed to succeed in his pernicious plot after all? Would my friend and the Inspector emerge from the laboratory, alive and unharmed?

After what seemed an eternity, two figures materialized through the smoke. Holmes's tall frame was half-draped over Lestrade's wiry body. Holmes still retained his clutch on some object in his hand, despite the coughing which racked his body. I ran to them and took Holmes's free arm; together Lestrade and I eased him to the ground.

When Holmes could finally open his eyes and speak, he whispered hoarsely to the Inspector, "Thank you, Lestrade. Had you been a few moments later, I suspect I would now be unable to say this to you."

"Thank you from me as well, Inspector," I added, much moved.

Lestrade nodded. "I'll help Queensley with the others."

Queensley had been least affected by the smoke, and was rendering what little aid he could to Mountjoy, Rosso, and Miss Killington. "Professor Queensley," I spoke to him, "is there somewhere we can take the others to recover?"

"My office is just in the next wing—there is a sofa there," Queensley replied, "and there is another in the reception room."

"Watson," Holmes said to me, his voice still rough from the smoke, "have Queensley go to the reception room with Mountjoy and Rosso. I wish to interview Miss Killington privately when she recovers."

I passed on Holmes's message, and we made our way to our respective destinations, the doughty Lestrade carrying Miss Killington's unconscious form, which he deposited on the sofa in Queensley's office. "She will be unconscious for some time yet," I told Holmes and the others. "Call me when she awakens. I shall be tending to the others; I fear Mountjoy and Rosso may have suffered some optical damage from the blast."

I had finished with Rosso and was nearly done bathing Mountjoy's eyes when Lestrade called me back. I returned to find Miss Killington partially conscious and coughing violently. With the assistance of myself and a quantity of cold water, she was soon fully conscious again.

"Are you all right, miss?" I asked.

She nodded, but was unable to answer. Holmes arose then and stood before her, holding out in his hand the object which he had brought from the laboratory. The lady blanched visibly and shrank back with a shudder.

Holmes looked down at her, and though his face was solemn, there was pity in his eyes. "Tell me, Miss Killington," he said quietly, "was it Professor Queensley's chess programme which finally drove you to this? Was this, the latest triumph of the Analytical Engine, so repugnant to you to compel you to wreak such a vengeance?"

"Holmes, what is this?" I exclaimed, taken completely aback by his sudden accusation.

"I believe the phrase you used earlier, Watson, was 'avenging angel,'" he said, turning to me. "She is the author of the message to Queensley."

"*She* is the Red Queen? But how? How could she have concealed a bomb on her person?" I asked, astonished. "You saw that she had nothing in her reticule."

Holmes handed me the object which he had held out before Miss Killington. "You have been a married man, Watson. You will recognise this bit of feminine apparel."

I turned it over in my hands. "What the——? Why, Holmes, it's—— it's a thingummy—the thing Mary used when she put her hair up in a pompadour. It's a rat!"

"Exactly," said Holmes. "If you recall, Miss Killington had quite a remarkable pompadour when she entered the laboratory."

"Look inside," he directed me. I found that one end of it was open, and there, packed in amid cotton wool, was a stopped-up bottle such as had been used in the other bomb.

"But what possible motive could she have?" I stared at the bomb, unable to believe what it was that I held.

"Her motive was revenge, Watson," Holmes replied gravely. Miss Killington had her handkerchief over her eyes, weeping silently. He drew me aside and went on in a low voice, "Consider, Watson, the events of Miss Killington's childhood; her mother died when she was a young child, so that the only real parent she has ever known is her father. You have seen how she feels about him."

"She all but worships him, true," I agreed. "But I still fail to understand her motive. On whom did she intend to take vengeance?"

"The Analytical Engine. It had become a tangible, ever-present symbol of her father's humiliation; every new triumph which Queensley achieved with it reopened the old wound, until finally the chess programme threatened to bring him public recognition. This she could not bear, for it would not be given to the man to whom she felt it rightfully belonged. The lady's naturally romantic spirit led her to devise what she would consider a proper revenge; she could, so to speak, slay her private Jabberwock. I imagine that Mrs. Queensley may have won herself an unwitting disciple in Miss Killington, for the girl could merge her true feelings with sentiments which Mrs. Queensley has ever been ready to provide."

"But how did you know that Miss Killington was the person we sought?" I persisted.

"I first suspected her from Killington's reaction to the decoy bomb," said Holmes. "There was indeed something about it which frightened him, for he recognised that his daughter had been responsible for its construction. He submitted to arrest too willingly; it was, of course, because he saw it as the only way to prevent his daughter's detection. Our call upon Miss Killington provided me the other clue: her devotion to her father provided her motive; her father's chemical laboratory gave her the means to construct the bombs; and I knew that she was familiar with the works of Lewis Carroll from her drawings, for many of them were copies of the illustrations which John Tenniel made for Carroll's books. When we found Miss Killington weeping upon our arrival, I had my clue as to what her father had recognised in her first bomb." He removed a scrap of cloth from his pocket and handed it to me. "This was what she proposed to use for the fuse for her bomb, Watson."

"It is apparently an old handkerchief which has been rendered into a rag," I said as I examined it. "Ah, there is a bit of embroidery left on the edge. A lady's handkerchief, clearly. But if you knew that Miss Killington had made the threat, why did you not say so at once?"

"I could not simply accuse her before Queensley and his wife," replied Holmes, "for they would certainly never have believed me without proof, which I lacked at the time. I had to catch her openly, Watson. Even now, Queensley will not be easily convinced that she has done this. As soon as the urn began to pour out smoke—a simple chemical infusion in the sand, Watson, which would ignite upon contact with heat. I watched to see what she would do. Instead of running out of the room, she ran *in* towards the Engine. By the time I reached her, she had the rat in her hand, poised to hurl at the Engine. When she saw me, she threw it into a corner and ran out. Even if I had not known before then, I might have guessed the identity of our would-be malefactor as soon as I caught the scent Miss Killington had spilled on herself to cover the odour of the gunpowder. That is, if I allowed myself to believe in the predictive power of coincidences."

"How so, Holmes?"

"That particular brand of scent, Watson, is called 'Spanish Queen.' The Spanish word for 'queen' is, of course, *la reina*."

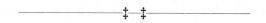

12.1   Can a Machine Think?

That is certainly a question that often brings an emotional response. But the answer is far from clear. What is "thinking?" How would we know if a machine *could* think? Look inside? Take a poll of interested observers? Is this a philosophical question or a pragmatic one? If one defines thinking as uniquely human then the answer is no. But there is another, more empirical view of the question, one that was taken by Alan Turing.

In one of the classic papers on computers ("Computing Machinery and Intelligence," *Mind,* October 1950), Turing addressed a number of issues central to the long-range implications of computers. He began by considering a simple game.

The Imitation Game

Suppose we have two persons, one a man and the other a woman, each sitting in a room. A third person, the interrogator, is located in a separate room. The interrogator can pose questions to the two persons, who are known to the interrogator only by labels, say X and Y. The interrogator's objective is to discover which of the two is the woman.

1890 Cover of Scientific American on the American Census

The woman's objective is to help the interrogator make the right choice, to identify her as the woman. The man's objective is to confuse the interrogator.

Obviously, hearing the voices of the man or woman would make the game a give-away. To prevent this, the interrogator can communicate with the persons by teleprinter or interconnected typewriters.

In questioning player X, for instance, a sample scenario might go as follows:

```
Interrogator :   Do you like to cook?
Player X     :   Yes, I certainly do.
Interrogator :   Tell me the name of your favorite poem.
Player X     :   I'm not interested in poetry.
Interrogator :   Well then, do you play chess.
Player X     :   No, but my husband does.
```

If say, player X is the man, his strategy would probably be to imitate the answers of a woman. If player X is the woman, probably her best strategy is to give truthful answers.

Now for the step up. Suppose the part of the woman is replaced by a computer. In the new game, illustrated in Figure 12.1, both the computer and the person have a typewriter connection to the interrogator. Can the interrogator now decide whether X is the man or the computer? The question "Can a machine think?" is now recast as "Will the interrogator fare no better in deciding between a man and a woman than in deciding between a man and a computer?"

In the new game, a sample scenario might run as follows:

```
Interrogator :   Tell me about your family.
Player X     :   Well, my wife is British. I have two children, Edwin and Helen.
Interrogator :   Do you like to cook?
Player X     :   Yes, I certainly do.
Interrogator :   Who was Charles Babbage?
Player X     :   I haven't a clue.
Interrogator :   How much is 14 times 15 times 16?
Player X     :   (pauses for 30 or so seconds, and then says) 3,260.
```

You would be right if you had some disbelief that player X was the computer. Programming a computer to give answers like those above is a herculean task, and at present, not even close to being achieved. But this is not our concern at the moment. It certainly is conceivable that a computer can be so programmed. Our interest here is our question "Can a machine think?" as expressed by this revised imitation game.

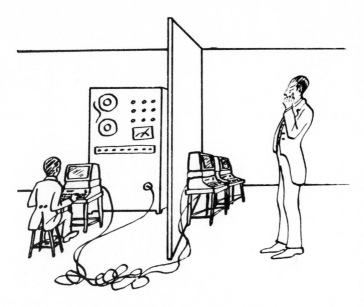

Figure 12.1   *Turing's Test*

Turing's rephrasing of the original question "Can a machine think?" disposes of a number of problematic issues. The theological or philosophical claim that thinking is a uniquely human activity is immaterial to the rephrased question. With the imitation game, we ask only if a machine can have the appearance of thinking. That is, the behavior of a human need only be successfully imitated.

The argument against machine thinking, that a machine is not conscious of its thinking, is also dismissed in the imitation game. It is certainly far-fetched to believe that a computer could compose a song or a sonnet and then feel pleasure at its success, or to believe that the computer would have feelings about the way it treated a human user.

It may be argued that a machine can be programmed to respond in a dialogue, but it certainly would not be able to be friendly, to know the difference between right and wrong, to get angry, to enjoy a sunny day, to make mistakes, or to develop a taste for vanilla ice cream. The basic argument here is that no machine could be programmed to exhibit the behavior that human beings do.

Some special remarks are in order here. Clearly the messages typed by the computer could be made to appear friendly. While most computers often give messages to the contrary, this need not be the case. As for making mistakes, it is certainly possible to program a computer to do precisely this. Perhaps it should err only occasionally, for example, by periodically reaching a faulty conclusion. Developing a taste for vanilla ice cream is much more difficult. Obviously computers don't eat. In the imitation game, however, this is irrelevant. It is only important that the dialogue exhibit the appearance of developing a taste.

The above issues, and others, are extensively discussed in Turing's paper. We offer here a few general points. First, the imitation game is a significant simplification of the original question, "Can a machine think?" Essentially the imitation game asks the question "Can a machine be programmed to give the *appearance* of thinking?" A positive answer to this question is certainly conceivable. But if we accept the rephrasing of the question, a new, more pragmatic, question arises, "Is it likely that sufficient machine resources and programming skills would be available for the computer to play the imitation game successfully?" "Successful" here means well enough to satisfy a good statistician that certain measures of performance have been met.

Some (see Dreyfus, 1972 and Wizenbaum, 1976) have argued that this is basically a foolish enterprise. The problem stretches computer technology to such an extraordinary degree that the energy, skill, and expense would be enormous. And what would the value be?

If we accept all this, a positive answer to Turing's question is not likely to be forthcoming. Will it happen in the next ten years? No. In the next 50? Unclear. In the next 100? Still unclear.

12.2   On Some Common Misconceptions

There is considerable public confusion about computers. This is not surprising. Almost any new and powerful technology brings an aura of mystery, a humbling lack of knowledge, and an inability to assess its ultimate impact. In the previous chapters we have attempted to explore relatively unadorned information about computers, their power, and their limitations. With our discussion of "Can a machine think?" we venture into nebulous territory. In particular, we now comment on some comments frequently heard about computers and try to put them in some perspective.

A computer never makes a mistake. Literally this is true. But it belies a deeper truth.

Of course a computer, like any other machine, may suffer a technical failure and make a mistake. But this kind of malfunction is quite rare. More often, a computer, like any well-operating machine, performs with regular predictability, and without technical error. It is in this sense that one can say that the statement above is literally true.

The misconception in the above statement is quite subtle, and is a matter of implication. Any computer that performs a task is programmed to do so. Such programs are, of course, designed and written by human beings. Like any human activity, one person makes assumptions about another. The development of programs is a very complicated task. Anticipating the needs of the user in any complete sense is often impossible. Even making good judgments about the requests likely to be made by the user is difficult.

When it comes to operating a computer, the user will undoubtedly make assumptions about the computer's behavior, or more precisely, about the performance of the program being used. If the user's assumptions differ from that expected by the program, a strange result can occur. This result can take the form of an error message, faulty output, avoidance of the user's request, or even a complete breakdown of the program. From the user's viewpoint, something has gone wrong. Many users are intimidated, some are frustrated, some are even unconcerned. But all will sense the inadequacy of the computer in meeting their needs.

Computers are fast. They certainly are; at least internally. But does this mean they can do what you want them to do in a time period that you would consider fast?

Suppose you are editing a document using a computer and wish to find the next line where the word "Sherlock" appears. Or suppose you wish to transfer the contents of a file from one place to another. Or suppose you wish to run a program that accepts a document as input and gives as output a reformatted copy of the document (for instance, with some specified page layout). Each of these operations is conceptually simple, and can be considered as a single operation.

From the computer's viewpoint, however, these operations can be very complex. Millions of machine instructions may need to be carried out. The result, often, is that a considerable time may be needed, from a few seconds to several minutes. If you are sitting at a terminal where the response time has been immediate, such delays can be annoying.

More generally, we have come to expect a variety of services from a computer. As our expectations grow, our demands upon the speedy servant also grow, taxing even the most sophisticated hardware.

The correct input always gives the correct output. Here again, the statement is literally true. A computer is certainly obedient to its programmed task. But the misconception creeps in with the word "correct." Correct according to whom?

Computer programs themselves may have errors. This is a serious problem for every software designer, every programmer, and every vendor of computer software. But this is not a problem we wish to address here. Let us assume that everyone who helped produce the software believes the software to be free of errors.

Now, from the computer's side, a program can have many inputs, and each gives some kind of response. If you enter a sequence of keystrokes, you will generally get some sort of output from the computer. The computer has no sense of "correctness," only a sense of "input" and "output." If you press the return key on your terminal and the computer responds by printing a question mark, what does correctness mean here? If you call for a report to be printed and some items are blank, again, what does correctness mean? From the user's viewpoint, the input is "correct," but the output is not.

What this means is that the correct-in, correct-out view of the situation doesn't help very much in explaining much of the behavior of the computer. Underlying this matter is, again, the fact that computer programs are designed by human beings. As such, and no matter how well-intentioned, many of the natural limitations in human-to-human discourse apply to human-to-computer discourse.

It is possible to change the computer's behavior by simply changing the software. Yes, of course, this is literally true. Just as you can change the music on your stereo system by simply changing the record or the tape, so, too, you can change the behavior of the computer by simply changing the software. But watch out.

First, it is often not easy to make modifications to the software. If you don't like the way the computer prints the time of day, that can be changed without too much ado. But if you don't like the grammar you use to print a file or run a program, changing the protocols may be very difficult. Generally the protocols for operating a computer are quite deeply embedded in its design. The entire system may depend on a certain regularity of vocabulary and punctuation. Changing a comma to a period or a space may be ruled out because of its effect elsewhere.

Second, there are some practical limits to what can be done. You can't really change your keyboard or screen (unless you want a new computer). If your keyboard has certain special keys or your screen only accommodates a half page of text, any software based on these properties may be nearly impossible to change.

Third, most users are not programmers. Even if they were, they would be unlikely to understand how to change the software they are using. This means that the matter of changing the software, no matter how good the idea, is not under your control.

Beyond all these points, there is a more subtle and pervasive issue. To use any computer system there are a great many procedures, conventions, security measures, and techniques that must be learned and developed. You have to learn how to use the keyboard, how the filing system works, how to read the manuals, what features are available, where to get supplies, and even whom to call when the machine breaks down. On top of this all of your files are recorded in a form that often only your computer recognizes. The result? Once the die is cast and you begin accommodating a computer, it is difficult to make changes.

12.3   Some Social Implications

There is no doubt that computers have profound implications in our lives. The technology is young, but not an infant, and we are already experiencing its effects. But unlike many technologies of the past, the impact of computers is not simply happening without concern for us, its users. The issue has been raised for years, and many of the public's fears are probably unfounded.

The first topic that comes to mind is privacy. Enormous amounts of data are routinely collected and stored in computer form. It is possible, for instance, to stop a person on the highway and in a matter of minutes verify whether a person has a record of criminal activity. The real question is whether such matters should cause concern.

The worst consequence of privacy invasion would probably come from access to data by an unauthorized person. This possibility arises, of course, even if data are stored in non-computer form. With computers, the problem is more severe. It is easy to copy data electronically or to get access to data from remote locations. Thus the potential for abuse is great. On the other side, elaborate safeguards can be used. These include issuing special codes to authorized persons, limiting access to special terminals, and coding data in a cryptic format. Such techniques are common and provide a good deal of safety.

It seems almost inherent in computer technology that people become identified with numbers—user identification numbers, special codes, special account numbers. For many, this number symbolizes the dehumanizing influence of computers. The feeling of impersonality is all too true. The ease with which computer printouts are generated, the mass of irrelevant information on them, and their puzzling appearance lead to distaste for the technology.

Perhaps the most striking symbol of impersonality is the form letter and its many variants. The computer-annotated brochure announcing that you may have won a prize, the sterile advertisement with the pretense of being written just for you, and the repeated letters telling you that your subscription is about to expire are persistent reminders of computer-age impersonality.

Much of the computer's impersonality can be simply ignored. But some of it cannot. Before computers, paychecks, bank statements, insurance forms, and customer bills were done by hand. If a question arose or a discrepancy appeared, you could depend on personal accountability. With the increasing reliance on computerized methods, a high degree of accuracy has been obtained, but not without a price. Because of computers, more elaborate options are available and the complexity of transactions has markedly increased. Much of this is to the good, but the personal accountability is vastly more difficult.

The promise of computer technology is layered with a new bureaucracy of forms and computer data that can be very difficult to comprehend. If you have a question about your computer-generated health insurance statement you may not like the process required to get an answer.

The technology need not be so unfair. It is, after all, human beings who write the programs and human beings who use the results. There is no technical reason why computers cannot be simple to use and humane in their treatment. The computer is, at its root, an amplifier of thought. Its benefit and promise have just begun.

Appendix A

ASCII Character Set

Binary Code	Value	Char	Common Use	Binary Code	Value	Char	Common Use
0000000	0	NUL	Null	0111111	63	?	Question mark
0000001	1	SOH	Start of heading	1000000	64	@	Commercial at
0000010	2	STX	Start of text	1000001	65	A	Uppercase A
0000011	3	ETX	End of text	1000010	66	B	Uppercase B
0000100	4	EOT	End of trans.	1000011	67	C	Uppercase C
0000101	5	ENQ	Enquiry	1000100	68	D	Uppercase D
0000110	6	ACK	Acknowledge	1000101	69	E	Uppercase E
0000111	7	BEL	Bell	1000110	70	F	Uppercase F
0001000	8	BS	Backspace	1000111	71	G	Uppercase G
0001001	9	HT	Horizontal tab	1001000	72	H	Uppercase H
0001010	10	LF	Line feed	1001001	73	I	Uppercase I
0001011	11	VT	Vertical tab	1001010	74	J	Uppercase J
0001100	12	FF	Form feed	1001011	75	K	Uppercase K
0001101	13	CR	Carriage return	1001100	76	L	Uppercase L
0001110	14	SO	Shift out	1001101	77	M	Uppercase M
			(turn cursor on)	1001110	78	N	Uppercase N
0001111	15	SI	Shift in	1001111	79	O	Uppercase O
			(turn cursor off)	1010000	80	P	Uppercase P
0010000	16	DLE	Data link escape	1010001	81	Q	Uppercase Q
0010001	17	DC1	Device control 1	1010010	82	R	Uppercase R
0010010	18	DC2	Device control 2	1010011	83	S	Uppercase S
0010011	19	DC3	Device control 3	1010100	84	T	Uppercase T
0010100	20	DC4	Device control 4	1010101	85	U	Uppercase U
0010101	21	NAK	Neg. acknowledge	1010110	86	V	Uppercase V
0010110	22	SYN	Synchronous idle	1010111	87	W	Uppercase W
0010111	23	ETB	End trans. block	1011000	88	X	Uppercase X
0011000	24	CAN	Cancel	1011001	89	Y	Uppercase Y
0011001	25	EM	End of medium	1011010	90	Z	Uppercase Z
0011010	26	SUB	Substitute	1011011	91	[	Left bracket
0011011	27	ESC	Escape	1011100	92	\	Reverse slash
0011100	28	FS	File separator	1011101	93	]	Right bracket
0011101	29	GS	Group separator	1011110	94	^	Circumflex
0011110	30	RS	Record separator	1011111	95	_	Underline
0011111	31	US	Unit separator	1100000	96	`	Grave accent
0100000	32	SP	Space	1100001	97	a	Lowercase a
0100001	33	!	Exclamation point	1100010	98	b	Lowercase b
0100010	34	"	Quotation marks	1100011	99	c	Lowercase c

0100011	35	#	Number sign	1100100	100	d	Lowercase d
0100100	36	$	Dollar sign	1100101	101	e	Lowercase e
0100101	37	%	Percent sign	1100110	102	f	Lowercase f
0100110	38	&	Ampersand	1100111	103	g	Lowercase g
0100111	39	'	Apostrophe	1101000	104	h	Lowercase h
0101000	40	(	Left paren	1101001	105	i	Lowercase i
0101001	41	)	Right paren	1101010	106	j	Lowercase j
0101010	42	*	Asterisk	1101011	107	k	Lowercase k
0101011	43	+	Plus sign	1101100	108	l	Lowercase l
0101100	44	,	Comma	1101101	109	m	Lowercase m
0101101	45	-	Minus sign	1101110	110	n	Lowercase n
0101110	46	.	Full stop	1101111	111	o	Lowercase o
0101111	47	/	Solidus	1110000	112	p	Lowercase p
0110000	48	0	Zero	1110001	113	q	Lowercase q
0110001	49	1	One	1110010	114	r	Lowercase r
0110010	50	2	Two	1110011	115	s	Lowercase s
0110011	51	3	Three	1110100	116	t	Lowercase t
0110100	52	4	Four	1110101	117	u	Lowercase u
0110101	53	5	Five	1110110	118	v	Lowercase v
0110110	54	6	Six	1110111	119	w	Lowercase w
0110111	55	7	Seven	1111000	120	x	Lowercase x
0111000	56	8	Eight	1111001	121	y	Lowercase y
0111001	57	9	Nine	1111010	122	z	Lowercase z
0111010	58	:	Colon	1111011	123	{	Left brace
0111011	59	;	Semicolon	1111100	124	|	Vertical bar
0111100	60	<	Less than	1111101	125	}	Right brace
0111101	61	=	Equals sign	1111110	126	~	Tilde
0111110	62	>	Greater than	1111111	127	DEL	Delete

Appendix B

Basic: Its Grammar and Meaning

This appendix summarizes some of the rules for writing computer programs in Basic. The intent of this appendix is to give you some idea of what programming languages are really like. Hence the appendix does not describe the complete language, but rather some essential features common to almost every commercially available version of Basic.

Keep in mind that, as programming languages go, Basic is a small language. Also, it is not especially useful for large-scale applications. Nevertheless, you can write some truly useful programs with what is presented here.

B.1 Some Preliminaries

At the most elementary level, a Basic program consists of a sequence of symbols. The arrangement of symbols is subject to numerous and sometimes complex conventions that you have to learn.

Names

A *name* is a symbol created by the programmer. A name consists of a letter, or a letter followed by a digit. If the name stands for a character, it must have a dollar sign ($) after it. Some examples are:

```
N     C
N$    C$
N1    C1$
```

In Basic, N and N$ are considered as different names.

Keywords

In Basic there are a number of words that have a special significance in a program. These are called *keywords*. A keyword is a special word that tells the computer what to do. For example, the keyword REM introduces a remark. Some other keywords are LET, IF, GOTO, INPUT, and STOP. You don't have to memorize all the keywords. The important point is that each has a specific role, as used below.

Numbers

Suppose you wish to compute the number of feet to the scene of a crime or an amount of money embezzled in a series of bank transactions. Basic, like any other programming language, has a rather fixed set of conventions for writing numbers.

The first kind of number you can write is an *integer,* which means a whole number. An integer is represented by a sequence of digits, possibly preceded by a plus or a minus sign, like so:

```
      0    10
   1776    +10
1000000    -10
```

Negative numbers can be used to represent things like a temperature of minus 10 degrees or a bank balance that is in the red.

The second kind of number you can write in Basic is sometimes called a *real number.* A real number has either a decimal point, a letter E followed by a scale factor (which means "times ten to the power of") or both. For example, you may write the numbers

```
12.34
1234E-2
0.1234E2
0.1234E+2
```

all of which stand for the same real number.

These are the only conventions you can use for writing numbers. Be careful, for as much as you would like, you cannot write numbers like:

```
1,000    -- you must write 1000
$123     -- you must write 123
```

Whatever number you have in mind, you must represent it as either an integer or as a real number. Normally you use integers to represent whole quantities (the number of suspects or the scheduled time of a train arrival, for example), and real numbers to represent things you measure (the number of feet to the scene of a crime or the weight of a molecule, for example).

Character strings

When you use a computer program, the computer asks you for some data and then prints some results. Since you will surely want to know what data are requested or what the results mean, your program should print messages telling you what is going on. You can do this with *character strings,* such as:

```
"ENTER YOUR PASSWORD:"
"THE MURDERER IS MR. POPE."
```

A character string consists of a sequence of characters enclosed by quotation marks ("). The characters that you can put in a character string can be any character that your computer recognizes, even such characters as ? and %. What if you would like to have a quotation mark itself as part of a character string? Usually you can't. If you want, you can use an apostrophe (single quote) instead. Thus we may have:

```
"THE MURDERER'S HAIR IS BROWN"
"NOTE THE APOSTROPHE ABOVE"

"STRINGS MAY CONTAIN SPECIAL CHARACTERS"
"LIKE ? AND %"
"as well as lower case letters in some implementations"
```

Each string must fit on the line in which it occurs.

Remarks

One of the most useful features of programming languages is the ability to annotate your program with *remarks.* For example, in the sequence

```
0010 REM  -- CALCULATE DISTANCE TRAVELLED
0020      LET D = 0
0030      LET N = 0
```

the first line is a remark.

A remark consists of the word REM followed by the text of a remark. The text of your remark may include anything you like, but must fit on a line. Thus we may have:

```
0010 REM  LONG REMARKS CAN BE WRITTEN, BUT
0020 REM  EACH LINE IN A LONG REMARK MUST
0030 REM  BEGIN WITH THE WORD REM.
```

As far as running your program is concerned, if execution reaches a remark statement, execution proceeds to the next line with no other effect.

Spacing and layout

It is much easier to read

```
0010 REM  -- ESTABLISH THE KNOWNS
0020      INPUT T, L, I, C
```

```
0030 REM
0040     LET D = 0
0050     LET N = 0
```

than

```
0010 REM--ESTABLISH THE KNOWNS
0020 INPUT T,L,I,C
0030 REM
0040 LET D=0
0050 LET N=0
```

The only difference between the two examples is simply the use of spacing. The computer will ignore blank spaces and blank remark lines, but the human reader will not. In fact, the proper spacing of programs can go a long way in making your intent clear.

There are a few restrictions on the placing of blank spaces. These restrictions need not concern you very much, as it is reasonably obvious just what these restrictions are. For example, at least one blank must be inserted between adjacent words, such as between the LET and N above. Generally speaking, you may insert blank spaces wherever convenient.

Unfortunately, some implementations make the use of program spacing difficult. For instance, your computer may execute more slowly when you put in extra spaces or remark lines. Some versions of Basic even remove all of the extra spaces you put in. If you have any of these problems, you will have to decide what you want to do.

B.2   General Program Structure

All programs consist of a sequence of lines. Each line has a *line number* and a *statement.* Depending on the version of Basic you are using, a line number usually consists of 4 or 5 digits. The line numbers must be in sequential order. Increasing line numbers are often given in increments of 10. This convention allows you to make small changes to a program without changing all the line numbers. The last statement in a program must be an END statement, such as:

```
0820 END
```

This statement signifies the end of the complete program text.
   The following lines,

```
0010 REM  -- THIS PROGRAM READS IN A NUMBER N AND
0020 REM  -- PRINTS TWICE ITS VALUE.
0030 REM
0040     INPUT N
0050     PRINT N + N
0060 END
```

form a correct program. It doesn't do much, but is, nevertheless, a program.

Sequence of execution

Next consider the following:

```
0010  PRINT "START"
0020  GOTO 0040
0030  PRINT "MIDDLE"
0040  PRINT "FINISH"
```

When this sequence is executed on the computer, the program will print

```
START
FINISH
```

and not:

```
START
MIDDLE
FINISH
```

The key line here is:

```
GOTO 0040
```

When this statement is reached, execution continues at line 0040, and not at the following line (line 0030).

More generally, a goto statement has the form:

```
GOTO  line-number
```

Whenever execution reaches a goto statement, execution continues at the given line number. The goto statement is one of the statements in Basic that causes a *transfer* of execution from one line to another.

Execution of a program terminates when a STOP statement is reached or, in its absence, when the END statement marking the end of the program is reached. A STOP statement consists solely of the word

```
STOP
```

and may appear anywhere in a program.

This leads us to the following rules about Basic:

■ Execution of a program begins at the first statement in the program, and normally, continues in sequence.

■ Execution of a transfer statement interrupts normal execution and causes execution to continue at a specified place.

■   Execution terminates when a STOP statement or END statement is reached.

Now let's turn to the means for making computations in Basic.

B.3   Variables and Assignment

A dominant feature of all programs is the use of names to refer to values needed in the course of the computation. For example, we may have:

```
D + 1       -- the value of D plus 1
D + C       -- the value of D plus the value of C
D + C*100   -- the value of D plus 100 times the value of C
```

In each of these forms a piece of information (for example, a distance) is associated with a name (for example, D). This piece of information is called a *value*. This value is not given directly (for example, the value may be 10.4), but instead is referred to by a name (for example, D). This name is called a *variable* since the value associated with the name will be established or changed during the course of the program.

An *assignment* is the means by which we establish or change the value of a variable. For example, we may have

```
LET N = 0
LET N = N + 2
LET D = D + C*100
```

In the first case, the value of N is set to zero. In the second case, the value of N is incremented by two. In the third case, the value of D is set to the value computed by the given formula.

The general form for writing all assignment statements is simple:

```
LET variable = expression
```

When this statement is acted upon by the computer, it means the following:

1. Compute the value of the expression
2. Then associate this value with the variable

While the rules are simple, you must be careful to obey them precisely.

Consider the following sequence of assignment statements, where the variables A and B have initially unspecified values.

```
LET A = 0     -- value of A is 0,  B is unspecified
LET B = 1     -- value of A is 0,  B is 1
LET A = 2     -- value of A is 2,  B is 1
LET B = A     -- value of A is 2,  B is 2
LET B = 2*A   -- value of A is 2,  B is 4
```

We see here that each statement in the sequence is executed step by step. Furthermore, each assignment establishes a new value for only one variable.

Basic, like all programming languages, has a number of rules regarding the use of variables. One such rule is that numeric variables can only be assigned numeric values, and string variables can only be assigned string values.

For instance, suppose the variable N is supposed to stand for a number of suspects, and P$ for a person's name. While you can say

```
LET N  = 4
LET P$ = "WATSON"
```

you cannot say:

```
LET N  = "WATSON"   -- error, N must be assigned an integer value
LET P$ = 4          -- error, P$ must be assigned a string value
```

If you do, the computer will complain, and it should.

Watch out, though, for the following anomaly. You can assign any kind of numeric value to a numeric variable, and any kind of string value to a string variable. Thus the computer will be perfectly happy if you say

```
LET N = 12.6
```

even though 12.6 is certainly senseless as a number of suspects.

B.4   Decision Making and Loops

The ability to make decisions is fundamental to programming. Depending upon one or more circumstances, we want to take appropriate actions. The basic mechanism for making choices in Basic is the IF statement. This statement has the following form:

IF *condition* THEN *line-number*

This statement means:

> If the condition is true, transfer execution to the statement with the given line number; otherwise do nothing and go on to the following statement.

The ability to include IF statements within a program has far reaching possibilities. While the basic mechanism is extremely simple, we can produce rather elaborate or even confusing effects. To use it effectively, we need to look at matters a little more closely.

Consider the following:

```
0010 REM  -- CASE 1
0020      PRINT "TEMPERATURE:"
0030      INPUT T
0040      IF T < 90 THEN 0080
0050         PRINT "MESSAGE DESCRIBING WHAT TO"
0060         PRINT "DO WHEN IT IS HOT."
0070 REM
0080      PRINT "ENTER HUMIDITY:"
```

Here the lines

```
0050         PRINT "MESSAGE DESCRIBING WHAT TO"
0060         PRINT "DO WHEN IT IS HOT."
```

describe an action to be taken. If T is 90 or greater, the action is performed, and execution continues at line 0080. Otherwise (the temperature is less than 90), the action is skipped and execution continues at the same line, 0080.

Next consider:

```
0010 REM  -- CASE 2
0020      PRINT "ENTER TEMPERATURE: "
0030      INPUT T
0040      IF T < 90 THEN 0080
0050         PRINT "MESSAGE DESCRIBING WHAT TO"
0060         PRINT "DO WHEN IT IS HOT."
0070         GOTO 0120
0080         PRINT "MESSAGE DESCRIBING WHAT TO"
0090         PRINT "DO OTHERWISE."
0100         GOTO 0120
0110 REM
0120      PRINT "ENTER HUMIDITY:"
```

Here the lines:

```
0050  PRINT "MESSAGE DESCRIBING WHAT TO"
0060  PRINT "DO WHEN IT IS HOT."
```

describe one action, and the lines

```
0080  PRINT "MESSAGE DESCRIBING WHAT TO"
0090  PRINT "DO OTHERWISE."
```

describe another action. If the temperature is 90 or greater, the first action is performed; otherwise the second action is performed. In both cases, execution continues at line 0120.

Looping

Now consider:

```
0010 REM -- COUNT THE CITIES UNTIL LONDON
0020     LET N = 0
0030     PRINT "ENTER FIRST CITY: "
0040     INPUT C$
0050     IF C$ = "LONDON" THEN 0100
0060        LET N = N + 1
0070        PRINT "ENTER NEXT CITY: "
0080        INPUT C$
0090        GOTO 0050
0100 REM
0110     PRINT "THE NUMBER OF CITIES IS", N
```

This simple sequence counts the number of cities until the city happens to be London. In particular, notice the sequence

```
0050     IF C$ = "LONDON" THEN 0100
...      ...
0090        GOTO 0050
```

This is called a *loop*. It is achieved by using IF and GOTO statements. In particular, the statements between lines 0050 and 0090 are repeated until some condition is met.

The ability to use IF and GOTO statements is what really turns Basic from a language of calculation to one of full algorithmic power. They should be used with care and caution, for as their power is great, so is their ability to confuse.

B.5   Reading and Writing Data

In almost every program you write, you are going to want to read in some data and print some results. Doing this is easy. Consider the statement:

```
INPUT T, L, I, C
```

When the computer executes this statement it will ask you for four values. You may give it something like:

```
28,  0.10,  0.06,  10.4
```

Notice that the values are separated by commas. When you give it these values, the four variables will be assigned the values that you typed in. This is exactly the same as writing

```
LET T = 28
LET L = 0.10
LET I = 0.06
LET C = 10.4
```

in your program. That is, reading of data is exactly the same as assigning values to variables.

The general rule for reading data is thus quite simple. You simply use the name INPUT followed by the list of variables whose values you want to read.

For printing your results, the process is just the opposite. For example, consider the statement:

```
PRINT M
```

When the computer processes this statement, it will simply print the value of M. If you want, you can say:

```
PRINT "DISTANCE IN MILES IS", M
```

In this case, your program will write the characters DISTANCE IN MILES IS followed by the value of M.

More generally, you may print out any character string or the value of any expression, provided that each of these items is separated by commas. Thus all of the following statements are acceptable.

```
PRINT "SOME INTRODUCTORY MESSAGE"
PRINT A, B, C
PRINT "D divided by 5280 is ", D/5280
```

When you are typing in data and give something the computer doesn't understand, for instance typing your name when the computer is looking for a number, the computer will either give up or ask you again for the data.

When you are using PRINT, the computer will print the output values so as to put several values on a line. Each printed line is divided into zones of a fixed size; the number of zones varies from four to eight, depending on your terminal or printer. A comma after an item causes printing of the next item to begin in the next zone. For instance, if you say

```
PRINT "SUSPECT", N, "IS THE MURDERER."
```

and N is 4, your output may look like:

```
SUSPECT        4               IS THE MURDERER.
```

If you want to control the situation a bit more, you can use a semicolon to separate the items given in a PRINT statement. Then the computer will print the items immediately after each other. Thus if you say

```
PRINT "SUSPECT"; N; " IS THE MURDERER."
```

your output will be:

```
SUSPECT 4 IS THE MURDERER.
```

Each PRINT statement causes printing to start on a new line. If you want to prevent this, you can put a comma or semicolon after the last item. Thus

```
PRINT A, B,
PRINT C
```

has the same effect as

```
PRINT A, B, C
```

and

```
PRINT "THIS LONG STRING WILL APPEAR ON A SINGLE ";
PRINT "LINE WHEN PRINTED."
```

has the same effect as:

```
PRINT "THIS LONG STRING WILL APPEAR ON A SINGLE LINE WHEN PRINTED."
```

The exact behavior of input and output depends upon the version of Basic you are using, and no doubt you will have to check your version or try out some examples to pin it down.

B.6   Expressions and Conditions

An *expression* is a formula for computing a value. Consider the very simple expression:

```
N + 2
```

This expression adds two to the existing value of the variable N. In this expression, we have an addition operator and two operands, N and 2.

This expression illustrates properties that are common to all expressions. First, an expression contains some special symbols like + and / called *operators*. Second, the operators are applied to the values of the *operands*. The operands may be numbers, variables, or other parenthesized expressions. Third, when an operator is applied to operands, a result is computed.

Some arithmetic operators available in Basic are the following:

+   addition
−   subtraction
*   multiplication
/   division

These operators are familiar; for instance, we may have:

```
14 + 7      -- result is 21
4.1 + 5     -- result is 9.1

14 - 7      -- result is 7
4.1 - 5     -- result is -0.9

7 * 5       -- result is 35
7.1 * 5     -- result is 35.5

7/5         -- result is 1.4
36/6        -- result is 6
```

There are a few little details you may want to know about. The first is called *rounding*. When you tell the computer to perform some arithmetic operation, it will only be accurate to some fixed number of digits. For instance, suppose your computer is accurate to six digits. If you write

```
PRINT 2/3
```

the computer may round out the result and print

```
.666667
```

or truncate the result and print:

```
.666666
```

The second point has to do with very large or very small numbers, which might arise if you are trying to calculate the distance between two planets or the weight of a molecule. In these cases, the computer will print results using the E notation (often called *scientific* notation or *floating point* notation). All of this means that

```
123000000000000
0.0000000000000456
```

will be printed as:

```
1.23E+14
4.56E-14
```

This saves you from counting zeros to the size of a number.

The operators plus and minus may also be used with a single operand. This is allowed only at the beginning of an expression, as in:

```
-10.0
+10.0
-10.0 + 3.14
```

Of course, you will often want to write expressions with several operands and operators, just as you do in conventional arithmetic. For example, you may wish to write

```
(D1 - 1) * 1440
```

or

```
A + B - C - D
```

To do things like this you have to remember a few rules. The rules are:

- Parenthesized operands are evaluated before unparenthe-sized operands.

- The operators * and / are applied before - and +.

- Otherwise, evaluation proceeds in textual order from left to right.

These rules are intended to make the writing of expressions easier. Thus if you write,

```
1 + N*2
```

and N is 3, the result is 7 (which is what you want) and not 8. This may look a bit tricky, but in normal practice you should have no problem. With proper parentheses or spacing you can write your expressions like

```
1 + N*2
```

or

```
1 + (N * 2)
```

so that you and the reader will have no doubt as to what you mean.

Expressions may not only contain variables and numbers, but calls to predefined functions available with Basic. For example, we may have

```
ABS (-4.6)     -- gives the absolute value, here 4.6
INT (4.6)      -- gives the integer part of a number, here 4
SIN (X) + 1    -- computes the sine of X and adds 1.
```

You will need to check your version of Basic for full details.

Conditions

Execution of an IF statement depends on the truth or falsity of some given *condition*. The simplest of all conditions is the testing of values to see if they are equal. For example, we may write:

```
IF S  = 0     THEN ...    -- test if score is 0
IF C$ = "BLUE" THEN ...   -- test if color is blue
```

In each of these constructs the condition has the form:

expression-1 = expression-2

A condition always evaluates to true or false.

Testing for the equality of two values is not the only operation we can perform in conditions. Each of the following operators may be used:

```
=    -- equal
<>   -- not equal
<    -- less than
>    -- greater than
<=   -- less than or equal
=>   -- greater than or equal
```

For instance, to see if one value is less than or equal to another, we may write:

```
N <= 10
```

This condition tests if the value of N is less than or equal to 10.

The operator <> appears particularly strange. This is the operator for testing for inequality. Thus, while you might be tempted to say

```
IF C$ ≠ "BLUE" THEN ...    -- Illegal
```

which looks perfectly logical, you can't. Instead you have to write:

```
IF C$ <> "BLUE" THEN ...    -- Legal
```

The rationale here is that a < followed by a > stands for "less or greater than," i.e. "not equal." So much for that.

B.7   An Example

This completes our summary of some of the rules for writing Basic programs. We close with a small program that illustrates many features discussed above. This program, given in Figure B.1, counts up an amount of change and computes the total number of dollars and cents. You will notice a loop in lines 0400 and 0430. This loop is used to subtract 100 from the value of the change C and add 1 to the number of dollars D until the value of C is less than 100.

In closing, consider the great detective's observation that "the simplest things are invariably the more important, the more powerful, and more often, the more difficult to bring home." Like Dr. Watson, you now have at your disposal the tools for solving some real programming problems.

```
0010 REM  -- THIS PROGRAM READS IN SIX INTEGER VALUES, RESPECTIVELY
0020 REM  -- REPRESENTING THE NUMBER OF PENNIES, NICKELS, DIMES, QUARTERS,
0030 REM  -- HALF-DOLLARS, AND SILVER DOLLARS IN COINAGE. THE PROGRAM
0040 REM  -- OUTPUTS THE TOTAL VALUE OF THE COINS IN DOLLARS AND CENTS.
0050 REM
0060 REM  -- DICTIONARY OF NAMES:
0070 REM  -- N  A NUMBER OF COINS, FOR INSTANCE THE NUMBER OF DIMES
0080 REM  -- T  TOTAL CHANGE
0090 REM  -- D  NUMBER OF DOLLARS
0100 REM  -- C  NUMBER OF CENTS
0110 REM
0120      LET T = 0
0130 REM
0140      PRINT "NUMBER OF PENNIES IS:"
0150      INPUT N
0160      LET T = T + 01*N
0170 REM
0180      PRINT "NUMBER OF NICKELS IS:"
0190      INPUT N
0200      LET T = T + 05*N
0210 REM
0220      PRINT "NUMBER OF DIMES IS:"
0230      INPUT N
0240      LET T = T + 10*N
0250 REM
0260      PRINT "NUMBER OF QUARTERS IS:"
0270      INPUT N
0280      LET T = T + 25*N
0290 REM
0300      PRINT "NUMBER OF HALF DOLLARS IS:"
0310      INPUT N
0320      LET T = T + 50*N
0330 REM
0340      PRINT "NUMBER OF SILVER DOLLARS IS:"
0350      INPUT N
0360      LET T = T + 100*N
0370 REM
0380      LET D = 0
0390      LET C = T
0400      IF C < 100 THEN 0440
0410         LET C = C - 100
0420         LET D = D + 1
0430         GOTO 0400
0440      PRINT "CHANGE IS "; D; " DOLLARS AND "; C; " CENTS."
0450 END
```

Figure B.1   *Counting Change in Basic*

Appendix E

Exercises in Basic

The following programming exercises are for beginning students of Basic. Many of the questions require only a short answer. Some require programs, most of which are a page or less in length. To really do the exercises, you should have use of a computer that supports Basic and a manual on Basic.

Exercise 1. *Printing a Big H*

Consider the following program, which prints a replica of the letter H:

```
0010 REM  -- THIS PROGRAM PRINTS A REPLICA OF THE LETTER H,
0020 REM  -- PRINTED WITH 14 LINES OF H'S
0030 REM
0040      PRINT "HH        HH"
0050      PRINT "HH        HH"
0060      PRINT "HH        HH"
0070      PRINT "HH        HH"
0080      PRINT "HH        HH"
0090      PRINT "HH        HH"
0100      PRINT "HHHHHHHHHHHH"
0110      PRINT "HHHHHHHHHHHH"
0120      PRINT "HH        HH"
0130      PRINT "HH        HH"
0140      PRINT "HH        HH"
0150      PRINT "HH        HH"
0160      PRINT "HH        HH"
0170      PRINT "HH        HH"
0180 END
```

Answer the following questions:

1. How many statements are there?
2. How many remarks are there?

3. What happens if line 0010 is deleted?
4. How many blanks are there in the string in line 0050?
5. How many lines of text are printed?
6. How many distinct characters are printed?
7. What happens if we omit the quotation marks in line 0070?
8. What happens if we change the name PRINT to DISPLAY?
9. What happens if we omit line 0150?
10. What happens if we add the line

```
0035 GOTO 0150
```

after line 0030?

Exercise 2.   *Learning the P's and Q's of Basic*

There are many little, and often annoying, details that must be learned in order to write a program. Some of these are covered in the following quiz. Try it.

True or False

1. The first character in a program must be a digit.
2. The last character in a program must be a D.
3. The identifier N$ may be used as the name of an integer number.
4. A period can be placed after every statement.
5. The following sequence of characters is a well-formed remark:

```
9999 REM  END
```

6. The Basic number 2.0 is an integer.
7. Spaces may be inserted between any two characters in a program.
8. Two statements, for example

```
PRINT "THIS"   PRINT "THAT"
```

may appear on a single line.
9. Parentheses can be placed around an item in a print statement, as in:

```
PRINT ("THIS")
```

10. The line

```
0110 GOTO 250
```

has the same effect as:

```
0110 GOTO 0250
```

Note: The answers to some of these apparently clear-cut questions may be debatable.

Exercise 3.   *A Little Error*

Consider the following simple program:

```
0010 REM  -- THIS PROGRAM READS IN A NUMBER N AND
0020 REM  -- PRINTS TWICE ITS VALUE.
0030 REM
0040      INPUT N
0050      PRINT N + N
```

Something is wrong. What is it?

Exercise 4.   *Numbers and Identifiers*

Classify the following as either (a) a valid identifier, (b) a valid number, (c) a valid string, or (d) none of the above. If your answer is (d) say why.

1. I2	6. –12	11. 4%
2. I2.2	7. –.12	12. R2D2
3. ""	8. 10 E+2	13. "LET A = 1"
4. " "	9. 1/2	14. .1
5. REM	10. $	15. "SHERLOCK"

Exercise 5.   *Writing Expressions*

The following expressions are written in familiar arithmetic notation. Write them as they would appear in a program. For example,

   A2 + B2

would be written as

   A*A + B*B

in Basic.

a. $B^2 - 4AC$	g. ½ BASE · HEIGHT
b. PI · r^2	h. $(A + B) / (C + D)$
c. square root of $A^2 + B^2$	i. $\sin^2(X + 1)$
d. 1,000	j. $\mid A - B \mid$
e. one million	k. $25,000
f. 6%	l. $X^2 / 2Y$

Exercise 6.   *Dealing with Expressions*

In dealing with computer languages, we must be careful of the order in which expressions are evaluated and the value of the result.

Assuming that A, B, C, and so forth are numeric variables, state what values are assigned to them.

```
LET A = 1 + 1
LET B = 1 + (1 - 1)
LET C = 2 * 3 * 4
LET D = 2 * 3 / 4
LET E = 2 * (3 / 4)
LET F = 2 / 3 * 4
LET G = ( -2) * ( -5)
LET H = 4 - 3 + 2
LET I = - 2 * 5 + 1
LET J = INT(30/7/2)
LET L = 2 * 4 / 2 * 4
```

Exercise 7.   *The P's and Q's of Assignment*

Like any feature in a programming language, assignment statements have their own peculiar conventions. For each of the following assignment statements, answer *True* if the statement could be valid in some program, and *False* otherwise.

```
 1.  LET A = B
 2.  LET A = A + A
 3.  LET X = INT + 1
 4.  LET S = ((N + 1))
 5.  LET P = A/B/C
 6.  LET I = + B*C
 7.  LET X = SQUAREROOT(Y)
 8.  LET R = A + B*C/(D) + 1.0
 9.  LET -X = A + B
10.  LET F(X) = 1
11.  LET Y = SINE(SINE(X))
12.  LET A = (A - (B - (C - (D - (X))))) + 1
13.  LET Z = Y + 1,000.00
14.  LET 1R = SQR(X)
```

Note: In making your decision, you must consider whether the statement could be valid in any program, no matter how strange. You should answer the questions using your version of Basic.

Exercise 8.   *Program Reading*

The following program is just about useless; nonetheless, it's simple to understand.

```
0010 REM  -- THIS PROGRAM READS IN THREE NUMBERS
0020 REM  -- AND OUTPUTS THE MAXIMUM VALUE GIVEN
0030 REM
0040 REM  -- DICTIONARY OF NAMES:
0050 REM
0060 REM  -- V1, V2, V3    THE THREE VALUES
0070 REM  -- M             THE MAXIMUM VALUE
0080 REM
0090      INPUT V1, V2, V3
0100      IF V1 > V2 THEN 0130
0110          LET M = V2
0120          GOTO 0160
0130          LET M = V1
0140          GOTO 0160
0150 REM
0160      IF M > V3 THEN 0190
0170          LET M = V3
0180 REM
0190      PRINT "THE MAXIMUM VALUE IS ", M
0200 END
```

How many errors are there in this program?

Exercise 9. *Entering Text*

Entering the text of a program is a task in itself. It is important that you become proficient at it. Unfortunately, most computers force you to learn a number of strange commands and cryptic notations to enter the text of a program. To do this, you may have to a use a "text-editor."

Now for your problem. Enter the text of this problem, word for word as it appears. If you make any mistakes, they must be corrected. The final result must be an exact (space for space, character for character) facsimile of these very lines.

Note: You may set your own line length.

Exercise 10. *Learning to Use a Computer*

Learning to use your local computer is usually a major problem in itself. You have to learn which buttons to press in which order, how to tell it whom to charge for using it, how to type in your program, and how to correct any mistakes. Often the conventions for dealing with these things are quite mysterious.

So be prepared for the worst, gather your manuals, and solve the following problem: write a program to print MY NAME IS followed by your name. A sample output might be:

```
MY NAME IS MYCROFT
```
It would be a good idea to bring along a friend who has used the computer before.

Exercise 11.   *Running a Program*

This problem is more difficult than it appears.

1. Enter the text of Holmes's program of Chapter V.

2. Run the program, and thus let the computer determine the distance traveled.

Why is it more difficult than it appears? First, of course, you have to face the computer with all of its complexities. Second, if the program you enter contains even one tiny mistake, it will not work. Third, you may have to make some changes to the program to suit your version of Basic.

Exercise 12.   *Time and Date*

Your version of Basic may allow you to obtain the time and date and display them on your terminal. If this is possible, write a program to do just that.

Exercise 13.   *Odd or Even*

Many people are afraid of computers. This may, in part, be because they think computers know too much. But you know that the only things a computer knows are what programmers put into their programs.

This is an easy exercise. Write a program that knows about odd and even numbers. The input will be an integer number, say 12 or 271. The output will be a message telling whether the number is odd or even.

Exercise 14.   *A Desk Calculation*

In some people's eyes, a computer is just a powerful desk calculator. Sure enough, we can perform common calculations with a computer.

One common application of calculations is the computation of averages. Suppose that you receive quarterly electric bills and wish to compute the average monthly cost. For example, if your quarterly bills in dollars and cents are

170.33   161.42   125.78   147.91

the average monthly cost would be:

50.45

Write a program to read in four real numbers representing quarterly bills and print the average monthly cost. Test your program with the above values.

Exercise 15.   *A Change Making Machine*

In a certain subway station there is a machine that accepts five-dollar bills and gives the change in coins for each of four possible fares. The fares $.65, $1.10, $1.75, and $2.10 are indicated by pressing buttons 1 through 4.

Write a program to read in one of the integers 1 through 4 and print the number of each coin given in change. The coins are half-dollars, quarters, dimes, and nickels. For each amount of change, the minimum number of coins is to be used. For example, if your input is

3

the program should print something like:

```
6   HALF DOLLARS
1   QUARTER
```

Keep an eye on singular (one coin) versus plural (more than one coin).

Exercise 16.   *Summing a Long Series of Numbers*

If you toss a coin you may get heads on the first toss. But then again you may not. The probability of getting your first heads on the first toss is 1/2. The probability of getting your first heads on the second toss is 1/4, on the third toss 1/8, and so on.

To get the average number of tosses needed to get heads you need to add the series of numbers:

$$1*(1/2) + 2*(1/4) + 3*(1/8) + \ldots$$

Write a program to find the value of this series as the number of tosses approaches infinity. A thousand terms should suffice.

Exercise 17.   *Printing Checks*

At some time or other, all of us have seen a computer-generated check. But have you ever wondered how the number gets printed in words? On a check, for example, $323 would be printed as:

```
THREE HUNDRED AND TWENTY THREE DOLLARS
```

Write a program to read in a one, two, or three digit integer and to print out the number in words.

Appendix H

The Halting Problem:
Proof of Unsolvability

In this appendix, we sketch the kind of argument needed to show that the halting problem discussed in Chapter X is not solvable. Here goes.

Suppose that an algorithm for solving the halting problem did exist. That is, given a machine M and tape T, the algorithm would compute Yes or No, depending on if the machine would halt or not. We could, of course, capture this algorithm in the form of a program for a Turing machine, as shown in Figure H.1. Let us label this machine as A. Here the description of M and T are placed on the tape, and the Turing machine A halts in one of the two states S_{yes} or S_{no}. Notice that we require A itself to halt, for otherwise we would not have a solution. Presumably A examines the description of M and T, does some calculations, and ends up in one of the two desired states.

Now, if A can solve the halting problem for any machine M and input tape T, it presumably can do so for a machine M whose input tape is itself the description of M. This is certainly far-fetched, but not unfair. For instance, if machine M prints a description of its input tape, applying M to a description of itself would simply print a copy of the program for M, ending up in state S_{yes}.

We can next devise a machine B that is just like A except that B's tape contains only a description of M. Before B attempts to solve the halting problem for M, it makes a copy of the description of M for use as an input tape. Then B decides if M will halt with an input tape that is a description of M. This setup is shown in Figure H.2. Notice that B, like A, must contain two halting states, S_{yes} and S_{no}; the first prints Yes if M will halt when given an input tape describing itself, the second prints No if the opposite is true.

The real step up comes next. We construct yet another machine, C, making a slight modification to B by adding two new states. If either one of the new states is reached, reading any symbol causes a transfer to the other state. One of the states moves the head left, the other right. The effect is that if either of these two states is reached, C starts looping back and forth forever. Furthermore, if C reaches state S_{yes}, control is switched to one of these new states. The net effect of this is: if M halts when applied to an input tape description of itself, then C does not halt, and vice versa.

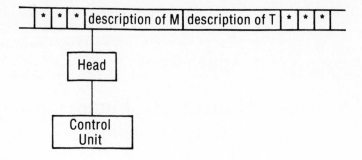

Tape symbols: As required for M and T

States: S_{yes}, S_{no}, plus internal states

Initial state: As required

Program: Assumed to exist

Figure H.1 *A Turing Machine A to Solve the Halting Problem*

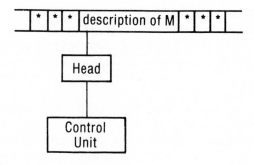

Tape symbols: As required for M

States: S_{yes}, S_{no}, plus internal states

Initial state: As required

Program: Same as *A*, except first makes a copy of the description of M

Figure H.2 *A Turing Machine B to Solve the Halting Problem for a Machine M Whose Input Tape is a Description of M*

Now for the final blessing. Suppose we take our Turing machine C and test it out, not with an arbitrary machine M, but with a copy of itself. This is shown in Figure H.3. If C halts when applied to a description of itself, then the machine of Figure H.3 will not halt, and vice versa. But the machine of Figure H.3 is C itself applied to a description of itself! So if C halts then C does not halt? Of course not.

Clearly C could not exist. Hence, neither could B, nor A. All of which means there could be no solution to the halting problem.

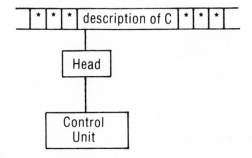

Tape symbols: As required for C

States: S_{yes}, S_{no}, plus internal states

Initial state: As required

Program: Same as B, except goes into an infinite loop if state S_{yes} is reached.

Figure H.3 *A Turing Machine C Applied to an Input Tape with a Description of Itself*

Appendix R

References and Further Reading

Byte (magazine)
Byte Publications, 70 Main Street, Peterborough, New Hampshire, 03458
   This is probably the most popular magazine on computers. It contains articles on almost everything. It is a bit more of a professional magazine than a personal computer magazine. It is loaded with advertisements.

Creative Computing (magazine)
Creative Computing, P.O. Box 789-M, Morristown, New Jersey, 07960
   This magazine is written primarily for owners of personal computers.

Hubert L. Dreyfus
What Computers Can't Do
Harper and Row, New York, New York, 1972
   This book takes a serious and questioning view of artificial intelligence. The author contends that progress in this area will be painfully slow. His arguments are both pragmatic and philosophical.

Edward A. Feigenbaum and Julian Feldman, Editors
Computers and Thought
McGraw-Hill Book Company, New York, New York, 1963
   This is a fine collection of articles on machine intelligence. Among others, it contains Samuel's original paper on playing checkers and Turing's article "Can a Machine Think?" Perhaps because it is an early work, the articles are fairly easy to read.

Frank Herbert
Without Me You're Nothing: The Essential Guide to Home Computers
Simon and Schuster, New York, New York, 1980
   This is certainly one of the most nicely written introductions to computers, with emphasis on personal computers. The topics covered are similar to our own, and include programming, the insides of a computer, and all kinds of witty advice about computers.

Douglass R. Hofstadter
Godel, Escher, Bach: An Eternal Golden Braid
Vintage Books, Random House, New York, New York, 1980
    This book, winner of the Pulitzer Prize, is a fairly sophisticated work. This book is not explicitly about computers, but is cleverly written and treats many computer topics — among them artificial intelligence, Turing's test, and some telling comments about what machines can and cannot do.

Henry Ledgard and Andrew Singer
Elementary Basic
Vintage Books, Random House, New York, New York, 1982
(student edition, with exercises, published by SRA, Chicago, Illinois, 1982)
    This work, and its companion, *Elementary Pascal,* provide an introduction to computer programming in Pascal using Sherlock Holmes. For those interested in programming, it is a natural sequel to this text.

Our Computerized Society with Basic Programming
Anaheim Publishing Company, Fullerton, California, 1979
    This book contains an extensive discussion of computer technology, with emphasis on devices for representing data.

Marvin Minsky
Computation: Finite and Infinite Machines
Prentice-Hall, Englewood Cliffs, New Jersey, 1967
    This textbook on theoretical aspects of computers has an excellent discussion of Turing Machines and the idea of computability.

Philip Morrison and Emily Morrison, Editors
Charles Babbage and His Calculating Engines
Dover Publications, New York, New York, 1961
    This book contains a number of original works of Charles Babbage. It includes notes on the design of the Analytical Engine. The book is nicely edited and easy to read.

Personal Computing (magazine)
Hayden Publishing Company, Rochelle Park, New Jersey, 07662
    This magazine is written primarily for owners of personal computers. Hayden also publishes many books on personal computing.

Ira Pohl and Alan Shaw
The Nature of Computation: An Introduction to Computer Science
Computer Science Press, Rockville, Maryland, 1981
    This text is an introduction to computer science for the serious student. As a text the book is all substance, with a blend of hardware, software and theory. It also treats number systems, programming languages,

and artificial intelligence. The text is the source of the small hypothetical computer presented in Chapter III.

Bertram Raphael
The Thinking Computer
W.H. Freeman and Company, San Francisco, California, 1976

This book provides a superbly written introduction to artificial intelligence. Topics include game playing, natural language recognition, and robotics.

Byron W. Stutzman
Data Communication Control Procedures
Computing Surveys, Volume 4, Number 4, pages 197-220, December, 1972

This early article is an easy-to-read introduction to a technology that is often mysterious to the layperson. It is also a good source of information about the ASCII control code characters.

Alan Turing
On computable numbers, with an application to the Entscheidungsproblem
Proceedings of the London Mathematical Society, Ser. 2-42, pages 230-265, 1936.

This is the original work by Alan Turing on Turing Machines. Definitely for the mathematically sophisticated only.

Computer Power and Human Reason
W. H. Freeman and Company, San Francisco, California, 1976

This is an unusual book, mainly about some social implications of computers. Its contents include how computers work, the role of psychology, and artificial intelligence. It is written with clarity and spice. The book is definitely opinionated (not to imply ill-founded) and thought-provoking.

Xerox Star Word Processor

This is not a text, but a product announced by Xerox in 1981. The Xerox Star stands out because of its outstandingly high attention to the human interface for word processing and other office tasks. This product, a result of years of research, sets a standard from which to judge other products. If you are thinking of getting a word processor, this is a fine place to calibrate your needs.

Appendix V

Vocabulary of Terms

Access time — An access time is the interval of time needed to locate an item from computer storage.

Accumulator — An accumulator is a special piece of circuitry inside a computer. It is used to hold temporary results.

Address — An address is a number specifying a location in computer storage.

Algorithm — An algorithm is a sequence of instructions for carrying out a task or solving a problem.

Arithmetic unit — An arithmetic unit is the collection of circuitry inside a computer needed to carry out arithmetic calculations.

Assembler language — An assembler language is a programming language whose form and meaning is close to the primitive operations built in to the computer itself.

Assignment — An assignment is an operation whereby a value is copied into a storage location. In a programming language, an assignment is usually made to a variable, which implicitly denotes a storage location.

Basic — Basic is the name of a popular programming language.

Binary — Binary is a number system with only two digits, 0 and 1.

Bit — A bit (short for *bi*nary dig*it*) is a single binary digit, i.e. either 0 or 1.

Bug — A bug is a colloquial term for an error in a computer program.

Byte — A byte is a sequence of binary digits taken as a unit. Most often a byte contains eight bits.

Card reader — A card reader is a piece of equipment that senses the holes in a punched card and thereby reads its data.

Central processing unit (CPU) — A central processing unit is the main piece of circuitry inside a computer. It houses the arithmetic unit, processing circuits, and other elements.

Character set — A character set is a selection of characters that is recognized by a particular computer. The characters normally include letters, digits, punctuation marks, and special symbols. Each character is given a binary code.

Code — A code is a sequence of binary digits. Codes are used to represent characters, data, operations, and other primitive elements.

Compiler — A compiler is a complex program used to translate other programs into the machine's own language.

Cursor — A cursor is a special symbol displayed on the screen of a video terminal. The cursor can be moved to various positions by pressing special keys. Its purpose is to work a specific piece of text, or more generally, an item of interest.

Debugging — Debugging is the process of finding and correcting errors in a computer program.

Disk — A disk is a medium for storing computer data outside the main memory of the computer.

Editor — An editor is a specialized computer program that allows a user to enter and modify text.

File — A file is a collection of data treated as a unit.

Floppy disk — A floppy disk is a small storage device about the size of a 45 rpm phonograph record.

Hardware — Hardware is a term referring to physical devices and equipment that make up a computer. It is often used in contrast to the term "software," the collection of programs and data needed to direct the computer's operations.

Input — Input is the collection of data entered to a computer program.

Keyboard — A keyboard is a typewriter-like panel of keys for entering requests to a computer.

Machine language — A machine language is the set of available instructions that are understood directly by a computer.

Magnetic disk — A magnetic disk is a synonym for disk; it is used to emphasize that the storage of data on a disk is achieved by magnetizing tiny regions on the disk.

Magnetic tape — A magnetic tape is a synonym for tape; it is used to emphasize that the storage of data on a tape is achieved by magnetizing tiny segments on the tape.

Memory — Memory is the collection of storage locations inside a computer. Memory is used to store programs and data.

Microcomputer — A microcomputer is a very small computer, often specialized for a given application. Microcomputers are used for personal computers. A wide variety of items (for example, a navigational system, intelligent terminal, or electronic cash register) have a microcomputer as one of their components.

Microsecond — A microsecond is one millionth of a second.

Millisecond — A millisecond is one thousandth of a second.

Minicomputer — A minicomputer is a small, general-purpose computer, often desk-top size.

Nanosecond — A nanosecond is one billionth of a second.

Off-line — Off-line is a term referring to an action performed by an auxiliary part of a computer system, not by the computer's central processing unit.

On-line — On-line is a term referring to an action performed directly by the computer's central processing unit.

Operating system — An operating system is the collection of programs and data.

Printer — A printer is a device that is connected to a computer and that can print characters on paper.

Program — A program is a series of interactions that can be understood by a computer.

Programming — Programming is the process required to produce a computer program. It refers to the process of designing, writing, and correcting a program.

Programming language — A programming language is an artificial language for communicating algorithms to a computer. Its grammatical rules are highly contrived and rigid, not at all like English.

Read-only memory (ROM) — A read-only memory, usually called ROM for short, is a collection of storage locations inside a computer. Once entered, the values stored in a ROM cannot be changed, and thus can only be read.

Real time — The term real time refers to a computer system that takes action simultaneously with the world around it. Airline reservation systems and video computer games are real time systems.

Software — Software is the collection of programs and data needed to direct a computer's operation.

Storage — Storage refers to a physical part of a computer where data can be kept for long periods of time. Main storage is for data to be used by operating programs. Secondary, or backup, storage is for data that is kept for later use.

System — System is a catch-all term used frequently in computers, for example, computer system, information system, programming system, and software system. The intent of the term is to emphasize a composite of devices, programs, and data.

Systems analyst — A systems analyst can mean almost anything, but it is meant to refer to a person whose job is to design computer systems. This includes defining the problem, solving it, making use of both hardware and software, and so forth. This kind of work is like that of an architect.

Tape — A tape is a continuous strip of material upon which computer data is recorded. With paper, tape holes are punched; with magnetic tape magnetized spots are used.

Teletype — A teletype is a typewriter-like device for entering and receiving data over long-distance communication lines.

Terminal — A terminal is a device, often with a keyboard and screen, for entering requests to a computer and receiving results.

Video computer — A video computer, or video game computer, is a computer with specialized features suitable for playing interactive games.

Word — A word is a unit of information around which a computer operates. A word is a sequence of bits (often of length 16 or 32) that is stored in a single location in memory.

POSTSCRIPT

It is sometimes hard to believe that Sherlock Holmes was a fictional character. His habits, wit, knowledge, and spirit seem as real as any person of Victorian times. This of course is due to his creator, Sir Arthur Conan Doyle. Sherlock Holmes would hardly be complete without his memorable appearance. For the most part this is due to his illustrator, Sidney Paget. To both Conan Doyle and Sidney Paget we are grateful.

CONAN DOYLE

A number of individuals contributed to this work. Linda Thompson provided creative drafts of "The Affair at the Golden Eagle" and "The Adventures of the Red Queen's Race." Sheila Paget served as general editor and expert on Victorian times. Both were a pleasure to work with.

George Forrest, during a visit to Oxford, suggested the title. Elizabeth Harvey suggested buying a Chamber's Victorian dictionary and Sari Stacey provided the clue in getting one. Christine and John Dunning provided splendid accommodations during research into original photographs.

Anne Freedgood provided a sharp eye in editing the manuscript. Gary Keenan and Marietta Rhyne performed a thorough final edit.

Jack Tracy, author of the *Encyclopaedia Sherlockiana*, provided some key advice. Gaby Goldscheider provided access to original Sherlock Holmes material. George Danziger, Jason Danziger, and Jason Woolf participated in the interviews on personal computers. Ed Judge, Helen Smith, and Peggy Farrell also kindly provided assistance.

SIDNEY PAGET

We also acknowledge the following photograph credits. The photographs of the Analytical Engine, Punched Card, "Mill" of the Analytical Engine, and the Underwood Typewriter, 1897 are courtesy of Crown Copyright, Science Museum, London. The photographs of Charles Babbage, Ada Lovelace, Hollerith's Sorting Machine, the Great Telegraph Room, Oliver Evans's Cornmill and the 1890 Cover of Scientific American are courtesy of the Science Museum, London. The photograph of the Wang Word Processor is courtesy of Wang Laboratories. The photograph of the Apple Personal Computer is courtesy of Apple Computer Inc. The ARPANET Geographical Map is courtesy of the Defense Communications Agency. Photographs of the "Beast" and the robotic arm are courtesy of The Johns Hopkins University Applied Physics Laboratory. Shakey the Robot is courtesy of SRA International and the Stanford Scheinman Arm is courtesy of Stanford University Department of Computer Science.

Linda would like to extend a special thank you to Drake Maher, our long-distance graphic artist, for his considerable talent.

Henry Ledgard
E. Patrick McQuaid
Andrew Singer

INDEX

abbreviation 149
access time 269
accumulator 42, 269
accuracy 5
Ada 77
adding circuit 44-49
address 269
Algol 77
algorithm 59, 62-65, 269
analog device 33
and gate 46
Apt 80
arithmetic unit 30, 42, 269
ARPANET 140-141
artificial intelligence 198
ASCII code 15, 18-19, 24-27, 138,
    239-240
assembler language 269
assignment 246, 269
automatic hyphenation 107
automatic paging 107

Babbage, Charles 5, 37
Basic 66, 73, 241, 269
binary 14, 16, 26, 31, 269
binary adder 44
binary table 17-18
bit 17, 269
Boole, George 28
bug 269
byte 19, 269

calculation 13, 34, 57
card reader 269
carry 45-49
carry signal 46
central processing unit 38, 270
character set 270
character strings 242

checkers 200
clock-and-control unit 42
Cobol 77, 79
code 270
communication 138-140
compilation 80
compiler 270
condition 64, 253
control characters 139
control unit 31, 168, 173
convertor 18
correctness 65
cost 119, 149
CPU 38
cursor 270

data 30, 44, 68
    external 19
    internal 19
    storing 20-27
debugging 270
decision 69
deleting a character 152
deleting a line 152
difference engine 6, 33
digital device 33
direct branch 69
direct cost 149
directory 155
disk 270
document 97, 98, 147
documentation 147, 149, 152, 156
draughts 200

ease of use 120, 151
EBCDIC code 19
editing 91, 98, 152
editor 270
electronic mail 142

275

error 4, 34, 139, 148, 149, 152, 183, 234
execution rules 245
expression 75, 246, 251
external code 19

feature syndrome 152
file 110, 270
floating point 252
floppy disk 20, 26, 101, 115, 125, 270
form letter 91, 96
Fortran 77, 78

game cartridge 125
garbage collection 155
gate 46-49
global replace 107
goto statement 245
grammar 147
graphics 126

halting problem 182, 263-265
hardware 38, 270
Hollerith, Herman 20
human engineering 151
human factors 151

ideal machine 170
if statement 247
imitation game 230
implementation 80
infinite loop 176-178, 183
input 38, 69, 74, 76, 249, 270
instruction 4, 5, 30, 31, 40, 57, 73
  counter 42
  register 42
integer 242
intelligence 198
intelligent program 200
internal data 19
interpretation 81
interview 118-124

keyboard 98, 107, 115, 126, 156, 270
keypunch machine 22
keyword 241

language 3-4
  cartridge 125
  machine 3-4
  natural 209
learning 188, 202, 207
  parameter 188, 208
  rote 207
light pens 126
light-sensing 15, 22
limited use 150
line number 244
location register 41
logical unit 42
look ahead 188, 206
loop 58, 63, 249
  infinite 176-178, 183
Lovelace, Lady Ada 5, 37

machine language 28, 40, 270
magnetic
  core 19
  disk 24, 101, 271
  tape 24, 271
magnetic tape 24
memory 19-20, 22, 38, 41, 42, 271
menu 155
micro-computer 271
micro-processor 20
micro-second 271
mill 30-35
millisecond 271
mini-computer 271
mini-maxi procedure 207
misconceptions 234
Morse, Samuel 20

name 70, 241
nanosecond 271
natural language 209
network 140
non-printing character 19, 139
not gate 46

off-line 271
on-line 271
operand 43, 251

operating system 271
operation-code 43
operator 251
or gate 46
output 38, 76, 155, 249
overflow 48
overhead 116

page 155
parameter 203
parameter learning 188, 208
partial result 30
Pascal 79
perfect copy 98
personal computer 115-118
photocell 23
physical characteristic 107
PL/I 77
printer 99, 121, 271
printing speed 107
print quality 107
privacy 221
procedure
  mini-maxi 207
program 4, 60, 67, 73, 76, 271
programming 4, 60-61, 78, 121, 271
programming language 73, 77, 271
punched card 5, 12-15, 17, 22, 30
punctuation 147

read-only memory 272
read-write head 173
real number 242
real time 272
register
  data 42
  instruction 42
  location 41
remark 68, 74, 243
representing knowledge 188, 202
representing data 16-19
rigor 5, 61
robotics 210-213
rote learning 207
rounding 252
rules, execution 245

Sam 40
screen, video 98, 107, 156
sensor 18
silicon chip 20
social implication 221, 226, 237
software 60, 101, 116, 272
solid state 20
state 167, 173
statement 244
  goto 245
  if 247
storage 272
storage device 98
switching device 30
symbol 173
system 272
systems analyst 272

table 97
tape 173, 272
  cassette 115, 125
teletype 272
television set 125
terminal 272
thinking 230
time sharing 135, 136-138
track 24
Turing, Alan 230
Turing machine 170, 173-176, 263-265
Turing's test 233
Turing's thesis 181

variable 68, 75, 246
video computer 272
video game 125-127
vocabulary 147, 154

unary adder 179-180
undo feature 152
unsolvable problem 182

weighting factor 205
word 19, 272
word processor 6, 97
word processing 96-105
work station 107

ABOUT THE AUTHORS

Henry Ledgard received his B.A. from Tufts University and his Ph.D. from the Massachusetts Institute of Technology. After a year at the University of Oxford, he joined the faculty of Johns Hopkins University and later the faculty of the University of Massachusetts. In 1977 he joined the Honeywell design team to develop a new computer language (Ada). In 1979 he started his own consulting, seminar, and writing practice. His is co-author of two other Sherlock Holmes books, *Elementary Basic* and *Elementary Pascal*, as well as a series of friendly books on programming style, known as *The Programming Proverbs*. He is also an author of *Ada: An Introduction* and *The Programming Language Landscape*. His primary research area is making computers more fit for human users. He lives and works on Drummer Hill Road in Leverett, Massachusetts.

E. Patrick McQuaid is an American journalist known mainly for his work in higher education. He is special North American correspondent to *The Times* (London) *Higher Education Supplement*, Northeast correspondent to the Washington-based *Chronicle of Higher Education*, and a political columnist for *Le Bulletin de l'Association canadienne des professeurs d'universite*, published in Ottawa. His reports on higher education have appeared in *The New York Times*, *The Boston Globe*, and a variety of overseas periodicals. His extensive knowledge of Sherlock Holmes, long a mild though amusing irritant among his friends, was first put to practical use during the programming series *Elementary Pascal* and *Elementary Basic*, for which he served as editor and Holmesian consultant. He is a resident of Cambridge, Massachusetts.

As a computer scientist, **Andrew Singer** has long been fascinated by the problems people have with computers. He is the co-author of a recent research monograph in this area, and his lighter comments on the subject have appeared in the personal computing magazine, *ROM*, for which he was a contributed editor. Mr. Singer is a well-known seminar leader and consultant and has been a member of the research staffs at New York University Medical Center, Haskins Laboratories, and the Department of Social Psychology at Harvard. Since 1979 he has been Vice President for Research and Engineering at E&L Instruments. Mr. Singer holds a Ph.D. and M.S. degrees in Computer Science from the University of Massachusetts. He lives in Woodbury, Connecticut.